# ADVENTURING on the EURAIL EXPRESS

# ADVENTURING
## on the
# EURAIL EXPRESS

*By Jay Brunhouse*

**PELICAN PUBLISHING COMPANY**
GRETNA 1989

*Library of Congress Cataloging-in-Publication Data*

Brunhouse, Jay.
    Adventuring on the Eurail Express / by Jay Brunhouse.
        p.  cm.
    Includes index.
    ISBN 0-88289-703-9
    1. Europe—Description and travel—1971—Guide-books.
    2. Railroad travel—Europe—Guide-books.  I. Title.
    D909.B777  1989                                    88-33370
    914'.04558-dc19                                         CIP

Maps by Brian Clarke

*Information in this guidebook is based on authoritative data available at the time of printing. Prices and hours of operation of businesses listed are subject to change without notice. Readers are asked to take this into account when consulting this guide.*

Manufactured in the United States of America
Published by Pelican Publishing Company, Inc.
1101 Monroe Street, Gretna, LA 70053

*To Mom and Dad*

# Contents

# Preface

You find many sensible reasons to take a train: you save money, you meet Europeans in congenial, give-and-take surroundings, you explore corners of the continent where scenery dazzles your eyes, you sleep and eat soundly and well, and you speed at unprecedented velocities from city center to city center and arrive fully ready to go. Alert travelers enjoy more than just a trip. They discover an adventure.

This book is for adventurers who plan to use their time in Europe confronting thrilling scenery and discovering wild and secret corners on exciting trains—the most comfortable and the most dazzling—for little money, little hassle, and much pleasure.

Take your pencil in hand. This guide covers train travel in eighteen countries, including Britain and Hungary, now that it is part of the Eurailpass network. Highlight the information to use and put this book in your travel bag.

This is an exciting time to adventure on the European trains. European trains are flexing their increased horsepower, providing tilting-train technology, and giving you more innovative personal comforts. High speed takes you comfortably from here to there. Adventuring takes you to the North Face of the Eiger, Midnight Sun in the most northerly station of Western Europe, teetering along the cliffs of the Isle of Man, through the feudal highlands of Sardinia, and down the Alpine ridges to the French Riviera.

You will find that adventuring on European trains is speedier, smoother, more convenient, and—with a cheap rail pass—your best value in Europe.

# Acknowledgments

Thank you to those who helped me gather and update information making this guide current and complete. Thank you Juergen Arnold, Hans Baumann, Kim Chisholm, Hank Fisher, Evelyn Heyward, Willi Isler, Linda Lang, Andy Lazarus, Francis Lucille, Joe Lustenberger, Patricio Fernandez Maillard, Annie Miller, Andre Moraillon, Jan Nijboer, Armond Noble, Alvaro Renedo, Nathan Sawyer, Dag Scher, Patricia Titley, Alex Townsend, Barbara Veldkamp, Heidi Wichmann, and Jens Wilhelmsborg. Thanks also to editor Nina Kooij.

# ADVENTURING
### on the
# EURAIL EXPRESS

# Introduction

Here is the feeling and thrill of *Adventuring on the Eurail Express*. The first chapter gives you useful tips to help you make the plans you want and to get you to Europe, well coached, with the right rail pass in your hand. You are guided aboard your train, into your destination, and back onto your train again so carefully a first-time adventurer will have no worries. Then it is up to you.

Experienced travelers know all national train systems have their quirks and secret rewards. Chapters taking you through Western Europe from Switzerland to the Midnight Sun to the Mediterranean show you how to profit from them. Adventurous trips to everywhere Eurailpass goes, and Britain, too, are described in loving detail to enhance your travels as you ride these trains. You are also alerted to adventurous trips that are not covered by Eurailpass.

Read the descriptions in the chapters for special trips and side options. The "Vital Tips" sections give you special information about traveling through the countries that most interest you.

Timetables follow each adventure to give you the latest schedules. Remember that summer and winter timetables change yearly. Times are shown using the same twenty-four-hour clock you see in Europe. Major cities and connections are capitalized, and dots in a time column indicate that the train does not stop at that station. Notes indicate special restrictions. Here is your first tip: when you can punch up a twenty-four-hour clock on your digital watch, use this mode when reading timetables.

3

# 4 ON THE EURAIL EXPRESS

Other travel books tell you where to stay and what to see. This one guides you through Europe and gives you tips to make your travel time exciting, social, and offbeat—every moment a pleasure.

# Vital Tips
## to Adventuring on
## the Trains of Europe

### *Arranging Your Itinerary*

*Study guidebooks—Milk tourist offices—Get free train information—*
*Use the Thomas Cook timetable—Plot your train travel strategies*
*craftily—Let travel agents fill in the blanks*

## Study Guidebooks

You can gather all your general and specific information about packing, hotel and hostel accommodations, air transportation, food, shopping, and sightseeing from guidebooks in your library and bookshops. Tailored for adventurers are the "Let's Go" guides edited by the Harvard Student Agencies (St. Martin's Press, 175 Fifth Avenue, New York, NY 10010) and "How to Europe" by John Bermont (Murphy & Broad Publishing, P.O. Box 3208, Newport Beach, CA 92663).

## Milk Tourist Offices

After you have a general idea of your plans, write to the national tourist office of every country you think you might possibly visit. Their addresses are in the Appendix. Don't simply ask for "information" or you will receive broad-brush propaganda. Ask specifically for details about your special interests, e.g., discount programs for hotels, subway savings and maps, castles to see, scenic bicycle routes, city "keys" or discount programs for museum admissions and city tours, regional maps and sightseeing in specific cities and areas.

## Get Free Train Information

Even when you are not considering buying a Eurailpass, write for their free information. Ask for all the following:

• "Through Europe by Train," a 160-page, pocket-sized timetable for the best European InterCity trains.

• "Eurail Traveler's Guide," a thirty-six-page illustrated booklet of wise tips to all aspects of train travel in Europe and an indispensable large foldout Eurail train map of Europe.

• "See Europe by Train," the promotional brochure giving you Eurail prices and rules.

Send your postcard to Eurailpass, P.O. Box 325, Old Greenwich, CT 06870-0325. In Canada write Eurailpass Distribution Centre, C. P. 300, Succursale R., Montreal, Quebec H2S 3K9. Also contact BritRail, GermanRail, and the French Railroads for additional information (see Appendix).

## Use the Thomas Cook Timetable

Check to see whether the reference desk of your public library has a copy of the Thomas Cook European Timetable. Should your library fail you, look for it in bookstores specializing in travel literature. If there is no travel bookstore near you, order the timetable from Forsyth Travel Library, P.O. Box 2975, Shawnee Mission, KS 66201-1375. (Write ahead for a free price list and order form.)

The Thomas Cook European Timetable helps you with detailed advance planning. When you buy one, carry it with you, or tear out the pages covering the countries you are visiting and take them with you, but in many train carriages filled with adventurers in Europe you will see one or more copies of the bright, orange-colored timetable, and the owner will be more than happy to let you look at it.

All European railroads publish complete timetables, but they are generally too bulky to carry around. In some countries they run into many volumes. You sometimes find complete sets on the reference tables in the railroads' information offices in Europe. Agents in the information offices will look up details for you.

Most railroads also publish pocket-sized timetables for their most heavily used routes and leaflets listing connections between popular city pairs or regions. These are available, free for the asking, in the information offices of the railroads (not the tourist office) in train stations. Pocket timetables are also occasionally available free in North America. Request them from the railroads' offices (see Appendix) before you leave.

## Plot Your Train Travel Strategies Craftily

Consider several travel strategies depending on where you decide to go and what you want to do. Adventurers traveling long distances prefer the circular trip plan. Start and end your train travel at your airline's European gateway and cover your stops with a circular plan that brings you back to your gateway city. (You can sometimes arrange an "open-jaw" airline ticket that allows you to return from a different city than the one in which you arrived.) When you want to see Europe extensively, you can see more using this plan.

You have best results when you plan at least one overnight following your arrival at your airline gateway city to allow for jet lag and familiarization, and at least two when you return there. This gives you flexibility to change your plans or cope with any unexpected delays during your trip.

Before you leave home, make a working itinerary. Using your timetables, select the best trains. Outline your day, city, and train connections. Carefully note the days of the week because some trains do not run on weekends or local holidays.

Make your itinerary loose enough so you can vary it depending on circumstances. Keep backup and alternative plans in the back of your mind. You can usually count on reliable train connections, but—for example—when you travel farther and farther south in Italy, trains run later and later. Strikes and natural disasters such as washouts can (and do) devastate split-second plans.

Some travelers save money by alternating nights in hotels and aboard trains. They travel on an overnight train, check into their hotel in the morning, shower, etc., do their sightseeing in the afternoon, and see the city by night. On the following day, they check out of their hotel, leave their luggage with the receptionist, top off their daylight sightseeing, dine, pick up their luggage, and leave on the late-evening overnight train for their next destination.

The second strategy involves locating in one city and taking day trips to nearby places of interest. You double your time on the train and return to your bed at the mercy of the train schedule, but you won't waste time packing, unpacking, and checking in and out of hotels. When you want to see an area intensively, this is the plan you follow.

When you are visiting both Britain and the Continent, schedule Britain either first or last. However, a Eurail Flexipass (see below) lets you sandwich some days in Britain into the middle of your itinerary.

## Let Travel Agents Fill in the Blanks

The right travel agent will save you a lot of time and effort and surprise you with good advice. Their computers handle rail passes. Let them buy for you your Eurail, BritRail, and national rail-pass products, hotel packages, and airline tickets because they also make reservations for seats, overnight sleeping cars, and couchettes in the trains. Make these seat and sleeping reservations at the same time you buy your rail pass, as soon as you can to avoid electronic glitches. Usually make them as early as two months in advance. You must pay telex fees for these reservation services, but in times when the dollar is weak, the lower price when you pay in dollars offsets the telex fee.

Be sure to pester your agent with questions on inexpensive charter flights, discount seats made available by consolidators, special promotional air transportation/rail pass combinations, and hotel "checks" or vouchers. (Confirm this by telephoning the airlines' 800-number international tour desks.)

It's not worth agents' time to write your letters for inexpensive hotels or pensions, and you are better off handling this yourself before you leave or, even easier, when you get there. Most adventurers like to have a confirmed place to stay for the day they arrive and then make their subsequent arrangements as they travel along.

## *Choosing the Right Pass for You*

*Eurailpass—Eurail Flexipass—Eurail Saverpass—Eurail Youthpass—*
*National rail passes—Rail/Drive passes*

## Eurailpass

Eurailpasses, now that the Hungarian State Railroads has been admitted to the Eurailpass association, cover unlimited travel on the national train networks of seventeen countries: Austria, Belgium, Denmark, Finland, France, Greece, Hungary, Republic of Ireland, Italy, Luxembourg, the Netherlands, Norway, Portugal, Spain, Sweden, Switzerland, and West Germany.

BritRail and some private lines are not affiliated. When Eurailpass does not cover a route in this book, you will read about it.

It is true that when you pay for all your transportation in one lump sum, it seems like a lot of money, but nothing approaches the value of a Eurailpass when you take total advantage of it.

• It is easy to use. No wasting your time standing in long lines at counters you sometimes can't find to buy tickets and surcharge coupons in unfamiliar currencies. No sorting through stapled and loose tickets and coupons to show the conductor. Just flash your pass.

• You can change your mind. When an acquaintance convinces you to go to Rome instead of Vienna, just board the next train. When it's flooding in Venice, get off the train in sunny Salzburg.

• It's cheap. You pay in low-inflation dollars. Fixed prices reflect last year's exchange rate.

• You pay at home and know in advance to the cent exactly how much your transportation will cost.

• Free Eurailpass information gives you a planning edge. Their map and pocket timetable guide you through Europe. Their booklet of tips smooths your way.

• If your pass is lost or stolen on the road, you can replace it at one of the forty-five Eurail Aid offices nearby.

Eurailpasses cover fast-train surcharges. You sit in first-class sections of the best trains of Europe without having to go to the trouble and expense of paying for that second charge.

Further, you have access to the handful of elite trains that are limited to buyers of first-class tickets, such as Italy's high-speed Pendolino between Rome and Milan, the Super Panoramic Express in Switzerland, business TGV (fast train) connections between Paris and Lyon, and EuroCity trains between France and Belgium.

In addition, you receive discounts on selected Europabus trips and 20 percent off Pullman and Altea hotels.

Your travel agent provides your Eurailpass with a tear-off stub and the line blank where your passport number is to be entered. Before you board your first train, you must have the clerk at the train station (any train station in Europe) validate the pass by entering your passport number and hand-stamping it or validating it with the clerk's validator. Keep the validation slip separate, perhaps with your traveler's checks receipts. You need it to prove your purchase for replacement if you lose your pass. When traveling, you should keep your passport handy so the conductor can check it against the passport number on the Eurailpass. In practice this happens very rarely, except in the Netherlands where rumor has it that forgeries have been found.

Reservation fees and charges for sleeping accommodations on trains or aboard ships are not covered by the pass. Book these through your travel agent at home before departure.

Treat a Eurailpass like a cow. Milk it every day. Eurailpass gives you free the kinds of things you would want to do even if you had no other reason to buy the pass itself. The bonuses cover some six pages in the "Eurail Traveler's Guide." Read how best to use them in each section of this book.

Buy your pass through your travel agent or any of the Eurailpass-issuing offices listed in the Appendix. Buy them the year before a price hike because you have up to six months to validate them at any train station in Europe—which you do before boarding.

In a pinch, you can buy a Eurailpass at one of the forty-five Eurail Aid offices in Europe, but you must present your passport proving that you entered Europe within the last six months, pay a 10 percent penalty, and—more expensive, yet—pay in local currency.

## Eurail Flexipass

There was a time when European trains were blooming with flower children holding Eurailpasses and knocking about carefree from Narvik to Naples, but those days are by and large past.

Modern Eurailpass purchasers (but not necessarily Eurail Youthpass purchasers) are more likely to stop longer at a single destination. Eurailpass offers a surprising concept in Eurailpass travel to this new breed of selective adventurers. See if it will save you money.

The Eurail Flexipass changes your planning. You have new ground rules. It allows you to stay as long as you want in one place without squandering money you invest in the pass. Concentrate your time in fewer locations and range less far afield with your travel adventures. You pay in advance only for the nine days out of twenty-one that you use.

Flexipasses are ideal for you when you feel you are frittering away your investment unless you are constantly on a train. By choosing nine travel days within a twenty-one-day period, you save your money even when you decide to stay in one place for a week. Use this built-in freedom to rent a car, stay with relatives in the old country, sunbathe on a Greek isle, ski in Switzerland, or cross the channel to Britain.

The Flexipass is a do-it-yourself pass. You enter the date on one of the nine lines provided when you decide to board the train—or aboard the train quickly when you see the conductor starting to pass through—and travel that entire day as much as you want until midnight.

If you start your trip between 7 P.M. and midnight, you validate until the following midnight. You ride overnight or journey by sea and use up only one validation date while avoiding the cost of lodging.

When you travel overnight on one of the international crossings covered by the pass, choose to validate your pass for either the date of arrival or the date of departure to take advantage of connecting trains at both ends.

There is one difference you need to know: you replace a Eurailpass if lost or stolen by taking the validation coupon (which you keep separate from the Eurailpass) to one of the forty-five Eurail Aid offices in

Europe. You cannot replace Flexipasses. There is no separate validation coupon.

A twenty-one-day Flexipass costs about one-sixth less than the conventional twenty-one-day Eurailpass.

## Eurail Saverpass

Eurail gives a bargain for three or more adventurers traveling together first class for fifteen days during the summer (only two are required during the rest of the year). The problem is traveling together. Your group can't break up and go traveling off in separate directions and still qualify for the discount, which is about 30 percent.

When you tailor your traveling to these restrictions, you qualify for the good deal.

## Eurail Youthpass

When you are younger than twenty-six, you want to save money by choosing the second-class travel pass. Like the first-class Eurailpasses, fast-train surcharges are included in the price of the pass. Most of your friends and young Europeans will be traveling this way.

When you are traveling with your parents or older adults requiring a first-class Eurailpass (especially when they need you to qualify for a Eurail Saverpass) or when you want the extra comfort and greater flexibility of being able to ride the few remaining first-class-only trains, buy a full-fare Eurailpass.

Second-class travel is more crowded but every bit as scenic as first-class travel. Only in Italy is first class markedly superior, but when this bothers you, upgrade to first class by paying the difference in fare.

You buy Eurail Youthpasses for one- or two-month durations for about two-thirds the cost of Eurailpasses.

## National Rail Passes

So many American travelers use Eurailpasses on long European express trains that conductors' eyes sometimes blur checking the passes. When a conductor sees an adventurer flashing the colorful rail pass of the conductor's homeland, he adjusts his eyeglasses, smiles, and mentally snaps to attention.

Most national railroads of Europe have their own all-purpose rail passes valid for unlimited travel within their borders. Some are good deals you buy in advance in U.S. dollars. The most popular ways to save money—and have lots of fun—are the best-selling passes of Britain, Germany, France, and Switzerland.

These passes save you money in several ways. You pay less per day, you have the option of traveling second-class at lower prices, you take juniors with you and pay as little as half for their tickets, and you receive useful side benefits that are different from Eurailpass's bonuses. Read the details of them all in their respective chapters here.

The national passes and regional passes do not let you travel across unlimited national boundaries like the continent-wide Eurailpass, but when you plan to travel in a single country (or primarily in a single country) or two or three at most, you do well to consider buying these special passes available only to visitors. (Residents have their own promotional pass programs for which you are ineligible.)

## Rail/Drive Passes

A Rail/Drive pass can be an ideal marriage, but leave the driving to your spouse.

Some of your friends report good results driving through Europe in rented cars. They argue fiercely with others who advocate train travel. Both cite the relative convenience, cost, and ability to learn about and appreciate Europe while traveling by their favorite means.

Rental auto advocates insist that you can visit villages not served by trains, and thus take advantage of cheaper lodging; that you can drive to the front door of your destination and make detours on a whim.

Everyone who has traveled by train will tell you that you get on and off just as easily, cut a great deal of red tape and bother, and see more than when you are behind a wheel cursing crazy drivers or buried in a road map sorting out lines that don't seem to exist. You don't have to suffer the quirks of foreign automobiles, strange and sometimes dangerous rules of the road, nor searching out parking places and walking even greater distances through pedestrian malls from a parking place than from the train station. You can stay in cheaper suburbs and commute by train, and—this is important—learn much useful information and insight from the Europeans you meet in your train compartment.

Eurailpass, GermanRail Tourist Card, France Railpass, and BritRail Pass sell combination Rail/Drive programs you prepay in dollars.

The brainchild offered by Eurailpass/Hertz (through the offices of the French National Railroads) and Eurailpass/Avis (through GermanRail) might combine the best of both worlds. The Hertz EurailDrive Escape gives you five days' unlimited use of an economy-class car (manual transmission) added to the features of a Eurail Flexipass. GermanRail's combination adds a Eurail Saverpass to an Avis rental car.

Rail passes give you the freedom to travel easily over long distances. Your car gives you local transportation, delivers you to doorsteps of relatives, and takes you to special, secluded hideaways.

Hertz and Avis have locations throughout Europe, many in or near train stations. On average their European fleets are less than six months old and English-speaking personnel are on call twenty-four hours a day.

BritRail's, GermanRail's, and French Railroads' plans in connection with their national rail passes work similarly in cooperation with Hertz and Avis.

## Boarding Your Train

*Using subway and rapid-transit services—Finding your departure platform—Locating your proper carriage*

### Using Subway and Rapid-Transit Services

All of Europe's major cities have either a subway or a rapid-transit connection to their principal train stations—and usually both. Subways save you steps by bringing you directly into the platform areas in many stations ("Bahnhof," "Estacion," "Gare," "Stazione"). Rapid-transit trains from the suburbs (which in all cases you ride free with a Eurailpass except for Paris's regional electric trains, the RERs) sometimes let you off on platforms parallel to the one from which you leave.

Almost all major cities have two or more train stations. Be absolutely certain you go to the correct one. You don't want to carry your luggage into Paris's Gare d'Austerlitz only to find out your train is boarding at the Gare de Lyon.

### Finding Your Departure Platform

When you arrive, especially when you are in a hurry, immediately look for departure information. This could be in the form of numeric signs, clacking digital signs, huge electronic BritRail displays, or most common, yellow posters—"Abfahrt," "Avgaende," "Avgang," "Depart," "Lahtevat," "Partenze," "Salida," "Vertrek" (not the white ones, or the ones printed in red in the Netherlands; those are for train arrivals) —which confirm your departure time and tell you the number of the departure platform or track ("Anden," "Bahnsteig," "Binario," "Gleis," "Plattaforma," "Quai," "Raide," "Spar," "Spoor," "Spor," "Via," "Voie").

### Locating Your Proper Carriage

While you are walking to your platform, look for posters or glassed-in bulletin boards ("Composition des Trains," "Composizione Principali Treni," "Var i Taget gar Vagnen," "Vognenes Placering i Perron Afsnit," "Wagenstandanzeiger") with color-coded cutouts of lined-up locomotives and train carriages (couchettes, dining, first- and second-class, etc.). You may see these anywhere, but most often right in the center of your departure platform. It is easiest to pick out your train by its departure time.

On these posters you identify the carriage in which you have a reservation by its carriage number. Often, vertical lines or strings are superimposed to form a grid, and a "sector" letter (A, B, C, etc.) indicates where your carriage now stands or will stand. When your long InterCity (domestic) or EuroCity (international) train arrives, you will avoid rushing down the platform when you are already standing at the stopping sector for your carriage. When you have no reservation and are traveling by Eurailpass—and don't care which carriage you board— still determine where the first-class ones to your specific destination come to a stop.

While you are looking at the train makeup, look to see whether your train is carrying a buffet or restaurant car and where it is located relative to your carriage.

In French-language Swiss stations, instead of composition boards, the digital departure signs above the platforms give you the entire train makeup at the bottom: an arrow indicates the direction the train travels, a "1" indicates each first-class carriage, a knife-and-fork dining symbol indicates the restaurant car, and a "2" indicates each second-class carriage. Below this shorthand is a note in French telling at which sector the car for children will arrive. (These carriages are marked with a teddy bear and a "Kinderwagen" sign.)

When your train sweeps in, watch for striping above the window line.
•A yellow stripe indicates first class (blue dashes on some Dutch trains, none on most Spanish and German trains). When your train slows to a stop, begin walking to your carriage—but be sure to check that the signboard fixed to the outside (another is usually posted in the vestibule) agrees with your destination.

When you are carrying heavy luggage, leave it in the space usually provided at the entryways of salon carriages, but guard it carefully at station stops. When it is light, hoist it onto the overhead rack above your seat.

When you sit in a compartment, you have overhead privileges. Etiquette requires that you pile your suitcases in the space in the overhead rack directly above your seat and not distribute them randomly. This makes it easy to see that your seat is occupied even when you leave for a moment.

With a reservation, you have an assigned seat. Without one, you must be careful not to sit in one already reserved. These are marked with paper or plastic strips (usually yellow) inserted in seat backs or on hallway doors. On the other hand, when there is no slip or it says "non reserve" or "nicht reserviert," it is available. When the seat is reserved from Hamburg to Cologne, you are welcome to sit in it between Mainz and Basel.

In a compartment, try to sit next to the window facing forward. In a salon car, you can appreciate the scenery better by sitting next to a window at the back of the carriage.

## Arriving in Your City

*Changing your money—Locating a hotel room—*
*Reserving your train connection—Getting to your hotel*

When you leave your train you often pass into an underground passageway. The direction toward platform one leads you to the main hall. Here you usually find a change bank, train information office, and—in most countries—a tourist office nearby.

### Changing Your Money

The very first thing to do upon arrival is to change for local currency. Most adventurers use traveler's checks and most have some currency from the country they just left.

In most large train stations, the change banks are open long hours and give you the same rate you find at large bank offices on the street. Even when you receive a slightly less advantageous rate, you need enough local currency to get around until you visit a larger branch. Beware of any office of a nonbank. You can expect poorer rates and/or a heavy service charge.

Look for these signs: "Bank," "Cambio," "Change," "Valuutanvaihto," "Vaxel," "Wechsel," or "Wissel." Sign your traveler's checks (changing one $50 check instead of two $20s and a $10 is usually cheaper) when you reach the counter and pass it to the teller with your passport or a photocopy of your passport. Changing currency usually requires no passport. (Some stations have machines to do this.) Coins are seldom accepted. Avoid getting caught with very high denomination coins by changing them into paper before you leave. Spend the lower-denomination coins for provisions.

Bank credit cards are accepted everywhere. Get cash advances at banks with those logos posted.

### Locating a Hotel Room

Your second order of business is locating a room for the night. Some tourists scrupulously follow hotel recommendations in travel guides, but the rule is simple: the more you pay the more you get, and vice versa. Competing hotels on the same block with equal amenities charge virtually the same. In fact, ones recommended in best-selling guides may be able to charge slightly more because of their popularity with guidebook-reading disciples. Beware of hotels that guidebooks describe as "clean." When writers say nothing more positive, look elsewhere.

It's often worth a few minutes after your arrival just to go outside the train station and look around. Frequently you see an attractive or suitable hotel nearby. Some railroads own and operate hotels in or near their train stations. From 500 major train stations in Germany you can book ahead InterCity hotels in Hanover, Heidelberg, Mannheim, Munich, Stuttgart, and Ulm. In Cologne and Zurich, you will see clusters of hotels outside the back entrances.

In many large train stations there are two information offices—one operated by the railroads ("Auskunft," "Information," "Inlichtingen," "Neuvonta," "Oplysninger," "Reise Zentrum," "Renseignements," "Travel Centre") and one by the city tourist office. The personnel in the train information office won't be happy answering your questions about hotel rooms. Those in the city tourist office send you across the station for train information.

You often find the city tourist office ("Bureau de Turisme," "Tourist Information Centre," "Turismo," "Syndicat d'Initiative," "Verkehrsverein," "Verkehrsburo," "VVV") by looking for the information sign: i. It may in fact be adjacent to the train information office, a few doors down the street from the exit of the train station, across the street, in a kiosk in the plaza in front of the train station, or nearby but indicated by an arrow. When the city tourist office does not have a location serving the train station, often a commercial, profit-making organization performs the function of finding you a room. In many Swiss train stations you find electronic consoles with photos of hotels, their prices, indications of whether they are filled, a city map showing you their locations, and automatic, free telephone connections with their room clerks to make reservations.

The best time to arrive at the tourist office for a hotel booking is about 10 A.M. When you arrive at popular or convention destinations late in the afternoon or in the evening, you will find it very difficult or impossible to find a good room unless you have made reservations in advance. You may have to reboard a train just to find a soft place to sleep.

At the tourist office counter, specify how much you want to pay and the area you want to stay in. Staying near the train station is often convenient, but sometimes an off-color neighborhood is also nearby. The tourist office personnel advise you. You are usually charged a nominal service fee. Sometimes you must also leave a reasonable deposit, which is later deducted from your hotel bill, and are told to check into your assigned hotel within a specified period of time. This time is negotiable when you have errands to accomplish first.

## Reserving Your Train Connection

Before you leave the train station, go back to make your reservation for your next train. Reservations are not required for slower trains, but you must make reservations for better trains, except in Germany and Switzerland where Eurailpass holders don't pay the surcharge and travel without reservations.

For long-distance travel, always select EuroCity (EC) or InterCity (IC) trains. ECs promise you English-speaking personnel to help you on the departure platform and serve you on the train; dining cars, cafeterias, or at least a refreshments trolley; a free timetable; and minimal wasted time at intermediate stops and border crossings. For your own peace of mind, you should reserve seats on international express trains during busy travel seasons on Fridays, Sundays, and local holidays, especially from Amsterdam and through Scandinavia.

Not all booking agents can or want to be bothered speaking English. You save yourself many headaches by giving to the reservations agent a piece of paper showing your date of travel (numerals for the day, month, and year, in that order), the time you want to leave (using the twenty-four-hour clock), departure city with arrow pointing to destination city, whether you prefer a smoking or a nonsmoking ("Nicht Raucher," "Niet rokers," "Non-fumar," "Non-fumeurs," "Non fumatori") compartment or section, and present your note simultaneously with your Eurailpass and—if you wish—your bank credit card. (To conserve cash, consider using your bank credit cards to make as many Europewide advance reservations as possible in these countries which accept bank cards: Austria, Britain, Finland, France, Ireland, Spain, and Sweden.) Present all three at once. The minimum credit-card charge in France is thirty francs.

Agents in some countries require train numbers. In these cases, go first to the train information desk to find the number of your train and then to the reservations counter.

Usually reservations counters are separated into domestic ("Binnenland," "Inland," "Interieur") and international ("Ausland," "Buitenland") reservations. Make sure you don't stand in a long line at the wrong counter.

## Getting to Your Hotel

Many large train stations are served by rapid-transit trains and/or subways. There are almost always discounts available on the subways ("Metro," "Metron/Metroon," "Underground," "U-Bahn," "T-Bana") including blocks of tickets ("carnets") or strip-tickets, and passes for a day, a week, or longer.

Rapid-transit but not subway trains are usually covered by your Eurailpass. In the Munich Hauptbahnhof you find parallel "S-Bahn" and "U-Bahn" lines. Eurailpass covers only the former.

## *Sleeping and Eating throughout Europe*

## Adventures in Train Lodging

One of the great pleasures of train travel in Europe is waking up in a brand-new city, yawning, stretching, and peeking expectantly out of the train window at bright, quaint, and different surroundings that promise fresh, new adventures. Feeling vigorous and eager after a good night's sleep, you are ready to conquer exciting new worlds.

Europe's long-distance trains offer you a worthwhile saving of vacation time and dollars usually spent sleeping in hotel rooms. Overnight express trains with famous names weave convenient international webs through western European countries. Respected names such as Wiener Walzer, Nord Express, Viking Express, Arlberg Express, and Sud Express pull seemingly endless strings of first- and second-class coaches, sleeping cars, and couchettes.

Fully equipped sleeping cars ("Bedplaats," "Place-Lits," "Schlafwagen") are designed for demanding business travelers, but couchettes ("Liege-wagen," "Ligplaats") give you an excellent value for your money. These mini-dormitories with four or six bunks are usually your best buy for overnight train travel. Their popularity with adventurers and European families is well deserved.

You sleep two to a side in first-class couchettes and three to a side in second-class couchettes. The lodging cost is the same in both classes. The difference is the train fare. You receive more room in first class because you pay more for your ticket (or pass).

Reserve sleeping compartments on EuroCity Night and most international trains first- or second-class. The most expensive is the "Single" (S), available in first class. This is a twin-bedded first-class compartment with only the lower bunk used. A first-class "Special" (Sp) is a smaller one-bed-only compartment. The larger first-class compartment is also available as a "Double" (D), with the top bed folded down. When you are traveling on a second-class ticket, the compartments are called "Tourist 2" (T2) with two beds, either one above the other or two upper beds, across from each other, and "Tourist 3" (T3), with three beds in a tier, one above the other.

Nordic and British railroads offer inexpensive domestic sleeping-car accommodations instead of couchette accommodations. Three-berth sleeping compartments in Nordic countries cost very little. Compared to hotel prices, two-berth compartments on BritRail are a steal.

When you want to save even more by not reserving a couchette, you still sleep very well. Most trains' seats slide forward so that you can pull them together and change a day compartment into a bedroom.

Such a large fraction of adventurers spend their nights sleeping in day-coach compartments on the long-distance expresses that a certain etiquette has evolved. Most seats recline partially or collapse together by pulling forward at the bottoms. It takes no practice to make three parallel beds by pulling forward at the bottoms. This is so practical the whole passenger list does it, but it's a nuisance when the claustrophobic person nearest the window crawls over two sleeping people to get off the train at 3:30 A.M.

Wise overnight adventurers sit nearest the corridor so they can step out to visit the washrooms or snack bar, or even get off to buy a sandwich from a platform vendor during a lingering, middle-of-the-night stop. Overnight trains are usually in no hurry.

When you are only two riding in a compartment overnight, it is more comfortable to fold up the arm rests, stretch full-length along the seats, use a parka or even unsnap the padded headrests for pillows, and sleep soundly until morning. However, when the train is crowded and the compartments filled, you won't be able to stretch out. You spend the night uncomfortably avoiding your fellow adventurers' space. It's not pleasant on crowded trains; your best bet is a couchette or sleeping compartment.

Couchettes can be reserved and paid for up to two months in advance through a travel agent in America. When the dollar is weak, this will often cost less, even if there is a telex fee. In Europe, you make reservations at most large train stations. All national railroads but Portugal's and Greece's have connected, computerized reservations systems, but the Nordic system does not interface with the one to the south. When couchettes are not completely sold in advance, you usually see a railroad agent selling couchettes at a reservations counter set up next to the train to accommodate last-minute arrivals. When making a couchette reservation, specify which level bunk you prefer. Some adventurers prefer top bunks because they are most private and give them space for their carry-ons; some prefer bottom bunks because they are most convenient. No one prefers middle bunks.

The glamorous Wagons-Lits sleeping-car system is a thing of the past, although you occasionally see a sleeping carriage still carrying an old Wagons-Lits logo. These have more or less been replaced by nationally owned trains and seven international trains classified as EuroCity Night Trains. The German, Scandinavian, and British railroads operate their own independent services and equipment.

Be on the lookout for the EC Alfred Nobel between Hamburg and Stockholm or Oslo, the EC Galilei between Paris and Venice or Florence, the EC Komet between Hamburg and Brig or Chur, the EC Palatino between Paris and Rome, and the EC Stendhal between Paris and Milan. These are the EC Night Trains.

The EC Barcelona Talgo between Paris and Barcelona, the EC Paris-Madrid Talgo, and the Barcelona-Madrid Talgo are upscale trains carrying only deluxe sleeping cars.

All the various sleeping-car configurations are not always on a given train or even in every country. Even international couchettes can be a surprise. A couchette originating in Zurich, Switzerland, for Amsterdam, the Netherlands, runs mostly through Germany, but uses an Italian Railroads' carriage staffed with a Danish porter.

When you board carriages fitted with couchettes, depending on the time of night, the standard bench seats usually have already been converted into bunks. Otherwise, passengers agree when it is time for them to convert them. All Europeans know how. Bright and early in the morning, train employees clear the bedding and reconvert the couchettes to regular seating for daylight travel.

Your porter leaves a plastic-wrapped package containing a blanket, a sheet-bag, and a pillow for every bunk. The sheet-bag is partially fitted like a bottom sheet to keep it from slipping, but there is no way to tuck in the blanket. It is always a tussle between you and gravity to keep your blanket from dropping to the floor. You stretch out quite comfortably, but undressing is discretionary in mixed company.

You would not expect such a difference in comfort between air-conditioned, first-class couchettes, and second-class ones (which may or may not be air-conditioned). The extra space created by removing two bunks and two people is astonishing. When you travel on a first-class pass or ticket on a French or Italian train (these two railroads offer first-class couchettes), the couchettes are a dream. On the other hand, many adventurers find it more comfortable to sleep in an air-conditioned first-class sitting compartment than a second-class, six-passenger, natural-ventilation couchette—unless the sitting compartments are crowded.

Couchette porters (who hold the passports to show at frontier crossings so you need not be disturbed) often have a case or two of cold beer and soft drinks they are happy to sell when the journey begins. Many make their private compartments available for a pickup party of talkative international adventurers.

Budget adventurers in France should also investigate an innovation called "Cabine-8." These specially configured sleeping carriages provide eight semireclining contoured bunks, four per side, per compartment.

## Dining on Wheels

Large train stations have some sort of travelers provisions or grocery store you should visit. One of the more important things to buy for long trips is a liter or two-liter plastic bottle of mineral water with a resealable cap. Some people bring canteens with them. A Swiss army knife with a bottle opener and corkscrew is even handier.

Dining on European trains ranges from white-tablecloth service on the best EuroCity trains, the TEE (Trans Europ Express train from Paris), Switzerland's Glacier Express, and InterCity trains in Germany, Italy, and Switzerland, to well-presented cafeterias on Scandinavian trains and German "Holiday" trains (where they are called "Quick-Pick"), to meals served at travelers' seats on BritRail's InterCities, French TGVs, Spanish Talgos, the Italian Pendolino, and Switzerland's Gottardo, and lastly, to wheeled refreshment trolleys (called "mini-bars") on most long-distance trains, overflowing with local specialties, sandwiches, pastries, and refreshments.

As you would expect, prices are higher aboard trains than in stations and higher in stations than in local supermarkets.

## Avoiding Problems

For simplicity, this book has dropped all the umlauts, accents, and other pronunciation marks you see as you travel. The Thomas Cook timetable retains all local spellings.

Will you have language troubles? None. Most of the words you need to know to travel by train are obvious. Pictographs (illustrated in the free rail pass reference materials you send for) are used throughout Europe—and you won't need them in Britain. You have found already most of the important word translations in this book.

City names are generally the same as in English. Just a few baffle: Copenhagen is Kobenhavn; Florence is Firenze; Venice is Venezia in

Italian, Venedig in German; Antwerp is Anvers in French, Antwerpen in Dutch; Geneva is Geneve in French, Genf in German; Munich is Munchen in German, Monaco in Italian; Vienna is Wien; Helsinki is Helsingfors in Swedish; the Danube is the Donau; Hauptbahnhof is German for main train station and Bahnhof refers to any train station.

It's advisable always to travel as though you were trekking through New York's Times Square, but it is never so dangerous. Except for areas of high drug activity and unemployment, most adventurers report smooth and safe travel. Paranoia is not worth your mental effort, but caution is. (One publicized incident where travelers on a night train were reputedly gassed and robbed sounds as likely as flying saucers.) Carry little cash, use traveler's checks, and keep separate the pink copy of your traveler's checks, the detached Eurailpass stub, and a photocopy of your passport and credit cards.

# Switzerland

## Vital Tips for the Trains
## of Switzerland

Swiss trains are best, according to travelers' votes. They are characterized by frequent service, punctuality, impeccable maintainence, helpful
personnel (who often speak English), comfort and cleanliness, and
service to the tiniest and most colorful villages.

Switzerland comes close to being a train travelers' paradise.

Keeping track of the Swiss train companies is like tabulating a can of
alphabet soup. The Swiss Federal Railroads has nine initials—three for
each of the three largest language groups: SBB (Schweizerische
Bundesbahnen) for the German-speaking region, CFF (Chemins de Fer
Federaux Suisses) for the French, FFS (Ferrovie Federali Svizzere) for
the Italian. Coaches carry all three designations but you'll see "SBB" in
this book. Nearly a hundred additional companies operating private
railroad lines, funiculars, ships, and cable cars advertise their particular
initials in one or more languages.

You need not worry. Swiss planners have efficiently coordinated all
schedules (usually with hourly departures), posted them for you to see
in every station, and grouped them in a single official timetable
("Indicateur," "Kursbuch," "Orario"), which for your convenience is
revised only once a year in two volumes, one for trains (with a winter
supplement for international connections) and one for buses. You can
buy it from the Swiss National Tourist Offices listed in the Appendix.

When you trace the outline of Switzerland on a map, it's all bulges
and squeezed-out extrusions. Vertically, it's even tougher—and the

23

Swiss have accommodated it with adventurous trains. In addition to the four described here, don't overlook adventuring on the Brunig line between Lucerne and Interlaken (SBB's only narrow-gauge line), the Gotthard route between Lucerne/Zurich and Lugano, the Lotschberg and Simplon Tunnel routes, the narrow-gauge RhB (Rhaetian Railroads) connections to Arosa, Scuol, and other mountain resorts, and the Centovalli line between Locarno and Domodossola, mostly on Italian soil but covered by the Swiss Holiday Card (see below).

Switzerland's flagship train, with meals served at your seat, is the two-class EuroCity Gottardo between Zurich's airport station and Milan. French TGVs from Paris reach Berne, Lausanne, and Geneva, with on-going deluxe Swiss trains to Milan.

A crossroads of Europe and a popular destination, thirty-three EuroCity trains take you to, or across, Switzerland. SBB, itself, has three kinds of trains: regional, fast, and InterCity. SBB's entire fleet of forest green and light gray IC trains is outfitted with "noiseless" carriages (50 percent less interior noise). They reach 100 mph between Martigny and Sion, 87 mph near Baden. When you ride them you will find they are utilitarian, but not flashy. All carry orange-colored, sit-down restaurant carriages with white linens, tables for two or four, waiters in white jackets, and excellent cuisine prepared in on-board kitchens.

## Airport Trains

You will find it very convenient to use SBB's excellent airport trains in Zurich and Geneva. Both airports are connected by long-distance IC trains not only to city centers but also directly to international destinations. At the Zurich airport, stop by train information (i) to have your Swiss Holiday Card or Eurailpass validated, then proceed via escalators (direction: "Bahn/Railway") using the escalator-friendly luggage carts. At Geneva's airport, you merely push your cart on ground level across to the adjacent terminus to catch your train.

Check your luggage through to your destination at special "Welcome Luggage" counters. This can be a convenience when you must change trains. Luggage checked at airport stations is given preference. You usually pick it up when you arrive at your destination. The cost is seven Swiss francs per piece. Normal checking of your luggage point-to-point will take more time than you expect.

Swissair allows their departing passengers to check in, receive boarding passes, and check their luggage at Berne, Lausanne, and Zurich train stations.

## Swiss Holiday Card

Swiss Holiday Cards are versatile. You receive travel on the SBB, most of Switzerland's privately owned railroads (more than the Eurailpass), most of the lake steamers, and all of the Swiss postal buses. In addition, you receive discounts on many mountain funicular and private lines. Further, you may ride public transportation (streetcars and buses) in twenty-four cities including Basel, Berne, Geneva, Biel, Zurich, Winterthur, Baden/Wettingen, Lausanne (including the funicular to Ouchy), La Chaux-de-Fonds, Fribourg, Lugano, Locarno, Neuchatel, Olten, St. Gallen, Schaffhausen, Solothurn, Aarau, Thun, Lucerne, Zug, and Montreux/Vevey.

You buy Swiss Holiday Cards for four, eight, fifteen days or a month, either for first- or second-class travel. Children from six to sixteen pay half-price. First class costs about 60 percent of a Eurailpass. You save still more when you buy the cards for shorter periods or second-class travel—still quality travel in Switzerland.

You often see parked in front of train stations yellow-and-white buses with bold red stripes and posthorns front and side. These are the famous Swiss postal buses you can ride free with a Swiss Holiday Card. Of the thousand or so routes you may wish to use, the most exciting include the transit of Italy from Lugano/Menaggio/Chiavenna/St. Moritz and the dazzling routes over the Susten, Furka, Neufenen, and Gotthard passes from Meiringen and Andermatt.

You may also take free cruises on Lakes Geneva, Constance, Zurich, Lucerne, Thun, Brienz, Neuchatel, Biel and Murten, on the Untersee, that segment of the Rhine River between Schaffhausen and Kreuzlingen, and on the Aare River between Biel and Solothurn. You will find it very enjoyable to break your travels with restful day outings on these big white steamers. The most beautiful way to enter Geneva is by lake steamer.

## Half-Fare Travel Card

The Swiss federal government subsidizes (on grounds to reduce air pollution) a card valid for half-fare travel on *all* public transportation (not city buses or streetcars) at extremely reasonable prices. One in four Swiss (on average, one person in every family) owns one. You buy them, valid for one month or one year, in U.S. dollars.

Although you pay half-fare for some trips that Eurailpass or Swiss Holiday Card holders ride free, you will frequently come out ahead when your travel is lighter than it would take for a Swiss Holiday Card to pay for itself or when you travel on routes not fully covered, such as to the Jungfraujoch, Schilthorn, and Gornergrat.

For longer stays or multiple visits to Switzerland, buying a year Half-Fare Travel Card is essential. Otherwise you would have to buy several Swiss Holiday Cards. Analyze your itinerary before making a purchase, but it is a good bet that a half-fare card will save you money.

## Using Eurailpass Bonuses

Most of the railroads and the same lake and river steamers listed above (50 percent off for crossings of Lake Constance) honor the Eurailpass, but with certain exceptions. Not participating in the Eurailpass program (but in the Swiss Holiday Card arrangement) are the Furka-Oberalp Railroad (FO)—which you will need to use on the Brig-Disentis segment on the Glacier Express and the Goschenen/Andermatt connection with the Gotthard line—the BVZ Railroad between Brig and Zermatt, and the Bernese Oberland Railroad (BOB) between Interlaken Ost and Grindelwald/Wengen.

Swiss Holiday Cards and Half-Fare Travel Cards are sold at the Swiss National Tourist Offices in New York, San Francisco, and Toronto (see addresses in Appendix). Eurailpasses are sold in New York and San Francisco, as well.

## Regional Holiday Season Tickets

When you are interested in traveling in only one particular region, it is worth investigating Regional Holiday Season Tickets. These are summer-season travel passes for one region, valid for fifteen days of which you choose five days for unlimited travel and ten days for travel at half-fare.

The regions participating in this discount program include: Montreux/ Vevey, the Vaudois Alps, the Bernese Oberland, Central Switzerland, Sargans/Wallensee, and Graubunden. In the Central Switzerland region, you may also buy a seven-day pass including two days of free travel. The regions of Locarno/Ascona and Lugano offer unlimited seven-day passes.

A 20 percent discount on the purchase of these regional passes is given if you already hold a Swiss Holiday Card or Half-Fare Travel Card. Purchase them at train stations of the regions you are visiting.

Now that you have your travel pass, all aboard for these four Swiss train adventures: the Glacier Express from Zermatt, the Bernina Express to the Italian border, the railroads of the Jungfrau Region, and the Panoramic Express from Montreux.

## Glacier Express
## Flowering with Adventurers

Glacier Express train service between Zermatt and Chur or St. Moritz has flowered since tourism officials discovered, with surprise, that an adventurous train trip could attract visitors without any additional expenditure or spoiling of the landscape.

One train a day since 1930 was sufficient until adventurers discovered the excitement of traveling above the Rhone and Rhine rivers along their valleys to their sources at the Furka Pass. The newest timetable shows Glacier Expresses *B, C, D, F, G,* and *K,* three a day in each direction. Glacier Expresses *A* and *H* are reserved for travel groups and feature three specially built panoramic dome cars similar to the ones on the Panoramic Express.

This train curiously has always been named "Glacier Express," in English and French, although you pass through three language regions (French, German, and Romansch). When the Furka tunnel was opened in 1982, the Glacier Express moved from summer-only service to a year-round delight.

Make reservations in advance, unless you only use the segment between Chur and Disentis carried by the Rhaetian Railroads (RhB). Seat reservations cost six Swiss francs.

Glacier Express trains *B, C, F, G* and *K* carry a dining car (the newest one seats sixty) serving lunch, but you should make dining reservations in advance. There are never enough seats to accommodate all travelers. The conversation piece is the Glacier Express wineglass (for sale) with a bent stem so that, in theory, you face it one way uphill and reverse it downhill. In fact, you worry more about your wine sloshing over when you are traveling horizontally. Train *D,* the late departure from Zermatt, carries a dining car from Andermatt to Chur, with service beginning at 3:20 P.M. This is sufficient for afternoon tea and drinks.

When you arrive at the Zermatt train station, you are immediately drawn into that magical square in front of it bubbling with enchantment and leading to the fairy-tale main street lined with hotels and shops designed in the characteristic architecture made fashionable by the Seilers, the family of hoteliers who established Zermatt in 1855. The Bahnhofplatz is dominated by horse-drawn carts and is filled with charm. You are welcomed by parties of bell captains and drivers in black hotel caps, ready to lead you in a horse-drawn carriage to your nearby hotel. In winter, riding in the horse-drawn sleighs gives you the feeling of being in a winter wonderland.

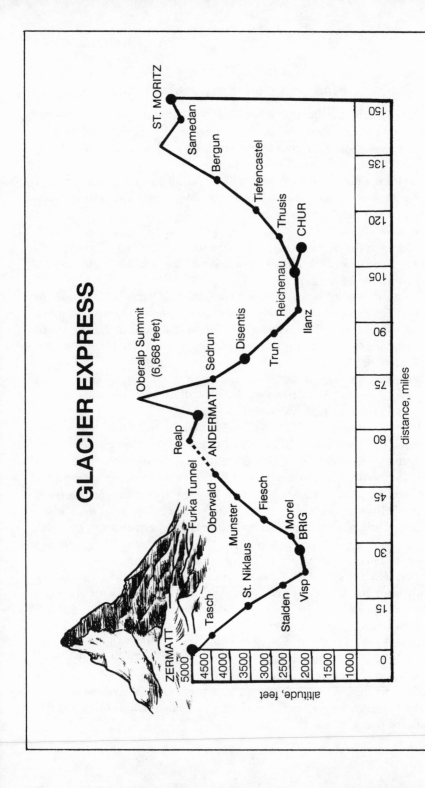

GLACIER EXPRESS

distance, miles

altitude, feet

When you clear the sparkle from your eyes, you see that Zermatt's modern Gornergratbahn station stands opposite the train station on one side of the Bahnhofplatz and a Swiss chalet housing the tourist bureau stands on the other. The tourist office is open 8 A.M. to 8 P.M., Monday to Saturday, and 4 to 8 P.M. on Sundays.

While you are in Zermatt, take a journey up the world's first electrified rack railroad, the Gornergratbahn, for one of the most rewarding mountain train adventures in Switzerland. The Matterhorn (and there is no competition) is one of the world's most-photographed natural wonders. It dominates the scene throughout most of your journey and you see increasingly magnificent views of the surrounding peaks as you climb.

From the Gornergrat (10,132 feet), extend your excursion still more by climbing farther to the east on the 2.8-mile cable line to Stockhorn (11,588 feet) on the highest open-air transport in the Swiss Alps.

Leaving Zermatt, the Glacier Express retraces your cogwheel train up, because there is no other way to Zermatt, but it is worthwhile revisiting the 1 1/2 hours of smashing scenery, passing cataracts, rushing waters, and tall, wooden Valais houses and storage barns, or Spychers, protected from rats by stones.

A powerful red BVZ railcar, required for the steep upward climb, pulls your Glacier Express train out of Zermatt. (The BVZ accepts Swiss Holiday Cards, but not Eurailpasses.) The red carriages are narrow, because of the slim gauge, but still offer ample space to first-class passengers riding two-opposite-one. Their interiors are bright, warmed by Scots-plaid, vinyl upholstery—red in the smoking section, green in nonsmoking.

You follow your path on diagrams inserted in the utility table below your window showing altitude relative to distance to St. Moritz. St. Moritz (5,822 feet) and Zermatt (5,261 feet) surmount each end, but on the way you climb to 6,668 feet at the summit, Oberalp Passhohe.

At Randa, seven miles down the Glacier Express route, you see the Dom rising up one side and the Weisshorn up the other. These are the highest peaks in the Alps after Mont Blanc and Monte Rosa. Descending another eight miles, you pass through Brattbach tunnel, 428 feet long, and a series of concrete avalanche shelters. Officials realized these were necessary to maintain Zermatt as a winter sports center when the winter avalanche of 1931-32 buried the line.

The BVZ lives in mortal fear of road building. Rail travel is profitable here. The BVZ is one of the few narrow-gauge railroads turning a profit. The renewals and reconstruction were undertaken on a guarantee from federal and cantonal authorities that no road would be built up the Visp valley above Stalden, but this promise lapsed in 1952. A highway from Tasch to St. Niklaus was authorized in July 1961.

When your train stops in Tasch, the point closest to Zermatt accessible by car, you look out on the parking lot. It is said that this is the largest parking lot in Europe. Since 1965, the BVZ has maintained hourly bus service between St. Niklaus and Visp and even runs a school bus between Stalden and Visp.

In Visp, your BVZ train stops in the street in front of the SBB station. Your final 5 1/4 miles of the meter-gauge BVZ parallel the tracks of the SBB. The BVZ segment makes it possible for you to travel by meter-gauge lines from the top of the Gornergrat, 211 miles to Tirano in Italy, with only two changes, at Zermatt and St. Moritz.

Brig is a major railroad junction of north-south and east-west trains. Your BVZ train runs into the south side of an island platform in front of the SBB station with road traffic rushing past on both sides. You can easily connect here between the narrow-gauge BVZ and Furka-Oberalp Railroad (FO) trains and those of the standard-gauge SBB and BLS (Berne-Lotschberg-Simplon Railroad) to Italy.

The FO takes over in Brig, but you do not need to change trains. You travel to Oberwald through the scenic and broad upper Rhone valley at 3,300 to 4,300 feet. The valley supports farms and farmhouses on both sides of the line. There is always one snowcapped peak at the end which is replaced by another when you reach there. Dense pine forests clothe the lower slopes of the mountains. Above, you make out high Alpine pastures and still higher summits covered with snow the year around.

Your train climbs steadily from Brig except for abrupt steps typical of glacial valleys, at Grengiols, above Fiesch, and below Gletsch. Above Grengiols, the valley is known as the Goms. At these steps, the valley also narrows, forcing your train to use loops, spirals, or a rack, or even all three, to overcome the height.

After you pass through the chestnut forests surrounding the village of Morel, you feel the cogwheels chattering as you climb to Fiesch.

Leaving behind the Rhone valley's picturesque villages, you reach the reddish-brown Oberwald station (4,480 feet) where your train swings into the all-weather Furka tunnel, the longest narrow-gauge train tunnel in the world, which permits the Glacier Express to operate all year round. Special flat cars transport automobiles through the Furka tunnel in winter when the Furka pass is closed, which is a great convenience for skiers, but it deprives you of views of the Rhone glacier. You must now take a postal coach to approach this azure glacier.

**Connections with Basel/Zurich**

| A* | B | C | D | | | F | G | H* | K |
|---|---|---|---|---|---|---|---|---|---|
| .... | 1427 | 1627 | 1827 | dep. | CHUR | arr. 0847 | 1041 | .... | 1133 |
| .... | 1550 | 1750 | 1950 | arr. | Zurich (Hbf.) | dep. 0723 | 0910 | .... | 1010 |
| .... | 1603 | 1803 | 2003 | dep. | Zurich (Hbf.) | arr. 0712 | 0900 | .... | 1000 |
| .... | 1702 | 1902 | 2102 | arr. | Basel (SBB) | dep. 0613 | 0758 | .... | 0858 |

## *Bernina Express*
## *The Impossible Takes a Little Longer*

You roar into the cliff of the black Landwasser tunnel, your Bernina Express throttled wide open, soaring high above the stream and over the treetops, riding the summit of an unseen viaduct without guard railings. It is like flying—or falling.

This climax of the 6 1/2-mile section from Tiefencastel to Filisur follows your crossing of two famous viaducts. First you pass the Schmittentobel viaduct, 6.1 miles out of Tiefencastel. Its seven arches rise 118 feet. Then, out of a 164-foot tunnel, you quickly glimpse ahead the five classic arches of the 1903 Landwasser viaduct curving to the right and the river far below. The viaduct's 400-foot span rests on 213-foot piers, and its celebrated southern arch plunges you directly into the Landwasser tunnel.

The Albula line is a triumph of creative railroad engineering. Your powerful, green, electric locomotive "Rhaetia" climbs through so many extraordinary spirals and tunnels up the Albula valley that it resembles a model engine racing through every complicated loop, tunnel, bridge, cloverleaf, and dramatic overpass that an ingenious toy shop display can conjure.

Your locomotive's speed of 30 to 35 mph seems heady, given the acrobatics, but your narrow-gauge coach swings around tight corners so smoothly that you don't feel frightened—even at the edges of sheer cliffs. You are too preoccupied watching the extraordinary views.

The Rhaetian Railroads (RhB) introduced the best train on this line, your Bernina Express, in 1973, for a one-day excursion through a rarely visited corner of Switzerland. It is also used for passage to Italy.

There are two Bernina Expresses southbound. Express *A* departs Chur at 8:47 A.M. in the summer only, stopping at just a few stations and not serving St. Moritz. Ten minutes later, the year-round Express *B* leaves with cars for St. Moritz which are separated in Samedan, so you must be sure to be on the right cars for Tirano. Past Pontresina, *B* operates almost like a local, stopping in twenty villages, which adds

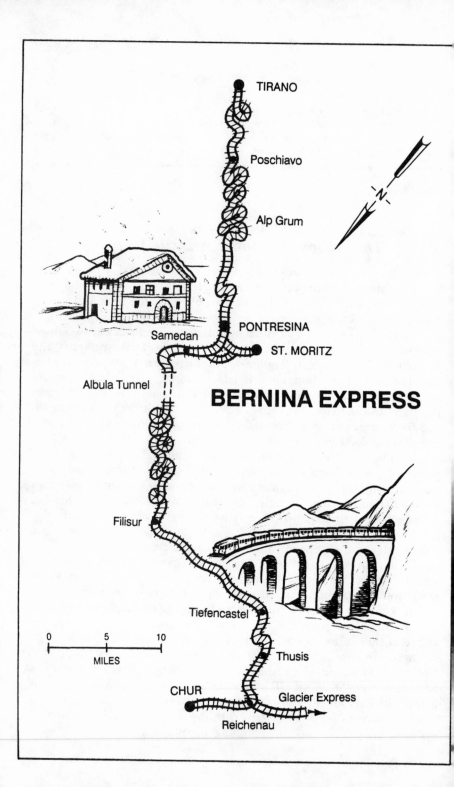

about forty minutes to your travel time but also to the enjoyment of your trip.

Northbound, Express *C* runs only during the summer and makes every stop from Tirano to St. Moritz, but does not run past St. Moritz, so you must change to *D* in Pontresina. Express *D*, also summer-only, runs the faster timetable, Tirano to Chur.

Passengers on fast trains *A* and *D* are charmed by English-speaking hostesses with information about the area outside, but single travelers must pay a surcharge of six Swiss francs which includes a seat reservation. Eurailpass and Swiss Holiday Card travelers are exempt, unless they want a seat reservation.

The red cars of the RhB leave from the front of Chur's SBB station. On the first stretch from the mountain capital of Graubunden canton, you will be traveling on the Albula line. Between Pontresina and the Swiss border across from Tirano, Italy, you will be riding on the Bernina line.

RhB is a private company serving the mountainous cantons of eastern Switzerland. To please both railfans and lovers of Graubunden canton, it is celebrating its one-hundredth birthday in 1989 with various events between April and October. Your seats in its first-class spic-and-span salon cars are comfortable, two-opposite-one, and highlighted by red (for smoking) or green (nonsmoking) Scots-plaid seat covers. RhB accepts Eurailpasses and Swiss Holiday Cards for free passage.

During your 2 1/4-hour, fifty-five-mile trip from Chur to Pontresina, you pass through forty-two well-engineered tunnels or galleries totaling more than ten miles (well over a quarter of the mountain segment). The line's 108 bridges and towering viaducts of arched rock and stone come to nearly two miles.

You leave Chur down a broad flat valley with forested mountains on both sides. You see corn; cows; big, busy factories; and churches with onion-shaped steeples.

Hikers push the panoramic windows down from the top to admit fresh mountain air. Photographers lean out, snapping photos nearly the whole length of the trip. In winter, skiers and beautiful people traveling to St. Moritz are warmly dressed. The train passes through the most agreeable summer and winter mountain climate in Europe.

The tracks paralleling your train's line are three-railed. This is so both the narrow-gage RhB and the standard-gauge SBB cars can share the same works and electric lines.

You first follow the Rhine valley to Reichenau where the Inner Rhine (Hinterrhein) comes from the south to join the Outer Rhine (Vorderrhein) beneath the Castle of Reichenau. The two rapid rivers churn together, mixing their chalky blues and cloudy whites of melted snow and glacier runoff.

You pass steep and thickly wooded slopes with villages and ruins of feudal fortresses secluded in green foliage. Bends are so sharp that you can see both the locomotive and the end of the train. Past the gray-plaster Thusis station house you travel eight miles through the Schyn gorges to Tiefencastel, one-third in tunnels and one mile over early twentieth-century viaducts. The sturdy, hand-built stone bridges complement the wonderful scenery rather than cheapen it.

The view here is very good from the left side, but the backseats of the carriage give a better panorama of the unfolding landscape outside. The nonsmoking section is longer and offers wider views. The murky tints of the blue-white waters of the Albula River run far below your twisting train on the mountainside.

The valley widens again and you see the Tinzerhorn mountain group ahead. Change to the right side for better views of the breathtaking scenes you are approaching. Past Tiefencastel, the Albula River runs fast and the valley becomes more and more wooded with fir trees, larches, and arolla pines. At this point you cross the Schmittentobel viaduct and roar into the Landwasser tunnel, as described at the beginning of this section.

Like many admirers of the Landwasser viaduct, break your journey at Filisur station (boarding a local train later on) to walk down the footpath and inspect the dramatic structure from below.

The most difficult terrain of your trip is on the 5.8-mile segment from Filisur to Bergun. You climb one foot for every twenty-eight traveled. The Albula valley becomes narrower and you become more steeply walled-in. In this short section, you pass through fourteen tunnels and over eight viaducts.

The next section to Preda is the highlight of your trip. "Slow but sure" is the watchword you appreciate during this stretch.

The direct distance to Preda from Bergun is 4 miles. Engineers have bent your line into such extraordinary contortions of loops and spirals that you actually travel 7.6 miles, including 1.7 miles through seven tunnels. If you climbed directly, you would climb one foot for every sixteen, but the expensive spirals and reversals of direction safely reduce your grade to one in thirty.

Plan to change from side to side to watch the elegant contortions. Look back for at least three extraordinary sights of the pleasing village of Bergun while your train climbs higher and higher.

You enter the Engadine region. Engadine architecture is so unique and bright that it sets the region off from the rest of Switzerland more distinctly than if you had crossed a frontier. The houses you see are white and thick-walled, with small, irregularly spaced windows widening outwards. Their most distinctive feature is their "sgraffito" (now you know where the word "graffiti" came from). Masons covered rough, gray plaster with coats of white limewash and then artfully scraped away the wash to bring out charming gray scrolls, interesting geometries, and fascinating embroideries.

From Preda, your Rhaetia picks up speed through the 3.6-mile Albula tunnel. It seems to go on forever. It is the highest (6,242 feet) principal tunnel through the Alps and the most expensive and difficult engineering work of the RhB.

When you emerge from the Albula tunnel at Spinas, clumps of larch have reappeared and your train is pointed downwards. You cross and recross the Beverin River at Bever and then run down the flat floor of the Inn valley above the Inn River. The colors of the glorious peaks of the Bernina massif ahead through the Pontresina Gap are vivid. The air is electrified with natural radiation.

Railroad hands separate Bernina Express *B* in the large, modern Samedan station at 10:45 A.M. One portion goes to St. Moritz. Your half goes to Pontresina and onto the Bernina line, the highest in Europe without cogwheel assistance.

Both St. Moritz and Pontresina—all the villages of the Engadine region, in fact—welcome tourists. The inhabitants speak Romansch, Switzerland's fourth national language, but the area is so international that English is widely understood. Bring extra money if you can, especially to St. Moritz, but if you can't, inexpensive lodging catering to adventurers is easy to find.

Besides more aerial acrobatics, the Bernina line presents you with another distinction: it is a joy to photograph. You are able to focus on the magnificent scenery through pulled-down panoramic windows while traveling along at only a snail's pace. Trains south of Pontresina average only 20.5 mph, including stops, which is slower than the Glacier Express.

Beyond Pontresina, the valley becomes wider with every mile. Panoramas open on every side while your train runs high on the mountainside on tracks that were laid to avoid spoiling the beauty of the Taiser Forest. Past the Berninabach Falls bubbling with froth in early summer, you turn your lens to the right for a splendid picture of the magnificent Morteratsch glacier and the most glorious peaks of the Bernina range, especially Piz Bernina itself, a double rocky summit of 13,261 feet.

Your Bernina Express reaches the summit at Bernina Hospiz (7,403 feet), where winter lasts seven months. You have climbed 5,973 feet by simple adhesion—even more than any Swiss rack railroad with cogs.

Lago Bianco to your right, covered by ice until late May, was originally four lakes but it was dammed to form a reservoir for Brusio power station, forcing the railroad to be moved some thirty feet higher. From here you descend through the 630-foot Scala tunnel, the Pozzo del Drago tunnel (a dragon is rumored to lurk in the nearby lake), and an avalanche gallery to reach Alp Grum (6,858 feet).

It is time for lunch. Your Bernina Express carries a refreshments trolley where most passengers buy snacks, but the brownstone Alp Grum station is an amazing place to disembark for lunch (and then continue on one of the four later trains). You enjoy vast views over the Palu glacier and its surrounding peaks. There is also an Alpine garden. Most thrilling of all is the view from above the tracks on the terrace of the upper restaurant down the Poschiavo valley to blue Lake Poschiavo, 4,231 feet below and only 6.8 miles away. The trains calling at the toylike station below look like those on a scale-model railroad.

Your climb from Pontresina has been relatively easy. Descending follows a route that required surveyors to perform near miracles. To reach Poschiavo, your train has to drop 4,034 feet through larch and spruce forests in a horizontal distance of only 4.7 miles. Engineers solved this problem by designing a series of cautious, cascading cuts, circular tunnels, sharp zigzags and astonishing loops.

First you descend to the right in a semicircle, passing below Alp Grum station to the 833-foot Palu tunnel, in which you make a three-quarter turn and emerge down the mountain. For a second time you pass below the restaurant terrace into the 948-foot Stabline tunnel, emerging on the back slope of Alp Grum before doubling back through the 745-foot Pila tunnel and returning below the terrace for a third time.

In less than ten minutes, you look up from Cavaglia (5,553 feet) to see the restaurant at Alp Grum, now 1,305 feet above you. The forests have turned to deciduous trees: hazel, aspen, alder, and birch.

Your coming descent to Poschiavo is the most miraculous of all. Your train makes four more zigzags and tunnel turnarounds. You see Poschiavo first on the left and then four more times on the right while your train loops above the towers of the city. Photographers race back and forth across the carriage in order to capture all of the kaleidoscopic scenery.

Past Miralgo (whose name, "Look at the Lake," refers to your view), you again descend steeply to Brusio. Here your train's crossing of the raised, looping stone viaduct having only a 164-foot radius—an open spiral—brings highway traffic to a stop.

Italian passport control at Campocologno is performed on the train. Then your Bernina Express continues down the valley past vineyards, fig trees, and tobacco plantations, across a steel bridge over the pressure pipes of the Brusio power station (which generate electricity powering the line), and past the Renaissance pilgrim's church of the Madonna di Tirano to the Italian frontier at Tirano, a pleasant little town of mountain houses and terraced vineyards.

You either return on the Bernina Express, or continue on Italian trains to Milan's Centrale station. Be sure not to arrive at Milan's inconvenient Porto Garibaldi station—you will have to ride the subway to the Centrale station for onward connections.

## Bernina Express Service

### Connections with Basel/Zurich

| | | | | | |
|---|---|---|---|---|---|
| 0554 | 0613 | dep. | Basel (SBB) | arr. | 2202 |
| 0700 | 0716 | arr. | Zurich (Hbf.) | dep. | 2100 |
| 0710 | 0723 | dep. | Zurich (Hbf.) | arr. | 2050 |
| 0841 | 0847 | arr. | CHUR | dep. | 1919 |

### Bernina Express

| A* | B | | | C | D* |
|---|---|---|---|---|---|
| 0847 | 0857 | dep. | CHUR | arr. | 1851 |
| .... | 0908 | arr. | Reichenau-Tamins | .... | .... |
| .... | 0927 | arr. | Thusis | dep. | 1822 |
| .... | 0930 | dep. | Thusis | arr. | 1820 |
| .... | 0947 | arr. | Tiefencastel | dep. | 1804 |
| .... | 0948 | dep. | Tiefencastel | arr. | 1803 |
| 0946 | 1001 | arr. | Filisur | dep. | 1750 |
| 0947 | 1003 | dep. | Filisur | arr. | 1749 |
| .... | 1016 | arr. | Bergun (Bravuogn) | arr. | 1737 |
| .... | 1033 | arr. | Preda | .... | .... |
| .... | 1045 | arr. | Samedan | .... | .... |
| .... | 1052 | dep. | Samedan | .... | .... |
| 1033 | 1059 | arr. | PONTRESINA | dep. | 1702 |
| 1042 | 1105 | dep. | PONTRESINA | arr. | 1628 | 1654 |
| 1124 | 1155 | arr. | Alp Grum | arr. | 1543 | .... |
| 1200 | 1232 | arr. | Poschiavo | dep. | 1503 | 1540 |
| 1201 | 1239 | dep. | Poschiavo | arr. | 1457 | 1538 |
| 1209 | 1248 | arr. | Le Prese | arr. | 1448 | 1531 |

**Bernina Express**

| A* | B | | | | C | D* |
|---|---|---|---|---|---|---|
| 1229 | 1312 | arr. | Campocologno | dep. | 1426 | 1511 |
| 1231 | 1317 | dep. | Campocologno | arr. | 1418 | 1506 |
| 1238 | 1325 | arr. | TIRANO | dep. | 1410 | 1458 |

*Summer only.

**Connections with Milan**

| 1240 | 1334 | dep. | TIRANO | arr. | 1225* | 1440 |
|---|---|---|---|---|---|---|
| 1322 | 1418 | dep. | Sondrio | dep. | 1150* | 1344 |
| 1508 | 1536 | dep. | Lecco | dep. | 1007 | 1230 |
| 1600 | .... | arr. | Milan (P. Garibaldi) | dep. | .... | .... |
| .... | 1625 | arr. | MILAN (Centrale) | dep. | 0910 | 1150 |

*Twenty minutes earlier on weekends and holidays.

---

## Railroads of the Jungfrau Region
## Top of Europe

### The North Face of the Eiger

After burrowing through the solid rock of the Eiger for several miles, Eigerwand station is startling. You hear "Ahs" as your train passes portals glowing with reflected white light. Folk music plays on the platform. It gives you an eerie feeling to be at this treacherous location where climber after climber tried and failed to scale the wall outside until finally, in 1938, the sheer face was conquered for the first time.

Passengers surge from the train to a set of twelve plate-glass picture windows—enough for everyone—revealing an amazing view of the Grindelwald valley, some 6,000 feet below. From the portals you look out onto the very center of the Eiger North Face.

The Railroads of the Jungfrau Region carry you to a land of snow and ice you cannot possibly reach otherwise unless you are a competent Alpine climber accompanied by guides.

Interlaken Ost (for "east") train station is your stepping stone to the Jungfrau region. The narrow-gauge Jungfrau Railroads' system departing from platform 2 takes you to the highest train station in Europe, a score of great mountaineering centers, and the spot where James Bond confronted his archenemy in *On Her Majesty's Secret Service*.

When you travel from Interlaken Ost to the Jungfraujoch, the highest train station in Europe, your route takes you through Grindelwald

# RAILROADS OF THE JUNGFRAU REGION

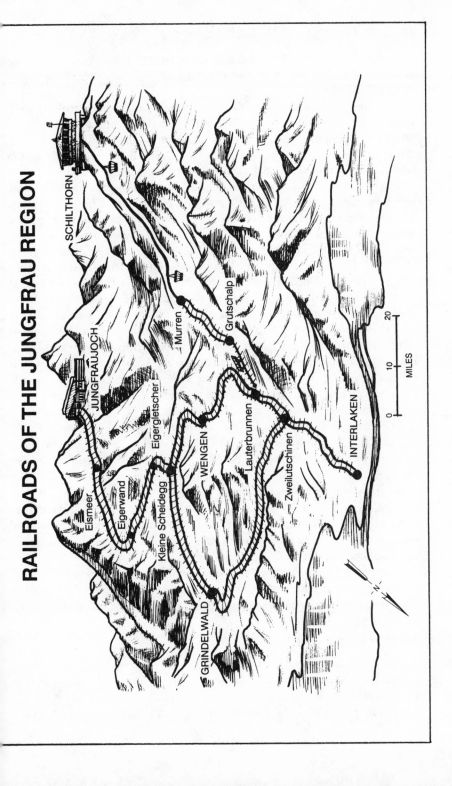

to Kleine Scheidegg, where you board the Jungfrau Railroad. Returning to Interlaken Ost, you descend through Wengen on the Wengernalp Railroad (WAB).

Traveling from Interlaken Ost to the Schilthorn takes you on four spectacular means of travel. You leave the WAB at Lauterbrunnen, board the funicular to Grutschalp, transfer to the mountain Murren Railroad, and top your adventure with a dramatic gondola ride to Piz Gloria, at the top of the Schilthorn (9,748 feet).

When you have taken both the Schilthorn and the Jungfraujoch trips, you judge the question: "Which is the more adventurous?" The Jungfraujoch is more famous and gives you things to do at the top—a museum, ice palace, "Toporama," and more. The Schilthorn gives you a stunning panorama, a thrilling ascent, and Piz Gloria of James Bond fame.

Your climb to the Jungfraujoch is expensive (the Schilthorn adventure is less expensive). Eurailpasses are not accepted past Interlaken Ost and Swiss Holiday Cards will take you only as far as Grindelwald (although the cards come in handy again during the Schilthorn trip). Because of the cost, do not invest in this trip when it is cloudy at the summit. The tourist office next to the extravagant Grand Hotel Victoria Jungfrau, a ten-minute walk from the Ost about halfway to the West station, will give you reliable advice before you set out. At the same time, check to see if there is currently an early-morning departure (before the connecting trains from Zurich and Geneva arrive) at reduced prices.

The brown-and-tan cars of the Bernese Oberland Railroad (BOB) marked for Grindelwald take the Grindelwald valley. Those in front marked for "Lauterbrunnen" travel up the Lauterbrunnen valley for Wengen, Lauterbrunnen, and the funicular to Grutschalp.

Your first stop is Wilderswil. Several Swiss with walking boots and Alpine walking sticks get off for the rack-and-pinion railroad to Schynige Platte.

Shortly before making your second stop, you get your first teasing view of the great white Alps in the distance. You feel a surge of anticipation.

Crossing a frolicking river to Zweilutschinen, you arrive in the yard where the two sections of your train are separated. Zweilutschinen is the meeting point of the two Lutschinen torrents, the White Lutschine and the Black Lutschine.

## To the Jungfraujoch

Your car to Grindelwald runs along the raging Black Lutschine, carefully banked with flagstones on the left. Contrary to its name, it is white with melted glacial runoff.

Climbing the Grindelwald valley, you see tall chalets scattered on the left. On the right you hear bell-tolling cows. Outside your pulled-down window you can almost pick a dazzling horticultural bouquet of delicate white wild flowers. A river on your right charges down over huge boulders and the waterfall dropping from above makes a rainbow arc from the sun.

Now you come round a bend, revealing a vision. The magnificent Eiger towers like a giant wall, its peak hidden in flying clouds. You look to the left and there is the Schweizerhof hotel with its red shutters. Now your train coasts to a stop in the brown-shuttered Grindelwald station (3,392 feet).

On an unforgettable site, Grindelwald, the "Glacier Village," is the center of the eastern Jungfrau Region, and looks like a Swiss village should look. Each chalet is neatly arranged and tucked under a tree, balconies are swept, geraniums are in full bloom and fuchsias flower from every window box. Firewood is corded neatly and stored symmetrically under the eaves. In the fields, hay is carefully stacked.

Grindelwald has changed with the times by adding a few key hotels and a modern indoor swimming pool, but it has not lost its essential mountaineering charm or its good mountain air. The tourist office (open 8 A.M. to noon and 2 to 5 P.M., closed Sunday) is three to four minutes to the right up the main highway from the station.

You quickly change to the waiting, thirty-one-inch-gauge, green-and-buff WAB train carriage which starts out down the mountainside past gardens filled with fruit and great dahlias of all colors before stopping at Grund station. Then it zigzags up the opposite mountain slope for its approach to Kleine Scheidegg.

This is a playground for long lenses. You see model farms, summer houses, hotels, chalets, churches, and cows with bells swinging on their necks.

At the Brandegg stop (4,272 feet), your ears pop. The clang of cowbells wafts through the lowered windows. The animals look uncomfortable on the steep mountainside as they take the last clumps of green grass.

Past Alpiglen (5,252 feet), your train enters a snowshed and then clanks through a double-tracked passing-point. The landscape has scattered trees, stubborn shrubs, and a marshy look. You pass through more snowsheds with extruded steel uprights for strength.

Kleine Scheidegg (6,762 feet) comes into view. From a distance, the big hotels look like those found on a game board. The sounds of a lilting alphorn serenade you as you climb off into a semicircle of hotels and restaurants. On this ledge connecting the Lauterbrunnen and Grindelwald valleys, you can cross to one of several large restaurants facing the station. Crowds of adventurers bask in the sun and enjoy the outdoor service on sunny days. Usually you will see a man in full Swiss folk costume playing an alphorn. You can order a nice lunch, a pair of sausages with potato salad, or just a beer while you listen to the melodious sounds of the alphorn and relish an incredible view of the Eiger, immense before you like a wall.

The shingled train station is more of an intersection where you board a thirty-nine-inch-gauge, chocolate-colored Jungfrau Railroad's carriage for your trip to the summit.

So formidable were the difficulties of working at this great altitude that sixteen years were required to complete the 5 3/4 miles upward from Kleine Scheidegg. Even then, the track ended at the Jungfraujoch, 1 1/4 miles and more than 2,000 feet below the summit of the Jungfrau, its intended goal.

Immediately after you start to climb, you have wonderful views back on Kleine Scheidegg and the Eiger glacier close on the right glaring brightly at you. When you near the glacier you see its detail, the scalloping and furrows caused by runoff, and you appreciate the vastness of it even more.

Your climb is so steep that those facing forward are thrown against their seat backs and those facing backwards brace themselves to keep from sliding out of their seats. Be sure to choose a forward-facing seat on the right side.

Your first stop is the stone Eigergletscher (Eiger glacier) station (7,612 feet). This is where the construction crew in 1898 established a colony of 150 workers just below the perpendicular North Face. Now you see the repair shop for the Jungfrau Railroad just below the entry to the long tunnel ahead.

Surging ahead, you enter the 4.4-mile tunnel gallery where you will spend some forty-one minutes in darkness. Travelers exclaim and push up the windows because of cold air suddenly blasting on them. Heat percolates from under the seats. You sit two-opposite-two in one-class, fancy seats more spacious than the other narrow-gauge trains of the Jungfrau region.

You climb so steeply that when you pass the horizontal sign "Open all year round," it appears cocked at an angle. The maximum gradient would be one foot in four on a direct route, so a corkscrew tunnel had to be constructed. The curved course allows you to stop at two intermediate stations with extraordinary views.

A gong sounds. Now you hear yodeling. Then an impersonal, recorded greeting in German and then French and English announces a five-minute stop at Eigerwand, the "Face of the Eiger" (9,400 feet).

From Eigerwand your train curves slightly more than ninety degrees in order to continue its climb. It runs through a tunnel scarcely big enough for one train only. You wouldn't dare walk alongside.

Less than a mile farther, now below the southeastern face of the Eiger and 10,368 feet high (a job which took the tunnelers two years to excavate), you reach the Eismeer (Sea of Ice) station. A hollow has been carved out of the rock big enough to hold a double track, so that ascending and descending trains pass one another. Once again you hear yodel music and an announcement for a five-minute stop. Here you see a view over the ragged surface of the glacier toward the Wetterhorn, the Schreckhorn, the Fiescherhorner, and the great crevasse under the Monchsjoch.

Your final segment lifts you only 970 feet, so the designers flattened the gradient from one in four to one in sixteen feet (except for the last 1,640 feet). For many years this stretch was carried by ordinary adhesion, at just more than eleven miles an hour, but now the line is rack-and-pinion throughout.

The Alpine world of the Jungfraujoch (11,336 feet) is decorated with the banners of many nations. Take the elevator to the Sphinx panoramic platform; visit the scientific exhibit. When you get hungry, dine in a restaurant or cafe. This is a wonderful complex of mountain restaurants, ice sculptures, husky dogs, mountaineering, the "Toporama" slide show, and breathtaking views at the Top of Europe.

Departures are half-hourly during the summer. If you miss one there is always another carriage waiting for you. You will be warm and satisfied after your magnificent day, and you won't be alone dozing on your way down.

## To the Schilthorn

For this adventure, board a BOB car in Interlaken Ost that is marked for Lauterbrunnen, or take the WAB to Lauterbrunnen from the Jungfraujoch. Remember that Eurailpass is not valid here. In Lauterbrunnen, disembark and cross the street to the sign over the "cave" opening: "Bergbahn Lauterbrunnen-Murren." Your climb in the stepped, sixty-passenger funicular will surprise you with its steep incline and length.

When you reach the upper terminus you immediately board the waiting Murren Railroad, a four-car brown-and-white electric tram which takes you 2 3/4 miles horizontally to Murren. You will see one of the grandest views of the world here. The magnificent presence of the Jungfrau seems only a stone's throw away across a precipitous chasm. On your return, a casual walk from Murren to Grutschalp will long remain one of your fondest memories.

When this tram reaches Murren, disembark and walk through the village fifteen minutes to the Schilthornbahn—there is only one street through Murren so you can't get lost. You pass every shop conceivable for a small village and carefully tended, flower-covered chalets as pleasant as any. Benches along the way offer places to break your walk.

You join the Schilthornbahn at its second stage. The first stage drops riders to the valley floor (free with the Swiss Holiday Card) in 100-passenger gondolas for a postal bus connection at Gimmelwald.

Your second-stage, swinging, eighty-passenger red gondola with white "Schilthorn Bahn" lettered in front (reduction with a Swiss Holiday Card) glides over the spacious Blumental ("Flower Valley") in a cable span of 3,038 yards supported by only two intermediate pylons. You appear simply to glide up a threatening rock face to a stop at the top of a towering bastion. You look down on unbelievable rock formations sculpted by snow and glaciers. Then you look down on the glaciers.

At Birg, you change gondolas. Birg (8,781 feet) has a restaurant and sun terrace. Your second gondola is a single-cabin for 100 persons. Between Birg and the summit, you see the scenery unfolding in all directions until you see the Black Forest and Mont Blanc appearing in the distance and the Jungfrau Alps face you. This span is 1,931 yards long—the longest unsupported span in the country. You notice even the gondola operators look exposed and weatherworn and wear dark glasses and sun creams. Finally you see some venturesome, hearty Swiss outside clambering down the snow. Your gondola swings to a final stop and you feel as daring as James Bond himself when he took those last few steps here to meet his archenemy in *On Her Majesty's Secret Service*.

As you saw in that film, Piz Gloria is a round building. The restaurant revolves in fifty-minute cycles past a continuous circle of picture windows that show off sectors of the 360-degree panorama. There are revolving restaurants and other revolving restaurants, but none have prepared you for the sense of the Swiss Alps rotating around you while you enjoy hearty Swiss specialties to the melodies of a mountain accordionist. Below, there is a self-service cafeteria with modest prices.

On the sun terrace, deck chairs are especially valued by travelers who have trouble with the high altitude. The red-and-white Swiss flag fluttering overhead seems planted as a backdrop for your photographs.

## Typical Service
## Railroads of the Jungfrau Region

Interlaken—Grindelwald—Kl. Scheidegg—Jungfraujoch

| | | | | |
|---|---|---|---|---|
| 0931 | dep. | INTERLAKEN OST | arr. | 1626 |
| 0936 | dep. | Wilderswil | dep. | 1621 |
| 0946 | dep. | Zweilutschinen | dep. | 1613 |
| 0953 | dep. | Lutschental | dep. | 1606 |
| 0959 | dep. | Burglauenen | dep. | 1559 |
| 1003 | dep. | Schwendi | dep. | 1555 |
| 1009 | arr. | GRINDELWALD | dep. | 1548 |
| 1015 | dep. | GRINDELWALD | arr. | 1525 |
| 1025 | dep. | Grindelwald Grund | dep. | 1520 |
| 1054 | arr. | KLEINE SCHEIDEGG | dep. | 1432 |
| 1102 | dep. | KLEINE SCHEIDEGG | dep. | 1421 |
| 1112 | dep. | Eigergletscher | dep. | 1412 |
| 1158 | arr. | JUNGFRAUJOCH | dep. | 1331 |

Interlaken—Lauterbrunnen—Wengen—Kl. Scheidegg—Jungfraujoch

| | | | | |
|---|---|---|---|---|
| 0931 | dep. | INTERLAKEN OST | arr. | 1600 |
| 0936 | dep. | Wilderswil | dep. | 1555 |
| 0945 | dep. | Zweilutschinen | dep. | 1545 |
| 0954 | arr. | LAUTERBRUNNEN | dep. | 1535 |
| 1005 | dep. | LAUTERBRUNNEN | arr. | 1520 |
| 1019 | arr. | WENGEN | dep. | 1503 |
| 1026 | dep. | WENGEN | arr. | 1457 |
| 1043 | dep. | Wengernalp | dep. | 1432 |
| 1051 | arr. | KLEINE SCHEIDEGG | dep. | 1423 |
| 1102 | dep. | KLEINE SCHEIDEGG | arr. | 1421 |
| 1112 | dep. | Eigergletscher | dep. | 1412 |
| 1158 | arr. | JUNGFRAUJOCH | dep. | 1331 |

Interlaken—Lauterbrunnen—Murren—Schilthorn

| | | | | |
|---|---|---|---|---|
| 1031 | dep. | INTERLAKEN OST | arr. | 1530 |
| 1036 | dep. | Wilderswil | dep. | 1526 |
| 1045 | dep. | Zweilutschinen | dep. | 1518 |
| 1054 | arr. | LAUTERBRUNNEN | dep. | 1508 |
| 1100 | dep. | LAUTERBRUNNEN | arr. | 1456 |
| 1111 | dep. | Grutschalp | dep. | 1445 |
| 1128 | arr. | MURREN | dep. | 1428 |
| 1140 | dep. | MURREN | arr. | 1420 |
| 1155 | dep. | Birg | dep. | 1410 |
| 1159 | arr. | SCHILTHORN | dep. | 1401 |

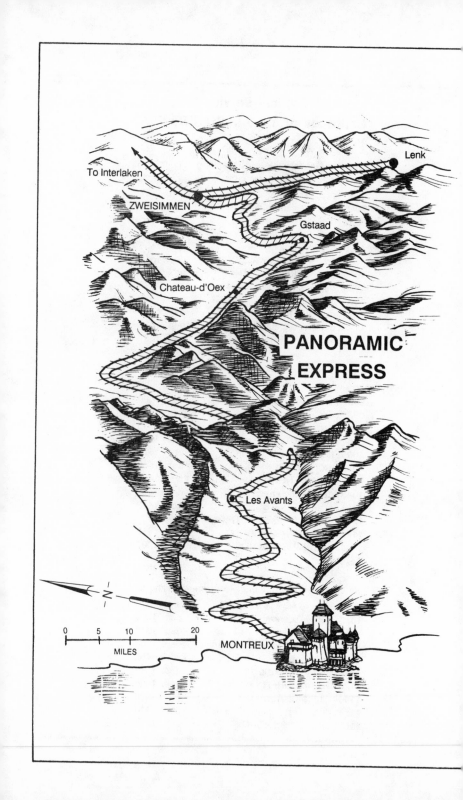

## *Panoramic Express*
## *A Taste of Gold*

Your blue-and-white electric power car curls back and forth, up through terrace after terrace of lush vineyards. You look down on Montreux's freshly whitewashed hotels, patina-green copper roofs, and brown wooden chalets getting smaller and smaller. The little strip of town set upon the only place the Swiss could find for it between the steep Vaudois Alps and the "Vaud Riviera" on the shores of Lake Geneva never loses its charm.

You have powerful views from the Panoramic Observation Car of the narrow-gauge Montreux-Oberland-Bernois Railroad (MOB). Daily Panoramic Express trains carry four panoramic cars with rooftop windows at forty-five degrees.

The Super Panoramic Express train will surprise you even more. It also carries a "chalet" car and a spectacular nose car in which twelve lucky passengers in three rows sit in front of, and below, the driver, with nothing between them and the rushing scenery but wraparound glass. The experience is the only one of its kind in Europe—but these seats cannot be reserved. You must arrive early to find a choice front-row seat.

When you ride the Super Panoramic Express from Montreux you ride in one of the best trains in Europe (and one of the few remaining first-class-only ones). These glassed wonders show you beautiful scenery in a way no other carriage can.

The "Super" runs only on weekends and holidays. If you can't fit the Super into your itinerary, the Observation Cars of the wonderful daily Panoramic Express still give you an outstanding show.

Although you can also start the Panoramic Express in Lenk or board it in Zweisimmen, the shimmering glare off Lake Geneva during a westward afternoon descent to lakeside blinds your view. It is always more scenic to make this trip going eastward from Montreux.

There is no better place to stay before beginning or after ending your Panoramic Express trip than Montreux. The flower-scented promenade here is one of Europe's most beautiful. Montreux occupies a lovely site sheltered from the wind on the eastern end of Lake Geneva and known for the mildest climate north of the Alps. Tourists enjoy excursions, water sports, tennis, and just strolling along the promenade. Snow in winter falls only a few hundred feet above the town.

Montreux's train station is oddly arranged on the side of a mountain. You reach platform No. 1 for the SBB to Lausanne/Geneva/Geneva Airport by climbing stairs or by elevator. Platform No. 5, where you board the Panoramic and Super Panoramic, is next to the MOB office. Climb the stairway to the left.

The tourist office is down the stairs in front of the train station; go to the promenade and 1,000 feet to the left (south). The steamers circling the Lake of Geneva dock nearby before proceeding around Chillon Castle. (They, too, are free on Eurailpasses and Swiss Holiday Cards—even for landings in France.)

To reach the train station from the lake steamers, walk left and up the steps. Agents at the tourist office will give you a free Panoramic Express color brochure and map to increase your pleasure. Of course, they will also make hotel arrangements.

Board your Panoramic Express in Montreux and enjoy this next adventure. As your train weaves farther up the mountainside, Lake Geneva shrinks and becomes dwarfed by gray, snow-streaked French Alps towering in the background. With a view like a satellite in the sky, you can pick out the casino and the red-and-white Swiss flag over the Montreux Palace Hotel. The tall building you see near the lake was built in 1964, when high-rises were the rage. It is a condominium boasting a twenty-sixth floor restaurant. The Eurotel to its right was built the same year. It is the second-tallest in town. You see lake hamlets like Vevey and Lausanne to the north, and the Rhone River valley to the south stretching toward the Simplon Pass.

The Panoramic Express has two first-class cars and two second-class cars. Traveling first class, passengers sit two-opposite-two with nine rows per carriage. Second-class passengers sit the same in fourteen rows per car. The difference is the amount of legroom and the comfort of the upholstery. Because about 90 percent of your car is glass, be thankful for the air-conditioning which overcomes the greenhouse heating.

The hillside above Montreux is famous for its trees and flowers. You pass through grape arbors to an altitude of nearly 2,000 feet, past walnut trees to 2,300 feet, and among fruit trees to 3,250 feet. Wild narcissus sparkle in springtime.

On your left you see the first of the charming chalets like those in the Bernese Oberland; they give you a warm first impression of the celebrated Golden Pass route, which rivals the Glacier Express for the most spectacular east-west route in Switzerland. (The Golden Pass route can be taken by disembarking the Panoramic Express at Zweisimmen for the train to Interlaken.) Looking up through the oblique windows reveals the crests of the Alps and gives you great depth of perspective. You feel inspired by the devastating height of the Alps above you.

Your final memory as you cross the crest is a long view down the valley to Chillon Castle, with a white Lake Geneva steamer gliding into dock.

Over the summit and through a long tunnel you enter the wholly different Sarine valley. Your Panoramic Express Observation Car picks up speed on the single, narrow-gauge track. The conductor with a blue-and-white MOB winged emblem pinned to his black cap (patent leather visor) accepts your Eurailpass or Swiss Holiday Card with a smile. The MOB is one of Switzerland's private railroad companies honoring both.

Now you are riding through cuts in the limestone mountainsides past Les Scieres. Brown-and-white contented-looking cows graze in the tall, green grass. Families harvesting hay wave at you with green handkerchiefs, glad of an excuse to lean on their wooden rakes. Most passengers wave back. The brown-and-white cows shake their heavy bells and more or less ignore them.

The valley is wild and green, but above, the limestone Vaudois Alps you see through the oblique windows form flat-topped ridges and throw long shadows. You regret that your train seems to rush. You wish it would slow down so you could study the rugged mountain crests, the peaceful valleys, and the randomly scattered, typical houses with broad, graceful eaves, intricate woodwork, and flower boxes overflowing with bright yellow and blue blossoms.

Looking at the homes, the dress, and the work, you form an impression of the way of life of these mountain people who speak French, are generally Protestant, and decorate their farmhouses profusely. They live in tidier versions of those you will see only a half-hour ahead in the Bernese Oberland, the region that gave our language the word "chalet" and this form of house synonymous with Switzerland the world over. They have low-pitched roofs and wide eaves on four sides.

Your Panoramic Express stops next in Chateau-d'Oex (say "Chateau Day"), at 3,083 feet. The traditional architecture here is magnificent. This is the typical family resort of the Vaudois Alps, with public pool and skating rink and a high lift to La Braye on the summit above.

You pass through Rougemont station (3,254 feet), remarkable for its carved wood decorations. The huge sloping roof below the train that catches your eye covers an early Romanesque church built on the site of an eleventh-century, Cluniac priory. Swiss from all over the country travel here to visit the church and the adjacent sixteenth-century castle.

The quaint Saanen station (3,364 feet) marks the point where you leave the Sarine valley and enter German-speaking Canton Berne. Some houses here, now adorned with climbing plants, date from the seventeenth century. Saanen's old-fashioned character makes a good contrast with that of its booming neighbor, pricey Gstaad, only three minutes ahead.

In Gstaad, buildings get bigger. The hotels do well here in this smart village, one of Switzerland's premiere winter resorts and a quiet summer destination.

When your express train winds up the mountain overlooking Gstaad, the view back is ideal for photographers. Passengers cluster to the windows to take advantage.

Saanenmoser's train station (4,043 feet), with green shutters and cutouts in the shape of hearts, must be the most filigreed in the world. The station's dark brown wood sets off the white detailing and lace curtains on the windows.

Picking up speed, you sweep down the Saanenmoser depression. Spiky Alpine peaks stand in the distance and farmhouses defy the pull of gravity on both slopes of the valley.

Your trip is nearly over when you arrive on the valley floor at Zweisimmen (3,090 feet). This is your junction for Lenk and Spiez/Interlaken, the route known as the "Golden Pass" leading onto the Brunig line to Lucerne. Tracks 1 and 2 (forty-two-inch gauge) are devoted to your blue-and-white narrow-gauge train from Montreux. Tracks 3, 4, 11, and 13 (sixty inches) lead SBB trains to Spiez. Construction underway will permit trains to continue to Spiez and on to Lucerne without change. This segment is due to open in 1991.

Almost everyone changes for the dark-blue-and-white carriages of the Bern-Lotschberg-Simplon Railroad (BLS) for the twenty-seven-mile run to Spiez. This private line also accepts Eurailpasses and Swiss Holiday Cards.

Those travelers to Spiez are back on big rails, but how disappointed they must feel when they look up for the view and realize they no longer have windows to see the high scenery.

Panoramic Express Observation Cars sit with the air-conditioning dead. After about five minutes, workers finish coupling on a new electric locomotive, the dispatcher waves his signal wand, and off they go—but in a surprising direction: not back up the mountainside. They travel twelve miles laterally, up the Simmental ("Tal" meaning valley) and arriving in Lenk fifteen minutes later.

The Simmen Valley is a showcase for beautiful farmhouses. Every year a panel of judges selects the most beautiful farmhouse in Switzerland and every year a farmhouse in the Simmental either wins or ranks high.

The village of Lenk (3,500 feet) is another of those wonderful summer and winter mountain resorts of which Switzerland seems to have no end. Whether for a lunch before continuing or for an extended vacation, Lenk is a pleasant stay.

## Super Panoramic and Panoramic Express Service

| (A) | (B) | (A) | (B) | | | | (B) | (A) | (B) | (A) |
|-----|-----|-----|-----|------|----------------|------|------|------|------|------|
| 0856 | 1000 | 1400 | 1420 | dep. | MONTREUX | arr. | 1144 | 1215 | 1702 | 1902 |
| .... | .... | .... | 1430 | dep. | Chernex | dep. | .... | .... | .... | .... |
| .... | 1024 | .... | 1444 | dep. | Les Avants | dep. | .... | .... | 1642 | .... |
| .... | .... | .... | 1503 | arr. | Montbovon | dep. | .... | .... | .... | .... |
| .... | .... | .... | 1504 | dep. | Montbovon | arr. | .... | .... | .... | .... |
| 0953 | 1057 | 1457 | 1519 | arr. | Chateau-d'Oex | dep. | 1043 | 1125 | 1604 | 1804 |
| 0954 | 1059 | 1459 | 1521 | dep. | Chateau-d'Oex | arr. | 1041 | 1124 | 1602 | 1802 |
| .... | 1108 | .... | 1531 | dep. | Rougemont | dep. | 1030 | .... | 1553 | .... |
| .... | .... | .... | 1537 | dep. | Saanen | dep. | .... | .... | 1547 | .... |
| 1010 | 1116 | 1516 | 1540 | arr. | Gstaad | dep. | 1020 | 1108 | 1544 | 1744 |
| 1011 | 1118 | 1518 | 1542 | dep. | Gstaad | arr. | 1018 | 1106 | 1542 | 1742 |
| .... | .... | .... | 1551 | dep. | Schonreid | dep. | 1010 | .... | .... | .... |
| .... | .... | .... | 1555 | dep. | Saanenmoser | dep. | .... | .... | .... | .... |
| 1036 | 1145 | 1545 | 1610 | arr. | ZWEISIMMEN | dep. | 0950 | 1041 | 1515 | 1715 |
| 1049 | 1150 | 1550 | 1649 | dep. | Zweisimmen | arr. | 0928 | 1018 | 1508 | 1708 |
| 1107 | 1205 | 1605 | 1707 | arr. | LENK i. S. | dep. | 0910 | 1000 | 1453 | 1653 |

### Connections

| | | | | | | (B) | (A) | (B) | (A) |
|------|------|------|------|-----------------|------|------|------|------|------|
| *1105 | 1221 | 1621 | dep. | ZWEISIMMEN | arr. | 0939 | 1039 | 1439 | 1639 |
| 1151 | 1257 | 1657 | arr. | Spiez | dep. | 0903 | 1003 | 1403 | 1603 |
| 1201 | 1301 | 1701 | dep. | Spiez | arr. | 0859 | 0959 | 1359 | 1559 |
| 1221 | 1321 | 1721 | arr. | INTERLAKEN (Ost) | dep. | 0839 | 0939 | 1339 | 1539 |

*Local train.
(A) Super Panoramic Express (Weekends and Holidays Only).
(B) Panoramic Express (Daily).

# Britain
# and Ireland

## Vital Tips for the Trains
## of Britain and Ireland

To understand how easy it is to get around Britain by train just realize
that Britain has more track per square mile than any other country.
More than 15,000 trains a day traveling over 12,000 miles of track take
you to more than 2,400 stations throughout England, Scotland, and
Wales. London has eight mainline stations accessible by Underground.
London's Underground takes you to and from Heathrow Airport.
British Railroads' (BritRail) Gatwick Express train speeds you to and
from Gatwick Airport.

Travel in Britain has until now centered on BritRail's core electrified
West Coast line from London to Glasgow and its East Coast line
featuring diesel-powered, 125-mph InterCity 125s between London
and Edinburgh.

You feel the effects of BritRail's biggest current project, the six-year
program electrifying the East Coast mainline between London and
Edinburgh. It is proceeding in three stages. BritRail has already opened
the London to Peterborough and Peterborough to Doncaster (with a *Y*
to Leeds) segments.

Electrification is due to be completed in May 1991, when the segment between Doncaster and Edinburgh opens and new electric trains
cut your time for the 400-mile trip between London and Edinburgh to
only 4 1/4 hours. Until then you will encounter some shifting about of
train scheduling between East Coast and West Coast lines. Some trains

are already being powered by a new class of locomotive, the 125-mph "Electra." Look for its sloped profile.

All of BritRail's name and InterCity trains carry first-class (look for the yellow stripe) and standard-class (BritRail calls its second class "standard class") carriages. Most of the locals consist of standard-class carriages only. Some of these are quaint, with separate doors leading to each compartment.

BritRail's blue-and-white Sprinter railcars—the latest in high-tech diesels—cut your journey times by about 10 percent. They are faster (up to 75 mph), more comfortable (standard class only), and more reliable than the older diesel railcars and locomotive-hauled trains they replaced. By 1990, you will ride nothing but Super Sprinters in Scotland.

Trainphones are common on BritRail's IC trains. You pay for your calls, national and international, by using a "Phonecard," which you buy in advance at train stations and elsewhere.

BritRail's premium trains are Pullmans, IC trains with tables preset with linens and bright flowers. Advantages include meals and light refreshments served at your seat, upscale speed, convenience, and punctuality.

American Express sponsors Pullman lounges at London's King's Cross and Euston stations, Leeds, Newcastle, Glasgow, and Edinburgh, but for entry you need an AMEX card or a Pullman card and a ticket.

## IrishRail

With a Eurailpass, it is not expensive to make Ireland your gateway to Europe. IrishRail, which honors the Eurailpass, is an arm of the Irish Transport Company, "Coras Iompair Eireann" (CIE), which also runs the CIE intercity buses, DART (Dublin's state-of-the-art electric regional transportation), and all city buses.

IrishRail is the most convenient way to go into the country for Eurailpass holders. Make Dublin your rail hub to reach all popular tourist centers. Dublin has three main train stations: Connolly, Pearse, and Heuston. Connolly and Pearse are connected by DART, which is free with your Eurailpass. Bus line No. 90 runs between Heuston and Connolly stations.

Travel times are short on IrishRail's modern, fully dieselized trains. Train journeys never take more than four hours—which is about the time it takes you to get from Dublin in the east to Tralee in the southwest. On mainline service you relax in comfort and watch the green Irish countryside. Waiters serve snacks or full meals—or even pints of Guinness—on the first-class service between Dublin and Cork.

To see completely the Republic of Ireland, supplement your train travel with the red-and-yellow CIE Expressway buses also covered by Eurailpass. Buses link every city and hamlet with mainline trains from stops usually in front of the train stations. Buy not only a train timetable but the Provincial and Expressway Bus Timetable.

## The London Underground

London's train stations, and Heathrow Airport too, are connected by London's busy subway system known as the Underground. When you buy individual tickets, remember to keep them to show the checkers when you exit.

The Underground's special unlimited-mileage subway pass for visitors, London Explorer, covers bus and subway travel over an area of 650 square miles and includes travel on the Heathrow Airbus and subway to the airport. With each pass, you get a guide to London and discount vouchers for tours of the Transport Museum, Covent Garden, Madame Tussaud's, London Dungeon, and London Zoo. When you visit London, use it to save money and avoid bunching at the electronic ticket vending machines.

Buy your London Explorer in London at the tourist information center at Heathrow Airport or major Underground stations in the city. You pay in pounds sterling for validities of one and seven days. In America, BritRail calls it the "London Visitor Travelcard." It is more convenient to buy it in the U.S., paying in dollars, at the same time you buy your BritRail pass.

For longer stays, buy in London a Travelcard for one-week, one-month, or one-year durations. A zonal system governs the cost and you supply a passport-sized photo.

The Underground system also boasts Britain's newest train (light railroad)—the Docklands, giving you views of London's old docks on the way to ancient Greenwich. Catch it at the Stratford Underground station on the Central line. It is covered by your Underground pass.

## Channel Tunnel

Construction of the Channel Tunnel between Britain and France is underway in both countries. You will be able to ride through it in 1993, in specially designed, high-speed trains running hourly from London to Paris in 3 1/4 hours and to Brussels in less than three hours.

## Airport Trains

The Piccadilly line on London's Underground is your access to Heathrow Airport (the London Underground has eleven lines). Travel to either of two stops: use the first stop for Heathrow terminuses 1, 2, and 3 (make sure you know which). The loop at the end of the line takes you to the second stop, terminal 4.

Wheel your luggage carts right up to Heathrow's train entrance. A straight trip between Heathrow and Piccadilly Circus takes about forty-five minutes, but when you must change from one subway line to the Piccadilly, your trip will take longer, especially on Sundays when service is less frequent.

To reach Gatwick Airport from London, board the Gatwick Express at Victoria station's modern Rail/Air check-in facilities on platforms 12 and 13. This area is equipped with elevator, escalator, and special escalator-friendly luggage carts.

The Gatwick Express is a gray-and-white, red-striped IC train specifically designed for air travelers. You ride in air-conditioned carriages, enter through wide doors, store your luggage on convenient shelves, and walk between compartments through automatically opening doors. You may telephone from the train and charge it to your credit card.

The Gatwick Express carries you nonstop at speeds up to 90 mph, cutting your travel time between Gatwick and Victoria station to thirty minutes. Quarter-hourly service begins at 5:30 A.M. from Victoria. After 10 P.M., standard train service continues around the clock. Use your BritRail pass or the voucher you receive in buying a "Capital Travel Pak" from BritRail (which gives you flexibility to travel outside the validity of your BritRail pass), or of course, buy a single ticket.

## Sleepers

BritRail's InterCity Mark III sleepers take you over all sleeper routes. First-class sleepers accommodate one passenger; economy-class accommodates two with an upper and a lower berth.

You can remain on your early-arriving trains in your sleeping compartment until at least 7 A.M., sometimes later, depending on the train. Your porter asks you whether you wish to be awakened early for arrival or after sleeping late. His call is always accompanied by the welcome coffee or famous English tea.

IC sleepers carry lounge cars as well as the sleeper units. BritRail converted first-class salon cars into pubs with bars, twenty-six lounge seats, and a public telephone. Located mid-train, this is where first-class passengers buy drinks, light meals, and snacks before and after their trip.

## Sealink

Sealink operates more ships to more places (France, the Netherlands,

Ireland, the Channel Islands) from Britain than any other company. It offers restaurants, shipboard pubs, comfortable lounges, spacious duty-free "Seashops," and even feature films on some ships. Make your reservations and buy your tickets in North America through BritRail Travel International (see Appendix).

## BritRail Passes

BritRail Passes are your basic go-everywhere, see-everything travel convenience. You travel free on every BritRail train in England, Scotland, and Wales, save the narrow-gauge private railroads in Wales and the Isle of Man trains.

Eurailpasses are not valid in Britain, so BritRail compensates by selling such an array of tempting train values that your head begins to swim. Write for their free color brochure, "Go BritRail," take it slow, and find the right combination for you.

BritRail sells first-class ("Gold") passes for rates about one-sixth more than Eurailpasses, but buy passes for second-class (the brochure prefers "economy-class") travel ("Silver") for more than one-fourth off the prices of the Gold passes. Buy them for eight, fifteen, twenty-two days or one month.

BritRail makes their passes especially attractive to those over sixty and those between fifteen and twenty-five by offering about one-sixth off on first- and second-class passes, respectively. There are no second-class Senior Citizen Passes or first-class Youth Passes. Children five through fifteen pay about half.

BritRail also offers BritRail Flexipasses which allow you leisure time, like Eurail Flexipasses. By paying for four days of travel out of eight, or eight days out of fifteen, you save about 15 percent of the cost of a standard first- or second-class BritRail Pass. Senior and Youth BritRail Passes are also available with the same Flexipass option and equivalent savings.

You buy BritRail Passes on the Continent, in Germany and France, for example, and in the Republic of Ireland, but you pay in local currencies, so it is more convenient to buy them before leaving America.

## Scottish Travelpass

When you travel extensively from March to October in the Scottish Highlands and Islands (Kyle of Lochalsh, for example), a seven- or fourteen-day Scottish Highlands & Islands Travelpass not only covers second-class travel on BritRail (called "ScotRail" there) within the region, but includes unlimited travel by Scottish Bus Group and Citylink buses, Caledonian MacBrayne's ferries to the islands off the west coast, and P&O's Scrabster to Stromness. Buy it in Scotland (Glasgow and Edinburgh gateways). It is not available through BritRail in America.

## BritRail/Drive

The BritRail/Drive plan combines a BritRail Flexipass for four or eight days with a Hertz rental automobile with unlimited mileage also for four or eight days.

Hertz has some 100 pickup stations at major BritRail stations, at 11 airports, and 89 more at practically any place you might venture.

You pay for the package in dollars and receive all instructions before you leave, making it very easy to use.

## Tours and Day Trips

BritRail offers a convenient and economical way to book a selection of luxury day trips and tours from London. These are detailed in "Go BritRail." They include day trips on the historic Pullman carriages of the Venice Simplon Orient Express like those used on the English leg of VSOE's opulent trip to Venice, a Britainshrinkers train/bus sightseeing calendar (BritRail Pass holders save up to 42 percent), and the round-trip "Great Britain Express."

## Using Eurailpass Bonuses in Ireland

Eurailpass gives you two bonuses that are valuable—essential—to seeing enjoyably the Republic by Eurail.

You can travel free on Expressway buses owned and operated by CIE (except the services to and from Northern Ireland operated jointly with the northern administration).

You can also connect with the trains on the Continent just by paying port taxes. The Irish Continental Line (ICL) gives Eurailpass holders free deck passage and Irish hospitality on its two car ferries, the *Saint Patrick II* and the *Saint Killian II* serving the Irish ports of Rosslare and Cork and the French ports of Le Havre and Cherbourg. You travel between Rosslare and Le Havre (21 hours) on four round-trip sailings per week during the summer and two to three per week during off-season. ICL's Rosslare-Cherbourg sailings (17 hours) take you twice weekly during the summer; once a week from October to February. Its Cork-Le Havre sailings (21 1/2 hours) occur once a week during the summer only.

ICL's ferries are large and comfortable—the equivalent of minicruises. You dine in a dining room or cafeteria, shop duty-free, gamble, go to the movies, and socialize in the bar-lounge and disco. You must pay extra for cabin accommodations, but by the time your Eurailpass credit is deducted from the overall charge, your costs for these are quite reasonable. For prices and reservations, contact CIE Tours International (see Appendix).

## Irish Rail Rambler Tickets

Rail Rambler Tickets give you unlimited access to IrishRail for eight days you choose out of fifteen or for fifteen consecutive days. In addition, to ride the Bus Eireann, buy a "Rail and Road Rambler Ticket," which adds bus to train travel for about 25 percent more. It is not honored on the city buses of Dublin.

When you wish to travel in both North Ireland (Ulster) and the Republic, buy an "Irish Overlander" ticket for fifteen consecutive days of unlimited second-class travel throughout Ireland and on the bus services of Bus Eireann and Ulsterbus Limited. It is not valid on the city buses of Belfast or Dublin.

You can buy these tickets at the principal stations and depots of IrishRail, Bus Eireann, Northern Ireland Railways, and Ulsterbus Limited (where applicable). CIE Tours also sells the Republic of Ireland tickets.

Adventuring in the British Isles takes you on Scotland's Kyle line from Inverness, on the Isle of Man trains, along the coast of Wales and through slate-mining Welsh countryside, and on an electric odyssey along Bay of Dublin.

## *The Gutsy Kyle Line*
## *Wild and Romantic*

While your Kyle train's gutsy diesel railcar, its face painted safety-yellow, climbs steeply into the sparsely settled northwest corner of Scotland, your fellow passengers prepare for the wildest and most romantic passage in all of Great Britain. For best results, sit on the right.

Featured on the television series "Great Railway Trains of the World," the Hebridean Heritage from Inverness to Kyle of Lochalsh reveals the essence of Scotland, exposing tough new images every moment. Your eighty-two-mile run shows peaks, headlands, forlorn islands and skerries, lochs and glens—and yet cries of protest from the local people were needed in 1974 to save this line much admired by train-lovers and adventurers.

When your train pulls in at one of the fourteen lonely stations along the line, villagers climb aboard, marvel at the new train, and greet friends. Postal workers collect the mail while passengers board from creaky wooden footstools still used because there are few boarding platforms.

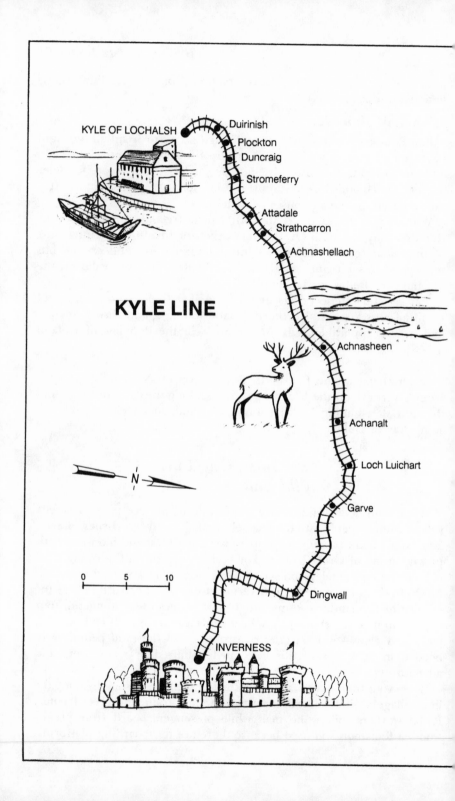

Your Kyle train is one of the new 75-mph Class 156 Super Sprinters especially designed for longer-distance, cross-country journeys. Five sets of panoramic windows, each with about six feet of anti-glare, tinted, and double-glazed glass, show you a changing picture of Scotland's Highlands.

You never lose sight of the views. The line twists so tightly that you see both the driver ahead and the carriages trailing you as you round the many curves.

The Hebridean Heritage runs every day from the brightly remodeled Inverness station, and BritRail Passes and Scottish Travelpasses are welcome. Be sure to pick up a free Kyle line color brochure at the Travel Centre. Maps and cameras are required equipment on this line.

Passing over the nine arches of the stone viaduct over the river Ness, you travel half an hour to Dingwall. In the green fields past Dingwall, try to picture one of the bloodiest clan battles in history, pitting the Mackenzies against the MacDonalds in 1429. It took place on Knockfarril (579 feet), near the vitrified fort built by King Brude of the Picts.

Now you climb steeply past Raven Rock, hunching 250 feet over the line to your left. At the summit of your first climb you see the dramatic contrast between the quieter green countryside dotted with cattle that stretches back below your train to Dingwall and the harsh Highlands ahead. Over the crest you approach brown, lifeless hills, wild woodlands, and rocky landscapes. Until the beginning of June, snow hugs mountains you see on your right.

Your modern Sprinter picks up speed on the downhill slope, crosses the Blackwater, and races beside Loch Garve on your right. Loch Garve, which means "Rough Lake," is mirror-smooth on calm days, and you see the reflection in the lake of pine-covered Little Wyvis (2,497 feet). The greater bulk of Ben Wyvis (3,297 feet) hulks behind it.

Your diesel coasts to a stop at Garve beside the tiny, tan, plaster station house surrounded in summer by cut wheat cropped in the fields. You see the pink Garve Hotel nearby. Garve, in the mountains of Wester Ross, is a camping center during the summer.

Puffing noisily, your Hebridean Heritage leads you from Garve through rolling countryside and past reforesting plantations. Passing over the Corriemoillie Summit (429 feet), you see heather-clad Loch Luichart with birches lined along its shores. The sky is incandescent with blue. The six miles of Loch Luichart join the weather systems east and west.

Loch Luichart was the first lake in the Highlands used to generate electricity in 1952. The hydroelectric project lifted the water twenty feet and submerged two miles of land, including the former track and station. Your train has been rerouted to the hastily built stone station house replacing the one sitting underwater.

You enter Strath Bran on the south side of Loch a Chuilinn, then cross quickly to the north side of sparkling Loch Achanalt (the two lakes are practically continuous) past marshy fields to Achanalt station.

Continuing along Strath Bran through wet, green grasslands, with desolate mountains in the distance, the scenery hardens. When you approach the tiny village of Achnasheen, meaning "Field of Rain," you have reached the bleakest bit of the line.

Your Sprinter comes to a stop. Post-office workers unload mail. Then your Hebridean Heritage climbs again. The treeless and rocky hills are especially attractive to a certain breed of moutaineer. Looking westward toward Glen Docherty you see the Torridon Mountains, old even in geologic terms. Liathach is the great barrel peak to the left, banded with hoops of sandstone and rising shear. To its right you see high-ridged Ben Eighe, looking white as snow but really covered with pale quartzite fragments for much of its height.

The summit of the line, Luib summit, lies only 700 feet above sea level between Loch Scaven and Loch Gowen, which drain into different seas. It is not high, but wild. You hear the crying of curlews and the loud, fluting calls of European sandpipers. Sometimes you see herds of deer, and golden eagles soaring on broad wings. In September, you may well hear great stags roaring at one another.

You almost hear your heated diesel sighing with relief as it heads downhill. At the Glencarron halt, some of the passengers with packs, ropes, and pickaxes climb off, planning to scale the cleft peak of Fuar Tholl (2,968 feet) on your right.

You then enter the deer-haunted Achnashellach Forest, thick with spruce, willow, birch, and holly. Watch for the splendid view of Glen Carron on your left before you glide into Achnashellach station.

Out of Achnashellach you pass Loch Dhugaill, surrounded with spruce. This is the country of the oldest rocks in the world, Archean gneiss forming its floor and Cambrian quartzite its walls, so that the predominant colors are pinks and grays.

At Strathcarron, the second double-tracked station, your Hebridean Heritage passes the return train. Your driver must stop to pick up a token to continue. You lean out the window and listen for the train coming from Kyle.

Impatient train-lovers and camera hawks rush outside to the head of the train and climb onto the iron overpass to snap photos of the imminent meeting. You cheer and applaud when the drivers meet. Then the photographers race back to their seats for fear of being abandoned at this remote stop. It is possible to take the train halfway to Kyle and then immediately travel back on the return train, but were you to do so you would miss the more spectacular half.

Past Strathcarron, a warm burst of air prompts you to remove your parka. You leave behind cold hills and enter the softer Gulf Stream climate.

Across the lake to your right, you see the whitewashed cottages of Loch Carron village gaily bedecked with roses. Loch Carron had good herring and salmon fishing before fishing failed about 1850, too early for the Kyle line to be of any help.

Loch Carron widens on your right, and the pressing question of the moment, as you look back at Fuar Tholl, is whether you really make out the famous profile of George Washington in the outline of the mountain.

You stop next at Attadale, meaning "Valley of the Fight." Here you try to imagine Vikings dueling and sporting. You run side by side with the highway between Attadale and Stromeferry through tall spruce forests on dangerously steep slopes.

Stromeferry, at the narrowest part of Loch Carron, was a short-lived terminus of ships to the Hebridean Islands, but piracy and shipwrecks abruptly terminated trading.

This last part of the Kyle line, past Duncraig, is the most spectacular. Look sharply, for the scenery dashes by faster than words. On level ground you race past the village of Plockton before finally slowing for Plockton's train station on the western outskirts.

Plockton is the gem of the Kyle line. Your train curves along the shore revealing gleaming white cottages across azure water and the striking, pink-rock Applecross peaks in the background. Plockton owes its size to the days when its schooners traded as far away as the Baltic. It looks like an island from your view but is actually on a thin promontory.

You see it best from across the water, a classic picture that sells well. You see paintings of this scene, complete with romantic yachts decorating the foreground, hanging in parlors and pubs throughout Britain.

When you run along the lakeside between tall mountains past Plockton, you become more excited than during any other section of the line. You see the western shore. You had not imagined such enchanting colors. Clouds, seaweed, and waterfalls suffuse in a soft, bluish light. Dozens of rivulets dash down. Granite chunks lie pink in the water, freckled with bright gold algae. Glorious views glow in changing shades of watercolor.

Past Duirinish, you travel inland through the Drumbuie crofting area. You realize your trip has to end soon when you cross the wild coast colored with orange lichen-daubed rocks, tide pools alive with sea creatures, and magnificent vistas of islands with pig-Latin names: Rassay, Scalpay, Loggay, Pabay, and the Crowlin Islands.

Breathe deeply the salty air when you step off in the Kyle of Lochalsh station. Kyle is Gaelic meaning "strait" or "narrows." It was simply "Kyle," population 600, until it took on its elegant new name on that historic day in November 1897 when dignitaries from all over Scotland came to declare the railroad officially open.

Photographers climb the hill behind the Railway Terrace next to the Tourist Information Centre for a big, sweeping picture of mountains, islands, and endless sea. The houses look like white miniatures ready to tumble into the sea.

Kyle is by no means the end of your travels. Free (for foot passengers) ferries shuttle on eight-minute crossings to Kyleakin on the Isle of Skye. From here, travel by bus across Skye to Armadale for the Caledonian MacBrayne ferry back to Mallaig and the return West Highland BritRail connection to Fort William on the Glasgow-London mainline.

Some schedule their Kyle visit to connect with one of the thrice-weekly Caledonian MacBrayne sailings to Mallaig.

The Lochalsh Hotel, an old-fashioned resort hotel at water's edge, offers overnighters magnificent views across the sound of the Isle of Skye, except of course when the famous Skye mist descends.

During the week the Hebridean Heritage carries a special, green-and-white "Hebridean Observation Saloon" attached to its rear where you can buy snacks and listen to a guide retelling dramatic history and pointing out sights of interest, but it is not a dome car. Its surcharge is about $10 out, $5 return. Book seats on this very popular carriage in advance at any BritRail Travel Centre.

---

## Kyle Line Summer Service

### Mondays to Saturdays Only

| | (1) | | | | | | | | (1) |
|---|---|---|---|---|---|---|---|---|---|
| 0655 | 1010 | 1110 | 1835 | dep. INVERNESS | arr. | 0946 | 1403 | 1735 | 1918 |
| 0715 | 1030 | 1130 | 1901 | dep. Muir of Ord | dep. | 0928 | 1345 | 1717 | 1900 |
| 0725 | 1040 | 1140 | 1911 | dep. Dingwall | dep. | 0919 | 1336 | 1708 | 1850 |

| | | | | | | | | | |
|---|---|---|---|---|---|---|---|---|---|
| 0751 | 1105 | 1205 | 1936 | dep. | Garve | dep. | 0853 | 1310 | 1642 | 1824 |
| 0801 | 1115 | .... | 1946 | dep. | Loch Luichart | dep. | 0842 | 1259 | .... | 1813 |
| 0809 | 1123 | .... | 1954 | dep. | Achanalt | dep. | 0834 | 1251 | .... | 1805 |
| 0825 | 1136 | 1242 | 2007 | dep. | Achnasheen | dep. | 0824 | 1241 | 1615 | 1755 |
| 0846 | 1157 | .... | 2028 | dep. | Achnashellach | dep. | 0802 | 1220 | .... | 1734 |
| 0857 | 1211 | 1314 | 2038 | dep. | Strathcarron | dep. | 0752 | 1210 | 1545 | 1724 |
| 0902 | 1216 | .... | 2043 | dep. | Attadale | dep. | 0747 | 1205 | .... | 1717 |
| 0912 | 1226 | .... | 2053 | dep. | Stromeferry | dep. | 0735 | 1153 | .... | 1709 |
| 0920 | 1234 | .... | 2101 | dep. | Duncraig | dep. | 0726 | 1144 | .... | 1656 |
| 0924 | 1238 | 1343 | 2105 | dep. | Plockton | dep. | 0723 | 1141 | .... | 1653 |
| 0928 | 1242 | .... | 2109 | dep. | Duirinish | dep. | 0719 | 1137 | .... | 1649 |
| 0940 | 1252 | 1355 | 2119 | arr. | KYLE | dep. | 0710 | 1128 | 1505 | 1640 |

## Sundays

| (2) | | | | (2) |
|---|---|---|---|---|
| 0925 | dep. | INVERNESS | arr. | 1641 |
| 0945 | dep. | Muir of Ord | dep. | 1623 |
| 0955 | dep. | Dingwall | dep. | 1613 |
| 1019 | dep. | Garve | dep. | 1547 |
| 1029 | dep. | Loch Luichart | dep. | 1536 |
| 1037 | dep. | Achanalt | dep. | 1528 |
| 1050 | dep. | Achnasheen | dep. | 1518 |
| 1111 | dep. | Achnashellach | dep. | 1457 |
| 1121 | dep. | Strathcarron | dep. | 1447 |
| 1126 | dep. | Attadale | dep. | 1442 |
| 1137 | dep. | Stromeferry | dep. | 1430 |
| 1145 | dep. | Duncraig | dep. | 1421 |
| 1149 | dep. | Plockton | dep. | 1418 |
| 1153 | dep. | Duirinish | dep. | 1414 |
| 1203 | arr. | KYLE | dep. | 1405 |

(1) The Hebridean Heritage (observation car, supplement payable).
(2) Observation car, supplement payable.

# Caledonian MacBrayne Summer Ferry Service*

| dep. Armadale | arr. Mallaig | dep. Mallaig | arr. Armadale |
|---|---|---|---|
| 0910 | 0940 | 0815 | 0845 |
| 1130 | 1200 | 1020 | 1050 |
| 1500 | 1530 | 1300 | 1330 |
| 1800 | 1830 | 1630 | 1700 |
| 2000 | 2030 | 1900 | 1930 |

(Mondays to Saturdays only)

| dep.<br>Kyle | arr.<br>Mallaig | dep.<br>Mallaig | arr.<br>Kyle |
|---|---|---|---|
| 1615 | 1815 | 1200 | 1400 |
| | (Tuesdays, Thursdays, and<br>Saturdays only) | | |

*Covered by Scottish High-
lands & Islands Travelpass
but not BritRail Pass.

---

## *Isle of Man*
## *Four-Ring Entertainment*

Your coastal car swings out to Laxey Head. A splendid view opens beneath you of Douglas's Victorian promenade, its pink-and-green horse trams, and the Irish Sea breaking on its strand. When your climb toughens and your frail car tilts upward more steeply from one in thirty-eight feet to one in twenty-four, you see the rugged coastline stretching out to far Maughold Head.

Your car labors at its effort. It vibrates, shakes, and rumbles. Wood rubbing on wood sings of excellent maintenance.

Your cautious pace gives you time to appreciate the view as you near Ballaragh, meaning "Place of the Rocks." You could not find a better name. Cliffs rise to more than 600 feet. While you run along the cliffside more than 500 feet above the frothy breaking waves of Bulgham Bay, you are traveling on one of the most spectacular railroad stretches anywhere in the British Isles.

When you near the end of your dramatic climb beside the cliff, you reach the highest point of Isle of Man's coastline, 588 feet above the crashing surf. Turning inland, your car descends more or less continuously through lush green countryside to Ramsey.

The Manx Electric Railroad's (MER) charming electric streetcars trundle through glens and atop cliffs. Aboard its cars you see some of the loveliest and most romantic scenery on the Isle of Man, the thirty-mile-long dot in the Irish Sea midway between the coasts of England, Ireland, Scotland, and Wales.

MER's three-foot-gauge electric fleet is admired by train-lovers the world around. Their pleasing cars have waged a continual battle against modernization and closure since their delivery and first use in 1893-1906. Now that they earn their keep by attracting visitors, they

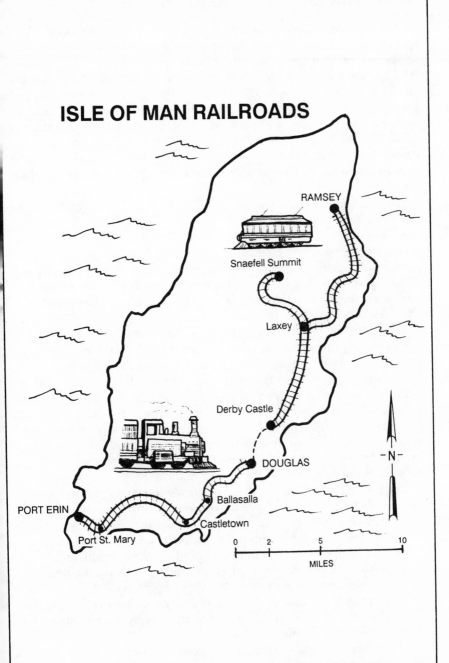

# ISLE OF MAN RAILROADS

RAMSEY

Snaefell Summit

Laxey

Derby Castle

DOUGLAS

Ballasalla

PORT ERIN

Castletown

Port St. Mary

-N-

| 0 | 2 | 5 | 10 |

MILES

receive funding adequate to ensure their safe running and meticulous maintenance.

The Isle of Man has been heavily hit by changes in vacation patterns. The railroads and the unspoiled environment used to attract workers from the industrial north of England (Birmingham, Manchester, and Liverpool). Brightly polished steam locomotives, colorful additions to the countryside, took them to deep Manx glens, patchwork quilts of fields, the breathtaking sea—places their friends in smoke-filled cities could hardly contemplate. Now, "sun holidays" on the Mediterranean lure away its visitors with cheap airfares and mass air transportation.

From 500,000 annual visitors after World War II, Isle of Man now welcomes only 200,000. The result is that you can take advantage of tremendous overcapacity and remarkable, well-maintained electric and mountain railroads and steam trains. With the drying-up of Man's traditional tourist market, a new breed of visitor has discovered this anachronism. The Isle of Man is known the world over as a train-lover's paradise. (For information visit or write the Isle of Man Tourist Board, 13 Victoria Street, Douglas, Isle of Man.)

You board the MER within reach of the salt spray at the north end of the Douglas promenade and climb to almost 600 feet along a precipitous ledge before returning almost level with the Irish Sea in Ramsey, 17 3/4 miles and seventy-five minutes to the north.

Derby Castle station lies at the northern end of Douglas's Victorian promenade. (The unique steam locomotive trip to Port Erin, from the Douglas Bank Hill station, is described later in this section.) Purchase your tickets at the whimsical ticket house designed with lacquered branches to resemble an illustration in a child's fairy-tale book. BritRail Passes are not honored on the Isle of Man.

One glance around the car reveals meticulous attention to preservation and detail. Your lacquered 1899 car shines with such a gloss that you can make out your reflection in the walnut paneling. Seats covered with flowery maroon plush have reversible backs for travel in either direction.

Leaving Douglas's promenade, anchored on the opposite end by the bright Gaiety Playhouse, your car crawls and squeaks up the persistent rise. Squealing wheels rounding the curves excite remarks from many of the younger passengers. Passing the ungated level crossings, your motorman sounds his air whistle or gongs loudly to tell automobile drivers that he is insisting on his right-of-way.

Soon after departure comes the spectacular stretch along the cliffs high above Bulgham Bay. When you near the stone-covered Howstrake station, look down at the splendid panorama of Douglas Bay to the east. To the west, the hedge-lined green fields are filled with grazing sturdy Frisian cows standing like plaster statues ignoring the rain. Black-faced sheep cluster together in the fields; none are the curious four-horned Loaghtans native to the island.

Your car levels and the motorman eases back on his brass handle before swinging sharply inland and starting his descent, one foot in twenty-four, along the wooded approach to Groudle, the terminus of the 1893 line. The long descent past Groudle into Laxey opens the lovely panorama of the Laxey bay and beach, the tiny harbor with its neat, white-painted lighthouses, and the headlands beyond.

At Fairy Cottage and South Cape stops you see the signs, "Alight here for the beach." In summer there is a mini-bus return.

MER shares the brown Laxey station house with the Snaefell Mountain Railroad, which runs daily during the summer. Their terminus lies in a romantic wooded glen in the center of the village, decorated by nearby Christ Church.

While in Laxey, walk down the convenient, well-marked path through the green, gorse-clad valley of Agneash to visit Lady Isabella. She's not a member of the British aristocracy but the name given to the celebrated Laxey Wheel, the largest waterwheel in the world at seventy-two feet in diameter. Built in 1854, the red-and-white wheel pumped the Laxey lead and silver mines until the 1920s. Now it is primarily a well-manicured tourist attraction.

Your car scrapes the white paint of the Mines Tavern leaving Laxey. It is a wonderful, old-fashioned British pub with needlepoint chairs, gleaming brass, shining glasses, darts, and an open fire.

You run parallel to the Snaefell Mountain train until it turns up the mountain and begins to climb at a gradient of one in twelve feet on its thirty-minute journey. When you climb Snaefell in that train, sit on the left side so you can see the rail of the Fell brake mounted on its side between the running rails.

The hardest part of your trip is over. Your MER car seems to fly past farms—sheep, cows, and green- and straw-colored meadows ringed with stone walls harboring scores of cats, not the tailless Manx breed, husbanded in Douglas's cattery, but the common alley variety.

About a mile past the green hut beside the Cornea halt, you pass Ballafayle, the residence of Sir Charles Kerruish. He is the Speaker of the House of Keys, the ancient parliament which celebrated its one-thousandth anniversary in 1979. Look for his Manx "Three Legs" flag fluttering in the breeze.

Descending steadily toward Ramsey Bay, you see the Victorian hotels lining the Ramsey waterfront, a smaller echo of Douglas, and you find this symmetry most satisfying. Your car formerly ran out on the 2,000-foot Ramsey Pier but now you complete your electric railroad run not far from the city center.

## Port Erin Line

The Port Erin line, the longest narrow-gauge steam railroad line in the British Isles, uses historic carriages pulled by one of the 2-4-0 engines—Loch (1874), Maitland (1905), Hutchinson (1908), or Kissock (1910)—from Douglas Bank Hill station in the Isle's capital city, to the southwestern hamlet of Port Erin. Remember, BritRail Passes are not honored on the Isle of Man.

The 15 1/2-mile stretch opened August 1, 1874. It is built now much as it was then. The train's story is one of evolution, with change sometimes for the better, often for the worse, but with a spirit of continuity for over a century.

The four steam locomotives still used are a fraction of the sixteen original ones. They are lovingly maintained and professionally cared for. Two are red, one is blue, and one is green, and they are named for original directors of the railroad. They look chubby because of the side tanks holding cold water, and they don't need a tender for supplemental fuel.

Buy your ticket for Port Erin at Douglas's red-brick train station at the head of the harbor. Arched ornamental gates sparkle with domes and pinnacles still glittering with the gold leaf applied in the railroad's more optimistic days.

You depart Douglas with a climb of one foot in sixty-five. You can feel your blue No. 12 engine, the Hutchinson (1908), working hard. Sitting in one of the original wooden carriages, you really know you are traveling by steam. Even the Hutchinson's modest climb produces loud puffing, smoke, soot, and flying cinders, leaving you little doubt that there is a steam engine up front.

You cross the Douglas River on the 1979 girder-span Nunnery Bridge. Past the Nunnery on your left, one of the Isle's "Stately Homes," you enter a narrow rock cutting where engines are prone to lose traction in autumn due to fallen leaves.

After a half-mile, you see spectacular cliff views opening out toward Santon Head in the south, and toward Little Ness in the Douglas direction.

Past Port Soderick station (3 1/8 miles, fourteen minutes), you run through the wooded Crogga valley—a treat in bluebell time. In season, dazzling displays of rhododendrons open up beside the line. Children reach from windows to catch wild flowers and the leaves brushing gently against your train as it passes.

Beyond Santon (5 5/8 miles, twenty-four minutes), the main highway runs below the track on your left but climbs up and passes over the train at the Blackboards. You don't see any black boards now, but when the road traffic was drawn by horse, a wooden screen was erected between the train and the highway to prevent horses from taking flight at smoke-belching monsters.

The airport you see on your left is Ronaldsway, site of the celebrated battle in Manx history. From here, Manx Airlines serves London, Liverpool, and Dublin.

Break your trip at Castletown (9 7/8 miles, forty-six minutes), the capital of the Isle until the 1860s, to explore Castle Rushen, one of the finest preserved medieval castles in Europe. Its Elizabethan clock with only the hour hand is still in use. You also see the Nautical Museum, the harbor, the beach, and King Williams College where Bragg, the Nobel-prize-winning physicist, was educated.

When the Hutchinson pulls you past Port St. Mary (15 3/4 miles, sixty-two minutes), you see Port Erin in the distance, nestling between ground rising to the south toward the Sound, which separates the Island from the Calf of Man, and the high ground of Bradda Head to the north. Crowned by Milners Tower, Bradda Head makes a popular subject for amateur photographers.

When you arrive at the red-brick Port Erin station (15 5/8 miles, sixty-five minutes), head for the beach or train museum. You will see there the locomotive that hauled the first train of 1873, a great sampling of historic locomotives, the coaches used by Queen Elizabeth in 1972, and those used by the Duke of Sutherland on opening day, 1873.

After the electric trams, mountain railroads, and steam locomotives, your four-ring entertainment is completed by returning to Douglas and riding its famous horse trams along the promenade. After being pulled by one of the nineteenth-century iron horses, you wonder which is more temperamental, the four-footed white trotters or the red, blue, and green steam locomotives.

Douglas is served by the m.v. *Tynwald* car ferry (3,630 tons) of the Isle of Man Steam Packet Seaways, with four-hour crossings to Heysham, Liverpool, Stranvaer, Dublin, and Belfast.

## Summer Manx Electric Railroad Service
### between Douglas, Laxey, and Ramsey (not Sundays)

| | | | | | | | | | | |
|---|---|---|---|---|---|---|---|---|---|---|
| 1000 | 1200 | 1400 | 1500 | 1700 | DOUGLAS* | 1145 | 1310 | 1445 | 1645 | 1745 |
| 1012 | 1212 | 1412 | 1512 | 1712 | Groudle | 1133 | 1258 | 1433 | 1633 | 1733 |
| 1020 | 1220 | 1420 | 1520 | 1720 | Garwick | 1125 | 1250 | 1425 | 1625 | 1725 |
| 1030 | 1230 | 1430 | 1530 | 1730 | LAXEY | 1115 | 1240 | 1415 | 1615 | 1715 |
| 1045 | 1245 | 1445 | 1545 | 1745 | Dhoon | 1100 | 1230 | 1400 | 1600 | 1700 |
| 1055 | 1255 | 1455 | 1555 | 1755 | Ballaglass | 1050 | 1220 | 1350 | 1550 | 1650 |
| 1103 | 1303 | 1503 | 1603 | 1803 | Ballajora | 1042 | 1212 | 1342 | 1542 | 1642 |
| 1115 | 1315 | 1515 | 1615 | 1815 | RAMSEY | 1030 | 1200 | 1330 | 1530 | 1630 |

*Derby Castle station.

## Summer Manx Steam Railroad Service
### between Douglas and Port Erin (not Saturdays)

| | | | | * | | | | | * | |
|---|---|---|---|---|---|---|---|---|---|---|
| 1010 | 1050 | 1145 | 1410 | 1610 | DOUGLAS | 1120 | 1310 | 1520 | 1635 | 1720 |
| 1024 | 1108 | 1159 | 1423 | 1624 | Port Soderick | 1108 | 1255 | 1509 | 1624 | 1707 |
| 1034 | 1118 | 1209 | 1433 | 1634 | Santon (R) | 1058 | 1245 | 1459 | 1614 | 1657 |
| 1046 | 1130 | 1220 | 1446 | 1646 | Ballasalla | 1046 | 1235 | 1446 | 1602 | 1646 |
| 1056 | 1139 | 1228 | 1455 | 1656 | Castletown | 1036 | 1228 | 1437 | 1553 | 1635 |
| 1100 | 1143 | 1234 | 1458 | 1700 | Ballabeg (R) | 1029 | 1220 | 1430 | 1546 | 1629 |
| 1106 | 1149 | 1240 | 1505 | 1705 | Colby | 1025 | 1216 | 1426 | 1542 | 1625 |
| 1112 | 1156 | 1247 | 1512 | 1712 | Port St. Mary | 1018 | 1209 | 1419 | 1535 | 1619 |
| 1115 | 1200 | 1250 | 1515 | 1715 | PORT ERIN | 1015 | 1205 | 1415 | 1530 | 1615 |

*Sunday through Thursday, July and August only.
(R) Request stop.

# Gwynedd
## Sea, Steam, and Slate

Hold on to your tongue. You struggle and stutter on the Welsh consonants of Blaenau Ffestiniog, Tan-y-bwlch, Betws-y-coed, and Llyn Ystradau.

Your adventure in Gwynedd, Wales' north county, takes you crashing beside the wild Irish Sea, below soaring thirteenth-century castles,

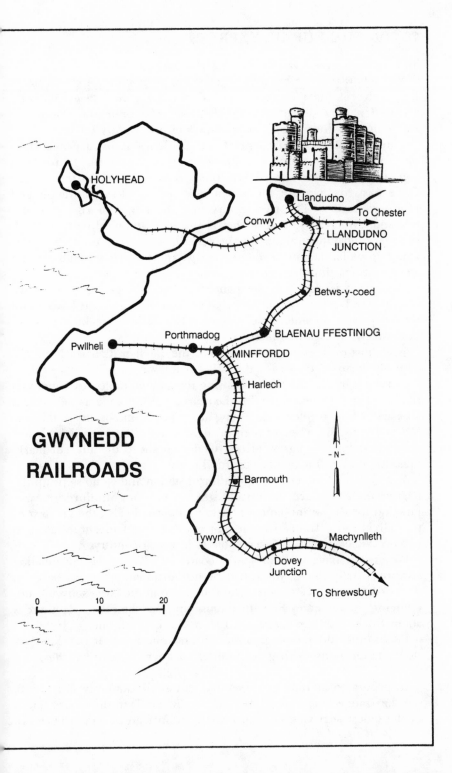

HOLYHEAD

Llandudno

Conwy

To Chester

LLANDUDNO
JUNCTION

Betws-y-coed

Porthmadog

BLAENAU FFESTINIOG

Pwllheli

MINFFORDD

Harlech

GWYNEDD
RAILROADS

-N-

Barmouth

Tywyn

Machynlleth

Dovey
Junction

To Shrewsbury

0    10    20

and through green valleys on a narrow-gauge, Victorian steam train.

You follow the Cambrian Coast of Wales on BritRail. A classic steam locomotive of the Ffestiniog slate railroad takes you on a volunteer-restored narrow-gauge line, and BritRail collaborates once more by sweeping you down the Conwy Valley line past Conwy Castle.

Entering Wales at Machynlleth on BritRail's secondary line from Shrewsbury (with mainline connections from London), guards split your train, so be sure you are in the correct segment. Sit on the left. Once past Machynlleth there is a new feeling—less cultivation and more wilderness. The river pours into the bay. You run past vast tidelands. Waterfowl of all feather are stalking the mud flats for food; boats are aground waiting for the return of the sea. Your train runs along an embankment, through cuttings and tunnels on high ground where the sea thunders against cliffs.

Your train is slow and the panorama great—over soft fine brown sand marked only with the footprints of fowl. Fishing boats have found the deepwater channel close to shore. High stone breakwaters show how violent the sea becomes.

Just short of Tywyn station, you pass the Talyllyn Railroad Museum. The sign reads: "Tywyn for the Talyllyn Railway."

Curving high on the cliff, you swing for a memorable vast panorama of the village of Fairbourne (for the railroad of the same name). This is an exciting line; you have the feeling of the power and beauty of the sea.

Stone walls, and none of them straight, divide the green fields below the mountains into jigsaw pieces filled with sheep of different markings. Rhododendrons bloom profusely.

You debark at the two-level Minffordd station and climb steps up the narrow path to board the private steam-train line. Minffordd is your junction for the steam-hauled Ffestiniog Railroad (FR), the greatest of the "Great Little Trains" that steam-train-lovers and adventurers use to explore Wales' normally inaccessible rich, green countryside.

When you have time to spare, board at FR's larger Porthmadog terminus. Beforehand, you can stroll on Porthmadog's sandy beaches, dine or snack in FR's station restaurant, shop in the large souvenir and model store, and enjoy FR's small museum—but the FR station there is about fifteen minutes across town from the BritRail one.

FR's Minffordd station is unstaffed and lonesome. It has a locked stone station house with green shutters, scattered green benches, and that's all.

Incorporated in 1832 and operated almost continuously since 1836, the slim-gauge (one foot, 11 1/2 inches) FR stands in the record books as the oldest surviving company in the train transportation business.

Now that the volunteers have renewed the operation and restored its antique steam locomotives to their original shine and vigor, FR is a point of pride for every Welsh person.

BritRail Passes are not accepted on FR, but you can buy a Great Little Trains Wanderer Ticket for eight railroads. Write to the Ffestiniog Railway Company, Harbour Station, Porthmadog, Gwynedd, Wales LL49 9NF.

You sit in first-class observation cars, with high-backed upholstered seats, or third-class two-opposite-one seats. FR won't let you be a second-class adventurer here. (First-class tickets cost about 25 percent more; children under sixteen ride free.)

Your coach is small but your fellow adventurers and the friendly staff give it a happy feeling. The best place to sit to see the rugged scenery is on the east, the same side as the platform at Minffordd. Elbow room is tight, but your interest is fun, not transportation, even while traveling from one end of Wales to the other by using the northern interchange with BritRail.

Your antique locomotive hisses steam and begins its sixty-five-minute trip at Porthmadog's harbor. It runs across the "Cob," an embankment for the toll highway and the railroad across the wide estuary. Its first request stop, Boston Lodge, is the location of the foundry works responsible for maintaining—and in some cases actually building—the rolling stock.

You see the panorama of Snowdonia opening on your left. On the right, you duck your head for a glimpse of Harlech Castle, one of the 700-year-old reasons for you to visit Wales.

Now your rattling carriage begins to tilt upwards for a narrow, tottering, almost continuous climb of one foot in every seventy you pass, sheer above the Vale of Ffestiniog and through the green Snowdonia mountain range with the Dwyryd River meandering below. You look for the pointed summit of Mount Snowdon (3,560 feet), the highest in Wales, barely visible in the distance.

Past Minffordd, your hissing locomotive pauses to take water beside the creeper-covered stationmaster's stone house in Tan-y-bwlch, 7 1/2 miles from Porthmadog. Tracks run around three sides of the parklike bowl in the mountains.

In a few minutes your train puffs through Dduallt and then you begin a spiral—the only one in Britain. A distant nuclear power station appears on your right, on your left, and then on your right again.

Engineers abandoned the original line and built the spiral to gain elevation when the reservoir of the coming Tanygrisiau pumped-storage hydroelectric power station flooded their first tunnel. You pass through a more recent tunnel in a spur of the Moelyn Mountains before you reach the shores of the new man-made lake. Below, you see the former roadbed looking like a grass-topped wall and running beside the reservoir (now a gravel highway).

From the reservoir, you descend to the Tanygrisiau station, crossing first a road to the parking lot and then Wales' highest road, leading to the top dam of the power station. The automatic traffic lights flash red, the bells clang, and traffic backs up fifteen car lengths, more or less. Some of the motorists take their children from the backseats to have a good view of your classic steam engine hissing past.

In Tanygrisiau look back to a mountain still covered with a shower of chips of slate. It seems more significant to you when you realize this slate is the reason for your train's existence.

It's downhill now. You pass a waterfall and wind between two-story, slate-roof houses built of the same stone as the craggy peaks around you. The calliope-like sound of your train's steam whistle announces your arrival in the FR/BritRail joint terminus in Blaenau Ffestiniog, the slate capital of the world. It was opened virtually on FR's 150th anniversary in 1982.

The Ffestiniog steam operation dates from the grimy times when handcrafted blue-gray slates were exported around the world for fancy roofing, paving, and fencing. The Welsh slate industry employed 16,000 workers—a quarter of them in the Llechwedd mines in Blaenau Ffestiniog.

Transporting large loads of finished slates became an acute problem by the 1820s. The roads were so rocky that slate had to be first carried in wicker baskets slung over the backs of mules and then transferred to horse-drawn wagons rented from local farmers at rates the slate entrepreneurs considered exorbitant.

After the horses pulled the slates down the Vale of Ffestiniog, the slate was reloaded into small sailing boats, each manned by two men known as Philistines and dressed in tall felt hats like the gamekeepers of the day.

In 1836, management began a simple rail operation. Tracks were laid and gravity-drawn trams loaded with slate were rolled down from the quarries to a new port facility. Horses hauled the empty cars back up (and then returned by riding down in so-called "dandy cars"). Passenger transportation began in 1865, two years after the horses had been replaced by steam locomotives.

To save the railroad, in severe disrepair in 1954, most of its shares were transferred to a charitable trust. More than 6,500 dedicated volunteers and an accomplished salaried staff turned it from near ruin into a top pleasure railroad. Any profit is returned for expansion and improvement.

There are six steam locomotives (the "Merddin Emrys" was returned in 1988 to Victorian-style service), including strange-looking "double" engines known as Fairlie Articulated. These pieces of machinery are polished, buffed, and lubricated to peak efficiency and luster. "Prince," one of the original six locomotives, is again in regular passenger service. Prince's twin locomotive is the highlight of FR's museum in Porthmadog.

Today FR carries only passengers on its 13 1/2-mile route, giving you an excellent way to see the wooded Welsh countryside once ripped apart by the Industrial Revolution.

The Blaenau Ffestiniog interchange requires crossing an overpass across FR and BritRail lines rather than simply changing platforms. A bus from the train station takes you to the Llechwedd Slate Caverns, Wales' largest working slate mine.

Be sure to sit up front, behind BritRail's driver, for the excellent view down the Conwy Valley when you continue to the North Wales scenic line at Llandudno Junction (where you see a splendid view of the magnificent thirteenth-century Conwy Castle). At this junction, board a diesel InterCity high-speed mainline train that will whisk you along the beautiful North Wales coast.

## High Season Service of the Ffestiniog Railway

| Dep. Harbor PORTHMADOG | Dep. MINFFORDD | Dep. Penrhyn | Dep. Tan-y-bwlch | Arr. BLAENAU FFESTINIOG |
|---|---|---|---|---|
| **Mondays to Thursdays** | | | | |
| 0845 | 0854 | 0900 | 0920 | 0950 |
| 0945 | 0954 | 1000 | 1020 | 1050 |
| 1045 | 1054 | 1100 | 1120 | 1150 |
| 1145 | 1154 | 1200 | 1220 | 1250 |
| 1245 | 1254 | 1300 | 1320 | 1350 |
| 1345 | 1354 | 1400 | 1420 | 1450 |
| 1445 | 1454 | 1500 | 1520 | 1550 |
| 1545 | 1554 | 1600 | 1620 | 1650 |
| 1645 | 1654 | 1700 | 1720 | 1750 |
| 1845 | 1854 | 1900 | 1920 | 1950 |
| **Fridays, Saturdays, and Sundays** | | | | |
| 0945 | 0954 | 1000 | 1020 | 1050 |
| 1100 | 1109 | 1115 | 1135 | 1205 |

| Dep. Harbor PORTHMADOG | Dep. MINFFORDD | Dep. Penrhyn | Dep. Tan-y-bwlch | Arr. BLAENAU FFESTINIOG |
|---|---|---|---|---|
| **Fridays, Saturdays, and Sundays** | | | | |
| 1215 | 1224 | 1230 | 1250 | 1320 |
| 1330 | 1339 | 1345 | 1405 | 1435 |
| 1445 | 1454 | 1500 | 1520 | 1550 |
| 1600 | 1609 | 1615 | 1635 | 1705 |

| Dep. BLAENAU FFESTINIOG | Dep. Tan-y-bwlch | Dep. Penrhyn | Dep. MINFFORDD | Arr. Harbor PORTHMADOG |
|---|---|---|---|---|
| **Mondays to Thursdays** | | | | |
| 1000 | 1025 | 1045 | 1050 | 1105 |
| 1100 | 1125 | 1145 | 1150 | 1205 |
| 1200 | 1225 | 1245 | 1250 | 1305 |
| 1300 | 1325 | 1345 | 1350 | 1405 |
| 1400 | 1425 | 1445 | 1450 | 1505 |
| 1500 | 1525 | 1545 | 1550 | 1605 |
| 1600 | 1625 | 1645 | 1650 | 1705 |
| 1700 | 1725 | 1745 | 1750 | 1805 |
| 1800 | 1825 | 1845 | 1850 | 1905 |
| 2000 | 2025 | 2045 | 2050 | 2105 |
| **Fridays, Saturdays, and Sundays** | | | | |
| 1100 | 1133 | 1150 | 1155 | 1210 |
| 1215 | 1248 | 1305 | 1310 | 1325 |
| 1330 | 1403 | 1420 | 1425 | 1440 |
| 1445 | 1518 | 1535 | 1540 | 1555 |
| 1600 | 1633 | 1650 | 1655 | 1710 |
| 1725 | 1753 | 1809 | 1814 | 1825 |

All trains call on request at Boston Lodge, Plas, Dduallt, and Tanygrisiau.

## *Dublin's Electric Odyssey*
## *A Nice Bit of an Outin'*

Irish know that Howth is a seaside place for fishermen, Dun Laoghaire for gentry, Dalkey for artists, Killiney for lovers, and Bray for all of the above.

From Dublin your Eurailpass takes you on an electric odyssey up and down Bay of Dublin aboard the Dublin Area Regional Transit (DART) system trains. DART runs north to the picturesque fishing village of Howth and south along the stretch of scenic coastline to Bray. You hop on and off to visit pretty coastal towns and yacht harbors, museums, and restaurants.

Dubliners, among the most critical of people, criticized DART when

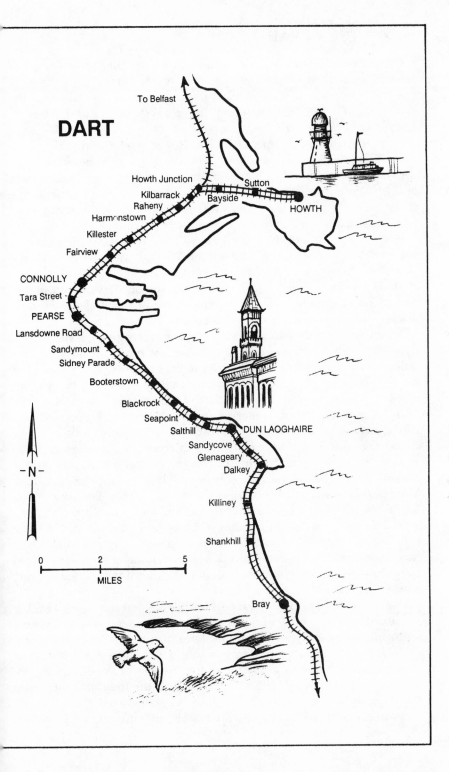

it was proposed. Now that it is running flawlessly, they have taken it to their hearts. They discovered that it is much more than a boon to commuters or a vast technological improvement; it has taken on the character of a leisure pursuit, giving to Dubliners and holders of Eurailpasses "a nice bit of an outin'."

At the northern terminus of DART, Howth (say "Hooth"; the name comes from the Scandinavian "hoved," meaning "head," as hovedbanegard for "head train station") is a mixture historic village, busy fishing port, and Dublin suburb. The sea gulls in Howth are the fattest in the northern hemisphere. One step out from Howth station and you smell why fresh salmon sell extremely reasonably.

From the summit of the Hill of Howth, 567 feet above the station at sea level, you can see Bay of Dublin, the Wicklow Mountains, and, on a clear day, the top of Mount Snowdon in Wales.

Stone buildings line the pier facing the station. Dry-docked green-and-white, blue-and-brown fishing vessels are propped above the pier, workers scraping and repairing their hulls.

Your DART electric railcar (EMU), appropriately green, leaves Howth past heather-covered islands to the west, across mud flats busy with sea gulls, and past shacks and fishing craft in dry dock. After you glide smoothly south past the rear of Parson's steel-fabrication works, you see across the main road to the east, on the high ground, the spire of St. Mary's Church of Ireland emerging above the trees, and below, almost in the shadow of the spire, the entrance gate to Howth Castle.

You pass the first of at least three golf courses—just as green as all Ireland in spring. Just south of Howth, Sutton station lies at the narrowest part of the isthmus connecting Howth with the mainland. Your next stop, Howth Junction, is the joining of mainline trains from Belfast to the DART corridor south to Dublin's Connolly Station.

At Killester, you reach the famous "Skew Bridge." Built in 1843, the bridge was regarded as a triumph of engineering at the time. From here you run on the original embankment, which was entirely surrounded by water a century ago but now is all but lost amidst the ever-expanding land reclamation.

From Killester you glide south past row houses and parks. You see red-sweatered men struggling with bad weather on the golf course to the west, and shipping cranes and storage facilities in the distance to the east.

Dublin's Connolly Station, formerly known as Amiens Street Station, is Dublin's major terminus in size but not in number of passengers served. You have access to the Mainline Booking Office, the Information Bureau, the cloakroom, the cafeteria, the central bus station, and taxis.

In 1980-81, IrishRail renovated Connolly in anticipation of DART's introduction. The platforms, roofing, underpasses, and entrances were rebuilt. DART platforms 6 and 7 are adjacent to the mainline trains using platforms 1 to 4. Use these platforms for trains to Belfast, Sligo, and Galway, and for the boat trains to Rosslare Harbor.

When your DART leaves Connolly, you glide almost noiselessly out onto the beginning of the Loop Line over Amiens Street. Take a look at the Italianate tower of the mainline terminal building facing Talbot Street and the fine old grimy and faded red-brick Victorian railroad offices with yellow brick window arches and dull-blue brick band. Inside, workers pilot the entire "space-age" computerized Central Control of today's rail system.

You pass through the rooftops past the new Irish Life Assurance building complex with golden windows. In front you see the Chariot of Life sculpture, "Look Ma, no reins!"

You travel on the elevated railroad to the stop at Tara Street Bridge over the Liffey River, but Tara Street station has no exit or entrance on Tara Street. The station opens onto George's Quay.

The stretch of the Loop Line between the Tara Street station and Pearse Station (formerly Westland Row) is the shortest distance between any two DART stations, yet for so short a stretch you see much: the notable spire of City Quay Parish Church, the more ponderous roofline of St. Mark's, Hawkins House, the darkly tinted glass of the Irish Press newspaper office, and the distinctive 130-foot watchtower of the Tara Street fire station. Finally you pass through Trinity College. Yours may be the only train actually to run through part of a university. The Loop Line viaduct curves gently across the Botany Bay area of the university, giving you a close-up of Trinity's Parade Ground and science buildings.

You arrive on the green ironwork bridge in red-brick Pearse station with antique girders and a glass arch overhead.

From Pearse Station you reach the interesting three-span skew bridge over the Grand Canal. To the west is the tall, gaunt Guinness malt store. Originally, in 1834, planners sketched a single bridge here, but engineering problems necessitated building two, the first almost square on, and the second a genuine "skew" bridge of thirty-three degrees— and both so low that in later years no double-decked streetcar or bus could pass under them.

At Landsdowne Road station, sports fans depart almost beneath a modern two-tier sports stadium straddling the station and the railroad line. This is the mecca of Irish rugby and a regular site for international and European Cup soccer matches.

The annual fair in Donnybrook nearby gave a new word to the English language. Established by King John in 1204, the fair was finally abolished in 1855 because more fistfights broke out outside the bareknuckle prizefighters' rings than within.

The new DART station in the pleasant seaside village of Sandymount, one of the line's most attractive stops, stands on the site of stations dating back to 1835.

Just after Sandymount, and before you stop at Sydney Parade, you see a fine view of Gothic St. John's Church across the green grass of Monkstown Rugby Club. On a late summer evening the church's warm sand-colored stones and its ornamental windows catch the last glow of the setting sun.

After Sydney Parade, you plunge suddenly into a panoramic scene of the bay. Your railcar, like a child dashing eagerly to water's edge, runs along the sands and as close to the seabirds fishing in the waves as prudent.

Past Blackrock, you watch clammers shoveling through the mud flats, filling their red plastic buckets to the limit. The coastline is alive with windsurfers steering their colorful craft and assembling their bright-as-buttons equipment in parking lots from Blackrock to Dun Laoghaire. Yachts dance in the harbor and seawalls protect oceangoing ferries.

Passengers on the overnight Irish Mail train/boat route from London get their first taste of the DART system at Dun Laoghaire (say "Dunleary"). Buses to and from Dublin's Heuston station are also available.

Dun Laoghaire, which was first called "Dunleary" and then "Kingstown" in honor of the visit of King George IV, is primarily a sea town, the only Irish port directly administered by the government and not by locally elected officials. Between the harbor and the DART station, look for the tiny brick office marked by the green i which combines the tourist information office, the "Bureau de Change," and the Sealink office.

DARTing south from Dun Laoghaire to Sandycove takes you beneath seven overpasses including three major road crossings. To complete DART, these either had to be lifted, rebuilt, and the highway approaches altered, or your train's roadbed had to be lowered by about twenty inches. As a result, you now pass over a one-mile stretch of continuously paved concrete railbed, the first in Ireland.

From your stop at Sandycove you see teams of windsurfers, canoeists, and water-skiers in Scotsman's Bay immediately outside Dun Laoghaire's east pier. Walk fifteen minutes from the station to Sandycove's premiere attraction, the Martello Tower, built in 1804 to withstand the Napoleonic invasion that never came.

From Dalkey's green cement station house, you, like George Bernard Shaw, see beautiful seascapes. Dogs play in waves. Anglers cast into the surf. The great playwright spent the happiest days of his youth here on Torca Hill, overlooking the splendid sweep of Bay of Dublin.

South of Dalkey, you travel on cliffs overhanging the sea. Mountains rise in the distance. At Killiney you have a chance to walk parallel to the DART line for breathtaking views, or to climb the steep lane opposite the station and in ten minutes reach a charming district distinguished by early Irish Christian architecture. Past Killiney and Shankhill you journey inland; white row houses separate you from the ocean. You pass through the middle of a golf course. All Ireland looks like a golf course in springtime, but this is probably the only golf course with a commuter hazard.

You now approach Bray, one of Ireland's premiere seaside resorts. The welcoming promontory of Bray Head stands high above the sea and Bray crowns the southern shore of Bay of Dublin.

At Bray station you see the original iron pillars bearing the logo, "Irish Engineering Co., Seville Works, 1853." "David's Diner and Market" sells fresh fruit and soft ice cream.

Bray, in County Wicklow, the only city outside County Dublin to be served by DART, is a fishing harbor, a holiday resort, a town of handsome urban architecture, an important shopping area, . . . and the honeymoon capital of Ireland.

---

## First and Last Dublin DART Services

### Mondays to Saturdays

| Morning | | Night | | | | | Morning | | Night | |
|---|---|---|---|---|---|---|---|---|---|---|
| | 0655 | 2255 | 2345 | dep. | HOWTH | arr. | 0750 | 0703 | 2345 | |
| | 0658 | 2258 | 2348 | dep. | Sutton | arr. | 0744 | 0657 | 2339 | |
| | 0700 | 2300 | 2350 | dep. | Bayside | arr. | 0742 | 0655 | 2337 | |
| | 0702 | 2302 | 2352 | dep. | Howth Junction | arr. | 0740 | 0653 | 2335 | |
| | 0704 | 2304 | 2354 | dep. | Kilbarrack | dep. | 0738 | 0651 | 2333 | |
| | 0706 | 2306 | 2356 | dep. | Raheny | dep. | 0735 | 0648 | 2330 | |
| | 0708 | 2308 | 2358 | dep. | Harmonstown | dep. | 0733 | 0646 | 2328 | |
| | 0709 | 2309 | 2359 | dep. | Killester | dep. | 0731 | 0644 | 2326 | |
| | 0715 | 2315 | 0005 | arr. | CONNOLLY STN. | dep. | 0727 | 0640 | 2322 | |
| 0700 | 0716 | 2316 | | dep. | CONNOLLY STN. | arr. | 0726 | 0639 | 2321 | 2351 |
| 0703 | 0719 | 2319 | | dep. | Tara St. | dep. | 0724 | 0637 | 2319 | 2349 |
| 0704 | 0720 | 2320 | | arr. | PEARSE STN. | dep. | 0722 | 0635 | 2317 | 2347 |
| 0705 | 0721 | 2321 | | dep. | PEARSE STN. | arr. | 0721 | | 2316 | 2346 |
| 0708 | 0724 | 2324 | | dep. | Landsdowne Rd. | dep. | 0719 | | 2314 | 2344 |

## Mondays to Saturdays

| Morning | | Night | | | Morning | Night | |
|---------|------|------|------|-------------------------|-----------|-----------|------|
| 0709 | 0725 | 2325 | dep. | Sandymount | dep. 0717 | 2312 | 2342 |
| 0711 | 0727 | 2327 | dep. | Sydney Parade | dep. 0715 | 2310 | 2340 |
| 0714 | 0730 | 2330 | dep. | Booterstown | dep. 0713 | 2308 | 2338 |
| 0716 | 0732 | 2332 | dep. | Blackrock | dep. 0711 | 2306 | 2336 |
| 0717 | 0733 | 2333 | dep. | Monkstown | dep. 0710 | 2305 | 2335 |
| 0719 | 0735 | 2335 | dep. | Salthill | dep. 0708 | 2303 | 2333 |
| 0721 | 0737 | 2337 | arr. | DUN LAOGHAIRE | dep. 0706 | 2301 | 2331 |
| 0723 | 0739 | 2339 | arr. | Sandycove | dep. 0704 | 2359 | 2329 |
| 0725 | 0741 | 2341 | arr. | Glenageary | dep. 0703 | 2258 | 2328 |
| 0727 | 0743 | 2343 | arr. | Dalkey | dep. 0701 | 2256 | 2326 |
| 0731 | 0747 | 2347 | arr. | Killiney | dep. 0656 | 2251 | 2321 |
| 0733 | 0749 | 2349 | arr. | Shankhill | dep. 0654 | 2249 | 2319 |
| 0739 | 0755 | 2355 | arr. | BRAY | dep. 0650 | 2245 | 2315 |

# Benelux

## *Vital Tips for the Trains of the Netherlands, Belgium, and Luxembourg*

The well-developed national railroads of the three Benelux countries make it easy for you to travel from city to city. The "Nederlandse Spoorwegen" (NS) carries 600,000 travelers daily on 4,200 passenger trains. The "Societe Nationale des Chemins de Fer belge" (SNCB) (called "Belgische Spoorwegen" in Flemish) and the "Societe Nationale des Chemins de Fer luxembourgois" (CFL) are nearly as busy.

Flat countrysides, dense train networks, frequent services, and short distances make it easy for you to see the Benelux nations by train. You can see any of these countries easily from wherever you make your base. You don't have to pack or unpack here.

### Trains of the Netherlands

NS runs some 2,000 coach units providing 135,000 seats. About 1,300 of these units consist of electric railcar units (or EMUs) made up of two, three, or four carriages.

The workhorse of the NS fleet is the blue-and-yellow railcar called "Dog's Head." Its distinctive profile says it all.

The Netherlands is one vast, efficient rapid-transit district. NS trains move you quickly and comfortably from one point to another not far away. NS has no long-distance trains with romantic names.

Your domestic transportation is carried out by "Stoptreins" (locals) and "InterCities." You can travel anywhere in the Netherlands speedily by a combination of the two. The yellow departure timetables posted in

87

the train stations are your key to finding your way about easily and quickly. There are usually four domestic sheets and one international one. Find the sheet showing your destination. The simple schematic route diagrams showing you the order of stations on your route make your planning easy.

Figure out what combination of InterCities and locals to take. The departure time and platform number followed by an *a* or *b* are printed beside every train's destination. Pay special attention to these letters, which refer to segments on the platform where your train boards. NS platforms are extraordinarily long in order to accommodate two or more trains at the same time. The train you want will be in the sector indicated on the timetable.

A new NS railcar is the IC-3. You can recognize it miles away by its raised driver's cabin. It is the 747 of the train world. You ride this 100 mph train between the Randstad (the high-population-density area stretching from Rotterdam to Amsterdam to Utrecht) and the east and north of the country.

You can tell the Sprinter train by its beveled profile. This electric railcar set was introduced in 1975 for fast acceleration and braking so it could decrease the travel time between nearby stations.

NS's latest acquisitions are the double-deckers. You ride these, in trains made up of multiple units of six or seven, during rush hour on the busiest commuter lines.

The Benelux Train (see the section on this adventure below) takes you between Amsterdam and Brussels. Ride German EuroCity trains to Germany and the French EC Etoile du Nord to Brussels and Paris (Nord).

For an offbeat trip to see the "new land," take one of the quarter-hourly trains to Lelystad. Of NS's twenty-nine-mile Flevoline, you travel for twenty-five miles on land newly reclaimed from the sea and descend from a high point of fifty feet above sea level to twenty feet below. Between Amsterdam and Almere, your first stop, you cross more than a hundred bridges.

Trains run from about 5 A.M. to 1 A.M. (on Sundays and holidays from about 7 A.M.), but trains on the Schiphol Airport line run all night, so count on hourly overnight service for Rotterdam-The Hague-Leiden-Schiphol-Amsterdam-Hilversum-Utrecht.

Round-trip tickets ("Retour") are less than twice the single fare ("Enkele reis"), but valid on the day of issue only. Children under three travel free; those four to eleven pay one guilder (about fifty cents) when accompanied by an adult over eighteen—limit three children per adult.

With a train ticket or pass, you receive a discount of almost 50 percent on bicycle rentals at train stations. Use this well in the Netherlands, where there are more bicyclists than voters, bike lanes are common, and the land is flat.

## Trains of Belgium

Brussels' North and South terminals were converted to through stations at the time of the 1958 World's Fair and a new, mainline station, Central, was built underground, allowing you to tunnel through Brussels' central district on all the mainline, crack trains such as the EC Etoile du Nord. EuroCity and international trains do not stop at Brussels Central but you reach it easily by one of the local trains passing through the North and South stations. The North and South stations are used for international connections.

When you arrive in Belgium, get a free copy of the pocket-sized brochure "IC/IR—1001 Fixed Interval Connections." SNCB's timetable is arranged for departures at fixed intervals, i.e., the same minute after the hour, every hour.

You ride four categories of SNCB domestic trains. InterCity trains give you fast connections between major centers of Belgium and foreign terminuses. InterRegional (IR) trains take you to more intermediate stops. Local (L) trains stop everywhere except stations where only peak trains (P-trains) stop. Peak trains are often double-deckers running at busy travel hours.

When you buy an ordinary single or round-trip domestic ticket (including those to the airport), remember your first segment must be used the day you buy your ticket. When you are buying your ticket in advance, be sure to say on what date you plan to travel. A round-trip ticket is valid for three calendar days.

## Trains of Luxembourg

Luxembourg City, the Grand Duchy of Luxembourg's enchanting capital, is so well connected to the rest of Europe by international and EuroCity trains that the tourist board is tempted to call it the "Heart of Europe." Once there you easily explore Luxembourg's green mountains and valleys by CFL's extensive bus network.

Luxembourg City's train station is one of the few with leaded glass windows and a striking, green patina steeple. The modern leaded-glass windows picturing the profile of Luxembourg Castle dominate the interior and cast colored southern lights on the central hall. A pleasant cafeteria adjoins the central hall. Use the coin-operated lockers in the main hall. When they are filled, check your luggage with the "Consigne des Bagages" down the hall. You orient yourself with city and regional maps protected in a glass case in front of the station.

CFL's international-standard trains have liveries of military green or green and white. Diesel railcars are purple. Locomotives are purple and yellow. Stripes indicating first class are orange.

The Place de la Gare is surrounded by hotels and banks for changing your money. Turn to your right as you exit for the bus stands where you board both the Luxair airport bus and the city buses to the airport. Past the bus stands, the Luxair terminus accommodates Luxembourg's tourist information office. Make hotel reservations and change money here. Everything closes tightly at noon for lunch.

Make Luxembourg City your base. CFL's two main lines and two secondary lines are centered here. Luxembourg lies on the mainline of the orange-livery EuroCity Iris, the EC Vauban, the Edelweiss, and the Riviera Express running along the Brussels-Namur-Luxembourg-Metz-Strasbourg-Basel route. You travel by EC Robert Schuman, EC Victor Hugo, and EC Goethe to Paris's Est station, Le Grand-Ducal to Brussels' South station, and L'Ardennais to Antwerp.

CFL's second mainline takes you between Luxembourg City and Brussels via Liege.

CFL's most scenic line, through "Luxembourgois Switzerland," takes you through the beautiful town of Esch-sur-Sure to Rodange and into France at Longuyon. CFL's other secondary line takes you across the Moselle River to Trier, in Germany.

Although the Eurailpass brochure doesn't say so, CFL's national bus system is included completely in your Eurailpass. Simply show your pass to the driver of the tan buses striped with Burgundy red. You can make a number of excursions through the delightful countryside into quaint villages, and because you use your Eurailpass, you visit the same sights as the tour buses without cost. Your bus calls at all small villages, enabling you to see the detail of the landscape and get on and off as you wish to explore.

## Airport Trains

When you arrive by air in Benelux, you have it easy.

Schiphol is one of the best train airports in Europe because of its mainline connections completed in 1986. InterCity trains take you to Amsterdam's airport from as far as Groningen and Leeuwarden in northern Netherlands, Hanover in Germany, or Brussels in Belgium, thus giving you a way to reach your plane from all over northern Europe without changing trains.

A second stretch of rapid-transit line takes you from Amsterdam's

RAI station (the convention hall), on Amsterdam's outskirts, to Amsterdam's Zuid station, to Schiphol, and to Leiden.

The train for the sixteen-minute trip to Brussels' airport (not covered by Eurailpass) is a blue-and-white railcar painted with an airport insignia. The worn two-unit shuttle power car and trailer departs from Brussels' Central station but you can also board in Brussels' North station.

You have two choices for travel between Luxembourg's Findel Airport and the train station. Most take the blue-and-white Luxair bus leaving every thirty minutes from the front of the airport terminal. Others walk across the small airport parking lot to the yellow sign marking the bus stop for Luxembourg city bus line 9, which departs every fifteen to twenty minutes and costs about one-fifth that of the airport bus. The city bus takes about ten minutes longer to the train station but stops near many hotels and the youth hostel.

From the train station, Icelandair provides its passengers with discounted train transportation to Switzerland and France, and free long-distance bus service to more than a dozen destinations in Germany, Belgium, and the Netherlands. Telephone Icelandair at 1-800-223-5500.

## Getting around Amsterdam

You are fortunate that Amsterdam has an excellent public transportation system. There are sixteen streetcar lines (five originate in front of Central station), thirty bus lines, and two Metro lines plus eight night bus lines.

Buy day tickets for one, two, three, or more days, but unless you intend to spend a day riding public transportation, a more flexible plan is to buy strip-tickets which are available in multiples of two, ten, and fifteen boxes.

Consider these strip-tickets as national currency. Use them for transportation not only on Amsterdam's public transportation, but for transportation in all of the Netherlands' major cities and even on NS trains for local transportation.

For one trip in Amsterdam's large "Centrum," you validate your ticket in the validating machines by folding and canceling two boxes. For more complicated journeys—because you are a tourist—the tram or bus driver will do it.

Save money by buying strip-tickets in public transportation offices (there is one across from Amsterdam's Central station) and in post offices. Here you receive fifteen-box strip-tickets for the same price as ten-box strip-tickets bought on a tram or bus.

## Crossing the Channel

Crossing the English Channel by steamship is certainly one of the most pleasant, or miserable, events of your European vacation. You avoid airport terminuses but face possible boredom or foul weather. It can be an overwhelming pleasure or a bloodcurdling horror.

Until the tunnel under the channel is completed in 1993, there are three ways of crossing: air, hovercraft, and steamship. (All steamships are motorships today, but the traditional name is still used.) Both Belgium and the Netherlands have important sea links to Britain. When you hold a Eurailpass, a Eurail Flexipass, or a BritRail Pass, taking the steamer is the most logical way although the ship fare itself (or cabin, when you travel overnight) is covered by none of them.

To reach London from Amsterdam, ride the Admiraal de Ruyter or Benjamin Britten to Hook of Holland for a day or night boat to Harwich (Parkeston Quai), where you take the nonstop IC to London's Liverpool Street station. Border formalities are fast and the transfer at Hook of Holland (where adventurers come from Germany and Austria aboard the Austria Express) is easy because moving walkways and luggage carts help you from train to boat.

The modern, 31,189-ton, Dutch *Konigin Beatrix* and Sealink's *St. Nicholas* (17,043 tons) offer duty-free shopping, three categories of restaurants, movie theaters showing recent American films, first- and second-class lounges, a disco, and space to waste. Warning: guilders are used on the Dutch vessel, pounds sterling on the British. Exchange banks are open aboard ship, but plan ahead to have the right currency.

Look for special, all-inclusive, bargain offers at the train and tourism offices when you visit Amsterdam, Brussels, or London, and also consult the free "Go BritRail" brochure available from BritRail offices (see Appendix).

You travel between Belgium and England either aboard air-cushion Jetfoils, or aboard the 3 3/4- to 4-hour crossing between Dover (Western Docks) and Ostende operated by Belgian Marine and P&O European Ferries.

Jetfoils are fast (one hour and forty minutes), but are often rocky and you see nothing. Your steamship's landing in Dover can be one of your fondest memories because of your views of the famous White Cliffs. When you arrive at Ostende at sunset, you'll see Ostende's surprisingly modern waterfront. The entire coast, lined with high-rise apartments and offices, is brilliant in the late sunlight.

Boat trains for Belgium take you via Dover from London's Victoria station, where you use their special ticketing and information office.

## Benelux Tourrail

The railroads of Benelux cooperate on a regional rail pass called the Benelux Tourrail. This gives you unlimited travel on the trains of SNCB, NS, CFL, and the bus lines in Luxembourg. You also receive more than a 25 percent discount on Panorama-Tours' city tour in Brussels and at the Antwerp Zoo, which is located next to Antwerp's Central station.

Similar to a Flexipass, the Benelux Tourrail is valid for travel on any five days of your choosing within seventeen. Why seventeen? So you can arrange travel over three weekends.

Buy it in the U.S. through offices of the Netherlands Board of Tourism (NBT) (see Appendix) or in Europe at the larger trains stations and many travel agencies in the Benelux countries. Second-class passes are about one-third less expensive than first-class ones. Those aged twelve to twenty-five buy a second-class Benelux Junior Tourrail for another 28 percent off. Children four to eleven pay half.

## National Rail Passes

You save a lot of green with passes on the yellow NS trains. From a general ticketing window in train stations in the Netherlands, ask for a day card ("Dagkaart") or three-day, week, or month cards ("3-Daagse-, Week-, or Maandnetkaarten") for unlimited first- or second-class travel. You can buy equivalent three- and seven-day passes from the offices of the NBT in America, which calls them "Rail Ranger" passes. When the guilder is strong, you save 20 percent by buying them before you leave.

In America you may also purchase a "Public Transport Link Ranger," a money-saving extension of (and only available with) the Rail Ranger pass that lets you travel on every subway, streetcar, city and provincial bus of the extensive Dutch public transportation system.

NBT also sells the Holland Leisure Card, which includes free first-class train transfers from Schiphol Airport to Amsterdam or The Hague; a 40 percent discount on a day pass for unlimited train travel in the Netherlands, on sightseeing, on car rentals, and on domestic flights; plus discounts on hotels belonging to the Golden Tulip, Novotel, and Cok groups. It's an offer you can't refuse. When you also buy a Eurailpass, you won't have to validate it until after you have exhausted the Holland Leisure Card's benefits.

SNCB offers a Belgium Tourrail similar to a Benelux Tourrail, but valid for travel in Belgium only. You buy these at Belgian train stations. SNCB also sells season, or "Runabout," tickets which are valid over the entire SNCB network or particular routes. These are sold for sixteen day- and longer periods for either first- or second-class travel.

The Luxembourg Billet Reseau provides a day's unlimited second-class travel on CFL's trains and buses. Senior travelers receive a 50 percent discount.

Adventure through the Benelux countries by boat across the Netherlands' Zuider Zee, the Benelux Train between Amsterdam and Brussels, and Dutch day trips.

## *Around the Zuider Zee*
## *Tamed Sea and Steam*

Have you ever wanted to sail across the Netherlands' Zuider Zee (now known as the Ijsselmeer)? Crossing this inland sea is smooth as peanut butter. When your train arrives in Stavoren, the *Bep Glasius* is unloading passengers and a line of bicyclists has formed to wheel their vehicles onto its deck.

When the ticket collector comes checking, just flash your Eurailpass. Even without a Eurailpass, the fare is modest.

The *Bep Glasius* is primarily a pleasure boat. Those without bicycles have backpacks.

The Netherlands has no rugged Alps or ragged fjords. Its charm lies in its tamed sea and in the fertile, flat farmlands crisscrossed with canals.

A one-day round trip through the north of the Netherlands, across the Ijsselmeer, and south through East Friesland samples the pleasing scenery of this low country. It is worth a day away from Amsterdam, especially when you are riding it free on a Eurailpass, taking advantage of Benelux's only advertised Eurailpass bonus—the free crossing of the Ijsselmeer during the summer.

Plan your departure from Amsterdam for an early hour so you have time to cross the Ijsselmeer, browse leisurely through the Zuider Zee Museum in Enkhuizen, and then travel on the "Bello" steam train. Be sure you board the right segment of your yellow-and-blue InterCity train at Amsterdam's Central station. It divides in Zwolle. One half goes to Groningen. You want to be in the half marked "Leeuwarden."

This train, the Netherlands, makes very few stops. The first is in Hilversum, the headquarters for Dutch radio. The second is in Amersfoort, the junction for trains coming from Hook of Holland and Rotterdam. By the time you stop in Zwolle, where your train splits, you are entering Friesland, the land of cows, cheese, and tall, blond people.

Your train proceeds as a local. By the time you approach Akkrum, the land is appealing. Broad fields are peppered with black-and-white

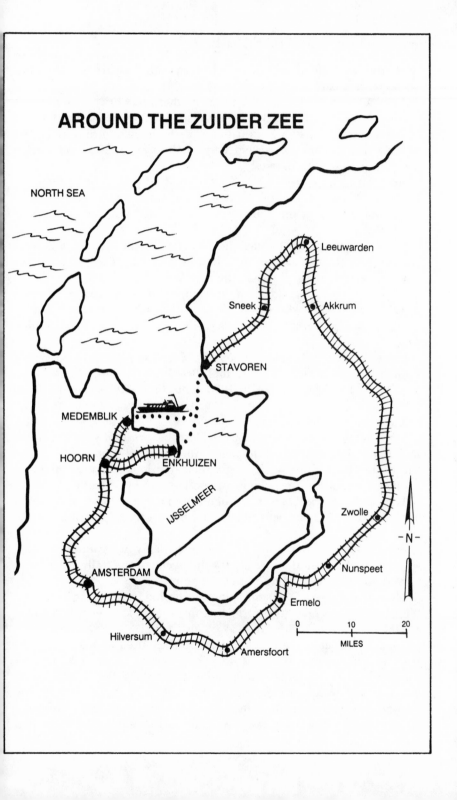

AROUND THE ZUIDER ZEE

cows. You pass ribbonlike, calm canals busy with pleasure motor yachts, sailboats, and barges.

After waiting almost a half-hour in the white-brick Leeuwarden station (you can lunch in the station restaurant or hire a bicycle), you board a second-class-only train for a 3/4-hour run to Stavoren. The driver revs its motor like an old Ford, and—clickety-clack—off you go past sheep, cows, and horses.

Some farms have black, glazed-tile roofs. This is a region of intensive farming. Of course, one of the dangers of traveling by train through farm country is that the window will be lowered and farmers will be fertilizing.

Herons stand sentry in stagnant, water-filled ditches. Most passengers get off at Sneek. The farm houses have acre-size red-tile roofs enveloping everything down to the first floor.

The canal running adjacent to your train is packed with small pleasure boats when you reach Workum. You often see curious sights along the tracks. Here you see a stack of bundled thatches for thatching roofs.

From Stavoren, the Rederij NACO Eurailpass service consists of summer-only crossings on the 12 mph *Bep Glasius*, a 300-passenger ship built by Peters' Scheepsbouw in 1966. The *Bep Glasius* sells sandwiches and fabulous Dutch fast food such as french fried potatoes and split pea soup in the luncheon area below deck.

From the deck you see a crazy, kaleidoscopic world of sails and ships: sailboats, cabin cruisers, schooners, very daring windsurfers, huge barges, and oddly masted fishing vessels that look like they might be manned by pirates. About halfway, you are met by a fleet of kayaks.

The afterdeck becomes one huge parking place for fully ladened bicycles. After an hour, you finally view the profile of Enkhuizen—the city hall and church.

When you land after your one hour and twenty-two minute crossing, you are greeted with the rare contrasting scene of the train station with a train and boat unloading at the same time.

This area of West Friesland is interesting for its seafaring tradition. West Frisian ships sailed the world's oceans from Enkhuizen, Medemblik, and Hoorn to trade with far-away countries.

Enkhuizen is lined with the old seawall which used to protect the city from storms on the former Zuider Zee, ending at the Old Harbor where you see traditional sailing vessels, the fishing fleet, and numerous yachts. Beyond the sea wall is the "living" Zuider Zee Museum, Europe's newest open-air museum, which gives you an interesting picture of the life and work of the people of the region who depended on this inland sea until 1932 when the Barrier Dam sealed the Zuider Zee from the North Sea.

From your landing near the train station, walk five minutes to the boat quay for your boat ride to the Zuider Zee showcase.

Leave the open-air museum on foot, pass through the town proper, and walk back to the train station in order to see the West Church and the South Church and to photograph the old fortified tower named "Drommedaris."

At Enkhuizen you rejoin the electrified lines of NS. It takes you slightly less than an hour to reach Amsterdam Central station by Dog's Head Stoptrein, and twenty minutes to reach Hoorn (the namesake for Africa's Cape Horn)—but there's a better way.

Steam-enthusiast volunteers come from all over the Netherlands to donate their time freely so you can travel on the twelve-mile steam-train line from Medemblik to Hoorn pulled by the restored steam locomotive "Bello," built in 1914. (You reach Medemblik by connecting boat from Enkhuizen—or you can travel in the return direction.)

In Enkhuizen, you begin the steam-train trip by boat at the quay; in Hoorn, you begin at the steam-train station across the overpass from the NS station. This is the same event as an NS day tour (see the "Dutch Treat" section below), but with a Eurailpass you save money because you don't pay for the NS transportation from Amsterdam.

At the midpoint, in Medemblik, you can visit the Dutch Steam Engine Museum. Many engines work regularly.

Most of your train trip back to Amsterdam from Hoorn takes you through heavily populated neighborhoods. Note the bright new stations at Zaandam and Amsterdam Noord. Shortly after Zaandam, you see the shipping and shipbuilding on Amsterdam Harbor.

---

## Rederij NACO Service

### Early July to Early September

| 0844 | 1144 | 1444 | 1744 dep. Enkhuizen | arr. | 1136 | 1436 | 1736 | 2036 |
| 1006 | 1306 | 1606 | 1906 arr. Stavoren | dep. | 1014 | 1314 | 1614 | 1914 |

**Middle May to Early July and**

**Early September to Middle September**

| 0944 | 1244 | 1644 | dep. Enkhuizen | arr. | 1236 | 1536 | 1936 |
| 1106 | 1406 | 1806 | arr. Stavoren | dep. | 1114 | 1414 | 1814 |

## Volunteer Steam Train and Boat Services

| (1) | (2) | (2) | | | (1) | (2) | (2) |
|-----|-----|-----|---|---|-----|-----|-----|
| 1100 | 1100 | 1500 | dep. Enkhuizen (Boat) | arr. | 1415 | 1415 | 1745 |
| 1215 | 1215 | 1615 | arr. Medemblik | dep. | 1300 | 1300 | 1630 |
| 1315 | 1315 | 1645 | dep. Medemblik (Steam) | arr. | 1215 | 1215 | 1545 |
| 1415 | 1415 | 1745 | arr. Hoorn | dep. | 1115 | 1115 | 1445 |

(1) May, June, and September: Tuesday to Saturday.
(2) July and August: Daily.

## Connecting Train/Boat Timings

InterCity trains, Amsterdam/Leeuwarden: Hourly
Diesel trains, Leeuwarden/Stavoren: Hourly
Stoptreins, Enkhuizen/Hoorn/Amsterdam: Half-hourly

---

## Benelux Train
### Dutch Yellow and Belgian Bordeaux Red

From Amsterdam's Central station you depart, not pulled by a locomotive in front, but pushed, by the locomotive in back. The driver controls from a special compartment in the front of the train.

Between Amsterdam's Central station, Schiphol Airport, Rotterdam, The Hague, Antwerp, and Brussels, you ride the Benelux Train—the crack train and namesake of the Benelux countries. The Belgian locomotives and Dutch carriages are painted in a shared, single livery—a combination of the NS yellow and the Bordeaux red of the Belgian railroads.

It is an impressive train: no-nonsense, comfortable, and most convenient for you to ride. It departs hourly, free to Eurailpass holders.

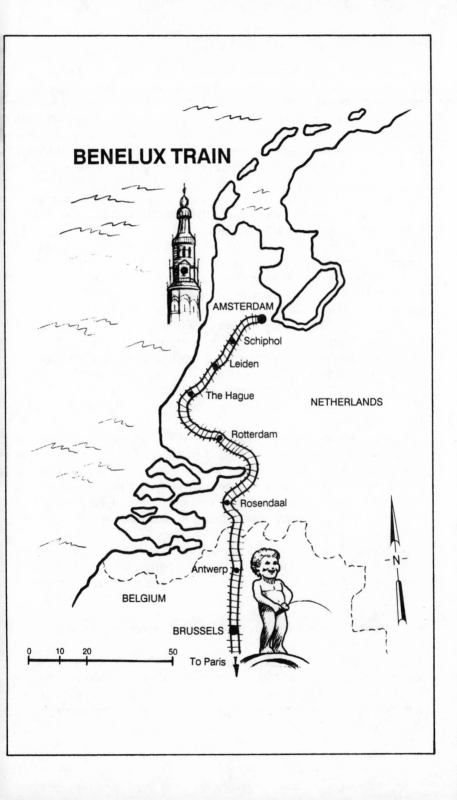

**BENELUX TRAIN**

AMSTERDAM

Schiphol

Leiden

The Hague

NETHERLANDS

Rotterdam

Rosendaal

Antwerp

BELGIUM

BRUSSELS

To Paris

-N-

0    10    20              50

The irony is that the proud Benelux Train is imported. The Belgian locomotive was manufactured in France; the Dutch carriages were made in Germany.

SNCB, the Belgian national railroad, procures its locomotives from France because the locomotives there share the same electrical characteristics, but the 100-mph Benelux Train locomotives, built in 1985, are convertible for running in the Netherlands as well as in Belgium.

The carriages were manufactured in 1986 by Waggonfabrik Talbot, in Aachen, Germany, because the Netherlands is too small to support a national train-carriage industry. The Benelux Train's carriages evolved from the design of NS's IC-3 coaches, which Talbot also built. You sit in orange-plush two-opposite-one first-class seats that recline a few inches when you press the orange armrest release; they have sturdy, fold-down tables in their backs. You look through panoramic windows that partially roll down. A clouded-glass partition separates smoking and nonsmoking sections. The interior doors open with a press of the lever. One first-class car is half compartments, half salon style; one contains a telephone booth; and one has a special compartment for bicycles. Linoleum floors and jet-type blowers for ventilation are used throughout.

Take a good look at the doors on this train. They are of a special Dutch design that quickly fly open into two halves to make it easier for you to get on and off faster—and are a boon for anyone bringing a bicycle with them.

Leaving Amsterdam's Central station (CS), you travel first over old track, then over new—past the futuristic elevated stop at Amsterdam-Sloterdijk. After a quick stop at the new Amsterdam-Lelylaan station (accessible by city streetcar line No. 1), you hear the announcement booming over the loud speaker: "Next station: Schiphol." Then you zoom underground, with lights zipping by you like lasers in a special-effects space movie.

At Schiphol, your train's doors open automatically. Schiphol train station has modern digital signs, marble flooring, an electric walkway going up, and abundant, conventional pushcarts (because walkways are used instead of escalators, there is no need for special pushcarts).

Out of Schiphol, refreshment trolleys are pushed down your train's aisle. Vendors wear Bordeaux-red jackets to match their train's livery. Catering is by Wagons-Lits.

Past Leiden, the university town, you stop briefly in the Netherlands' seat of government. The Hague's Central Station is a modern rectangular hall which makes it easy for you to find your direction. The tracks are located along one of the longer sides below an enormous digital departures board.

Rotterdam Central is a bright, airy station. Buses to North Sea ferries depart from the side door. City information (VVV) and train information share a yellow kiosk in the main hall. Cut flowers usually sold in Dutch stations brightly overflow an entire corner of the main hall.

Passengers disembarking here scurry down the stairs to Rotterdam's Metro station. The streetcar and bus circle is on the plaza in front. (Your national strip-tickets are valid.) The bank and information office ("NS Inlichtingen Bureau") can be found in the entrance hall.

Your train then passes through Dordrecht, a charming town on the Meuse which offers visitors an interesting church. At the red-brick Roosendaal station house, the border crossing, you see a whole carnival of NS equipment, including double-deckers—some blue-painted—on different tracks.

Antwerpen Centraal, remodeled in 1988, is an end station. A fresh locomotive pulls you south in the reverse direction.

When you enter the Belgian capital city's environs, before reaching Brussels' North station, you see to the west the giant aluminum Atomium representing a molecule of iron magnified 200 million times, symbol of the 1958 Brussels' World's Fair. In the same glimpse you see the first of Brussels' many Gothic churches.

Brussels' North station is a large station connected to a modern Metro station. Brussels has two Metro systems, and a twenty-four-hour tourist ticket takes you over the entire city.

The North station's information office is located in the departures hall; make your hotel reservations here. Nearby is a change bank and two restaurants, the "Edelweiss" and the "Hermes." There is also a waiting room in the underground passage between tracks 9 and 10, but adventurers traveling to Luxembourg have no time to waste, for they have only ten minutes before their InterCity leaves. You also board railcars to Brussels' Zavandam Airport here (not covered by Eurailpass) from various platforms shown on the yellow departure signs.

When the Benelux Train leaves the North station, it tunnels underground to Brussels' Central station, an underground station built on the side of a hill so that its entrance is at street level. It is quite like a busy subway stop.

Use Central station as your entrance to Brussels because of its location. From Brussels' Central station's platforms, you climb a gracious stairway below an imposing statue honoring the fallen of the two world wars. "Taverne Stephenson" honors George Stephenson, the British railroad pioneer.

Walk five minutes downhill toward the town hall's spire to the Grande Place. Brussels' tourist information office, for hotel bookings and abundant information, is one block north, at 61, rue du Marche aux Herbes.

Riders to Brussels' airport need to look for the signs "Bruxelles National-Aeroport/Brussel Nationaal-Luchthaven" and an airplane pictograph pointing to Track 1a, across the subterranean station from all the rest. It is poorly designed, poorly lit, and a dead end.

Continuing south from Brussels' Central station, your Benelux Train emerges into the sunlight at Brussels' Chapelle station, bypassed by express trains, and you see Brussels' Royal Palace to the east.

Brussels' South station also has Metro connections, a bank, a full-course "Pullman" restaurant, and a pleasant "Iris" cafeteria. A EuroCity Club, open to Eurailpass holders, is located in the departure hall at the center of the station's south side. The post office is next door.

## Benelux Train Service

| | | | | | | | | | |
|---|---|---|---|---|---|---|---|---|---|
| 0622 | 0724 | 0826 | ......2026 | dep. | AMSTERDAM (CS) | arr. | 0910 | 1008 | 2309 | 0013 |
| 0633 | 0733 | 0835 | 2035 | dep. | A'dam Lelylaan | dep. | 0900 | 0958 | 2259 | 0001 |
| 0642 | 0742 | 0844 | 2044 | dep. | Schiphol Airp. | dep. | 0851 | 0949 | 2250 | 2352 |
| 0658 | 0758 | 0900 | 2100 | dep. | Leiden | dep. | 0835 | 0933 | 2234 | 2332 |
| 0712 | 0810 | 0912 | 2112 | dep. | The Hague (HS) | dep. | 0823 | 0921 | 2222 | 2321 |
| 0731 | 0831 | 0931 | 2131 | dep. | Rotterdam (CS) | dep. | 0805 | 0902 | 2204 | 2302 |
| 0748 | 0848 | 0948 | 2148 | dep. | Dordrecht | dep. | 0745 | 0846 | 2148 | 2246 |
| 0811 | 0911 | 1011 | 2211 | arr. | Roosendaal (NL) | dep. | 0724 | 0825 | 2127 | 2225 |
| 0814 | 0914 | 1014 | 2214 | dep. | Roosendaal (B) | arr. | 0721 | 0822 | 2125 | 2222 |
| 0843 | 0943 | 1043 | 2243 | dep. | Antwerp (C) | dep. | 0654 | 0754 | 2057 | 2154 |
| 0852 | 0952 | 1052 | 2252 | dep. | Berchem | dep. | 0646 | 0746 | 2049 | 2146 |
| 0907 | 1007 | 1107 | 2307 | arr. | Mechelen | dep. | 0633 | 0733 | 2036 | 2133 |
| 0921 | 1021 | 1121 | 2321 | arr. | BRUSSELS (N) | dep. | 0619 | 0719 | 2022 | 2119 |
| 0926 | 1026 | 1126 | 2326 | arr. | BRUSSELS (C) | dep. | 0614 | 0714 | 2017 | 2114 |
| 0930 | 1030 | 1130 | 2330 | arr. | BRUSSELS (S) | dep. | 0610 | 0710 | ......2013 | 2110 |

. . . and then every hour until:

## *Dutch Treat*
## *Netherlands by Day*

Netherlands by day. Amsterdam by night. NS has a program for you to maximize your pleasure and minimize your cost.

Take advantage of NS's well-conceived, economical program to see all of the Netherlands by train, learn about the complex customs and history of this small exciting country, and come to understand the Dutch way of life. NS sells all-inclusive tickets to the best things to see in the Netherlands.

Buy individual day-trip tickets (these are not the same as the day cards described earlier) at any train station ticket office. These include the round-trip train journey (originating from any station), the price of the attraction, connecting bus or streetcar fare, and sometimes coffee and cake. You receive a substantial discount, you know the total cost in advance, and you determine your departure times yourself.

If you already have a special train ticket such as a Rail Ranger or a Eurailpass, use it for the train journey and buy an "Attraction Ticket" at your departure or arrival station. An Attraction Ticket gives you the benefit of NS's planning and lets you see the same day trip you select but without paying for the train. The money you save on day-trip tickets won't in itself justify buying a Eurailpass, however. To spend as little as possible, plan your itinerary to take these day trips before you validate your Eurailpass or after it expires.

The total program is set out in the booklet, "Er op uit," in Dutch, which is available from ticket offices at stations and from NS's information offices.

To gain a thorough impression of the Dutch way of life, modern and past, take day trips to Rotterdam, Arnhem, Enkhuizen, the Hague, Volendam and Marken, Zaandam, and Maastricht. Railfans enjoy Utrecht's Railroad Museum and enthralling music box and barrel organ museum (as who wouldn't?) and the volunteer steam train between Hoorn and Medemblik.

In Rotterdam, you sail in a motor launch from Willemsplein Quay for a round trip through the city's large, modern port complex. You climb the "Space Tower" in a glass-enclosed lift winding slowly up and around Euromast's steel extension to the very top of the television tower. Your ticket includes the train ride to Rotterdam, the round trip of the harbor, admission to the Euromast and Space Tower, and a day Rail Ranger ticket for the subway, bus, and tram.

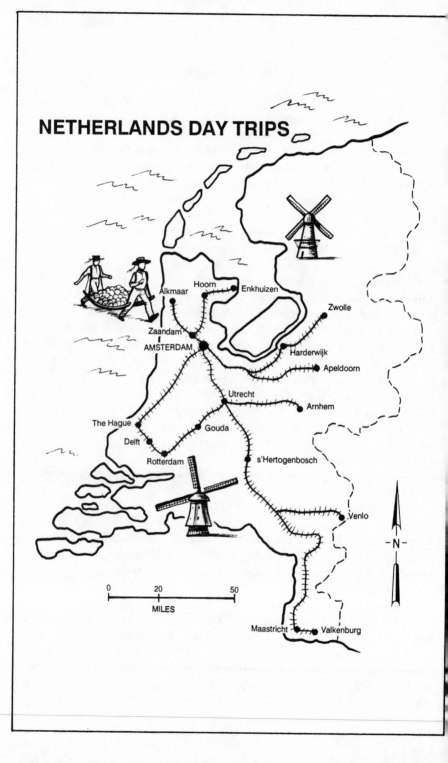

# NETHERLANDS DAY TRIPS

Alkmaar
Hoorn
Enkhuizen
Zwolle
Zaandam
AMSTERDAM
Harderwijk
Apeldoorn
Utrecht
Arnhem
The Hague
Gouda
Delft
Rotterdam
s'Hertogenbosch
Venlo
Maastricht
Valkenburg

0    20    50
MILES

-N-

In Enkhuizen, visit the preserved Zuider Zee houses and travel by ferry from Enkhuizen's train station to the Zuider Zee Museum and return. Your ticket includes the train, the ferry, and admission to the museum.

At Monnickendam, board the "Marken Express" boat to the Island of Marken, see the cottages built on piles in the IJssel lake, dams, dikes, and fishing boats with colored sails, and then continue by boat to Volendam. Your ticket includes the train, bus, and Marken Express boat.

The scale-model town of Madurodam in the Hague shows you how classic Dutch architecture looks to birds with broad wings. Then you visit Scheveningen, one of the Dutch people's favorite seaside resorts with a new pier and sea pool. Your ticket includes the train, admissions to Madurodam and Scheveningen Pier, and a day Rail Ranger ticket.

Curators of Arnhem's Open-Air Museum carefully gathered, rebuilt, furnished, and preserved a magnificent collection of complete farms, houses, cottages, and windmills so you can appreciate how the Dutch used to live. Your ticket includes the train, the museum bus, admission, and a Dutch pancake with coffee.

In Zaandam you see the 1948 village called Zaanse Schans, constructed from threatened windmills and houses. You visit the Windmill Museum to see how windmills work and cruise on the river Zaan. Your ticket includes the train, a brochure, admission to the Windmill Museum, the river cruise, and a Dutch pancake with coffee.

Another day trip is a walking tour of Maastricht to magnificent churches, historic public buildings, city walls, period houses, and Roman ruins. You cruise on the river Meuse (Maas). Your ticket includes the train, the river cruise, a grotto tour, admission to St. Servaas Church, and coffee with a Limburg open fruit pie.

When you have determined what dates you are going to be in the Netherlands, take out your pencil and note some of the following attractions. Seasonal events are some of the most interesting.

• Keukenhof Lisse—Between the end of March and the end of May tulips are in full bloom.

• Kaasmarkt Alkmaar—On Fridays only from the beginning of June until the middle of August, board the "Kaasmarkt Express" from Amsterdam to Alkmaar for the colorful cheese market.

• Schagermarkt—On Thursdays only from the end of June until the end of August, in Schager's market you can enjoy a folkloric color pageant with dancing and music.

• Hoornsemarkt—On Wednesdays only from the beginning of July until the end of August, ride to Hoorn to see the 600-year-old town present the famous old-time Dutch market and bring the medieval guilds of trade and artisans back to life.

• Kaasmarkt Gouda—On Thursday mornings only from the end of June to the end of August, take the train to the Gouda cheese market in the interesting city that gave the cheese its name.

Write the NBT (see Appendix). Ask for their free color brochure "Touring Holland by Rail" and their free pocket timetable "Main Train Connections."

## Selected Schedule of NS Day Trips

- The Hague, Madurodam and Scheveningen Pier or sea pool
- The Hague, Mauritshuis
- Delft
- Volendam and Marken
- Paleis Het Loo, House of Orange royal palace
- De Hoge Veluwe nature reserve
- Enkhuizen, Zuider Zee Museum
- Flevohof polder
- De Haar Castle near Utrecht
- Zaanse Schans settlement near Zaandam
- Historic triangle by steam train and boat
- Stormvloed barrier, Delta plan, Oosterschelde
- Rotterdam, Europort or Seven Rivers tour
- Rotterdam, Botlek and Euromast
- Utrecht Railroad Museum and Music Box Museum
- Arnhem Open-Air Museum
- Efteling recreation park
- Castle gardens, Arcen
- Maastricht
- Valkenburg
- Giethoorn, the Venice of Holland
- Burgers Zoo and Safari Park
- Anne Frank House, Amsterdam
- Amsterdam Museums

# France

## *Vital Tips for the Trains of France*

Base your travel in Paris. Paris is the heart of the network of the French National Railroads ("Societe Nationale des Chemins de Fer Francais," or SNCF). Because trains radiate from Paris, you have difficulty traveling long distances without returning to Paris for connections. Trains traveling circumferentially are so rare that they have a special name: "transversales."

You seldom travel through Paris without having to change train stations. There are six mainline train stations, serving five separately administered "Reseaux" or networks, each of which is subdivided into "Regions."

France is known for comfortable, convenient, and fast trains. SNCF's long-distance trains are a joy to ride. Two TGV networks ("Trains a Grande Vitesse") take you at the fastest speeds in the world and the last remaining TEE (Trans Europ Express) train carries you in great comfort.

TGV Southeast stretches from Paris's Gare de Lyon to Switzerland, French ski country and the Riviera. The TGV Atlantique, new in fall 1989, takes you between Paris's Montparnasse station and Brittany, Bordeaux, and Spain.

The last remaining deluxe TEEs run between Paris and Strasbourg—large stainless-steel, first-class-only coaches. You will also see shiny modern diesel railcars (TER, "Trains Express Regionaux") such as the ones from Strasbourg that take you throughout Alsace.

EuroCity trains from Paris take you into all neighboring countries. Choose between the EC Moliere, EC Parsifal, EC Goethe, and EC Victor Hugo for Germany; the EC Le Corbusier, EC L'Arbalete, and the EuroCity TGVs for Switzerland; the EC Etoile du Nord, EC Ile de France, EC Rubens, EC Brabant, and EC Robert Schuman (and the ECs Vauban and Iris through Alsace) to the Benelux countries; and the EC Catalan Talgo from SNCF's Geneva station to Barcelona.

Be sure to double-check from which train station your train departs. Gare de Lyon, Paris's origin of the TGV Southeast network, takes you to Lyon, Marseille, Grenoble, the Riviera, Italy, and French-speaking Switzerland. The Gare Montparnasse is headquarters for your TGV Atlantique service to Brittany, Bordeaux, Lourdes, and Spain via Hendaye. Go to the Gare d'Austerlitz for Toulouse, Limoges, Orleans, and Spain/Portugal. The Gare de l'Est serves Strasbourg, Luxembourg, southern Germany, and German-speaking Switzerland via Basel. Trains from the Gare du Nord take you to Belgium, the Netherlands, north- ern Germany, Scandinavia, and the Channel ports for England. The Gare St. Lazare serves Normandy, Le Havre, and Cherbourg for ferry crossings to the Republic of Ireland.

## Getting around Paris

Paris has perhaps the most convenient, efficient, and surely the least expensive public transportation system of any capital. There are two independent underground train systems with separate ticketing sys- tems. Plan to use both. You already know about the famous Paris Metro. Its lines are connected with SNCF's RER (Regional Electric Network) full-size (some are double-decked) rapid-transit trains. You ride RER trains between Paris's airports and the city center. Another takes you to Versailles.

Stop at the Paris Tourist Office (127, avenue des Champs-Elysees) for details on public transportation, system maps, and purchase of tourist tickets. Neither Metro nor RER trains are covered by Eurailpass but a France Railpass gives you limited privileges on both (see France Railpass section below).

To transfer between Paris's train stations, the Metro is the easiest and cheapest way. You ride the second-class cars (although many riders don't observe the distinction) unless you hold a first-class "Paris Sesa- me" ticket issued in connection with a France Railpass. Between Gare du Nord and Gare d'Austerlitz, you will save time by taking the RER and changing at St. Michel/Notre Dame (this takes less than thirty minutes).

You save substantially by purchasing single-ride Metro tickets in a block of ten (ask for "un carnet"), but you save even more with unlimited ride schemes. A "Formule Une" is a one-day Metro pass. Paris Sesame tickets provide you with unlimited transportation for two, four, or seven days. A "Carte Orange" allows you to use the system for one week but requires a passport-type photograph.

## Airport Trains

Use the convenient train connections from Paris's airports on SNCF's RER system (not covered by Eurailpass). Prices vary with distance, but a single ticket purchased at either Charles de Gaulle or Orly Airport will connect you to more than a hundred RER stations in the Paris area.

From Charles de Gaulle Airport, board the free shuttle bus between CDG's two terminals to the SNCF Roissy-Rail station. Then take the direct RER train, a high-speed, minimal-stop express which runs above ground outside the city and then underground within it. It departs every fifteen minutes for interchanges at Gare du Nord, Chatelet-les Halles, Luxembourg, and St. Michel/Notre-Dame stations.

From Orly, board the shuttle from Orly Sud to the SNCF Orly-Rail station, then the high-speed RER train running every fifteen minutes to the Austerlitz train station, St. Michel/Notre Dame, Musee d'Orsay, Invalides, and Boulevard Victor.

## Overnight Trains

SNCF's overnight equipment is so good it is exported. You can hardly resist riding overnight on the long routes from Paris because with a Eurailpass you pay no more to sleep in a four-bunk compartment than second-class passengers pay for six-bunk couchettes.

EuroCity Night trains from Paris include EC Stendhal to Milan, EC Palatino to Rome, EC Galilei to Venice or Florence, and upscale Barcelona and Paris-Madrid Talgo trains.

Budget adventurers may also investigate the Cabines-8 found only on SNCF. These specially configured sleeping carriages are designed for young people who prefer not to pay for sleeping accommodations. Each carriage contains twelve compartments with eight semireclining contoured bunks, four per side.

The bunks are treated as seats for reservations purposes so you pay no supplement. If the threat of claustrophobia does not bother you, these second-class bunks carry the right price. You only need to pay for a simple space reservation, as you would for a seat on any long-distance train. These travel nightly on the following routes: Paris-Hamburg,

Paris-Amsterdam, Paris-Strasbourg, Reims-Nice, Paris-Brest, Paris-Quimper, Paris-Ventimiglia, Paris-Briancon, and Metz-Nice.

## Using Eurailpass Bonuses

In France, take advantage of two of Eurailpass's best bonuses: the Chemins de Fer de la Provence and the Irish Continental Line crossings to the Republic of Ireland.

The Chemins de Fer de la Provence (CP) is a private, narrow-gauge line running between Digne and Nice. Read below about this way of entering the Riviera on its diesel railcars.

The Irish Continental Line takes you to Rosslare or Cork from Le Havre or Cherbourg. See the section about Ireland.

## France Railpass

As flexible as a Parisian tart's affections and as thrifty as a Gascon goatherd, the France Railpass makes seeing France by train cheaper, easier, and more fun.

With a four-day France Railpass, you can travel anywhere you choose on SNCF for fifteen days for only slightly more than the round-trip fare on TGV between Paris and Lyon. The nine- and sixteen-day passes are good for travel anytime within a month. All passes must be validated at any French train station (which may be done up to six months after issuance in the U.S.). Fast-train surcharges are covered but you must pay for the required reservations.

First-class prices cost about two-thirds of a Eurail Flexipass; buying second-class travel gives you an additional one-third savings. Children four to eleven pay about 60 percent of the France Railpass price. Those under four ride free.

Structured like the Eurail Flexipass, your France Railpass lets you save your days when you decide to stay in one place. Similarly, it is a do-it-yourself pass. You validate your pass yourself. When you start your trip after 7 P.M., enter the next day's date and travel overnight using up only one validation day.

France Railpass has a format different than a Eurailpass's. It is made up of pasteboard flaps folding down vertically. The front is the blue-and-green rail pass good for unlimited travel.

You exchange the first of the coupons at either of Paris's airports for gratis RER transportation to midtown Paris.

You exchange the second coupon at either airport, Paris's Gare de Lyon, Gare d'Austerlitz, Gare du Nord, Gare St. Lazare, or commuter Gare d'Orsay for a free magnetically encoded Paris Sesame transportation card valid for travel on Paris Metro and bus lines.

When you buy a four-day France Railpass, the Paris Sesame card you receive is valid for a day's travel anywhere in Paris. If you buy a nine- or sixteen-day France Railpass, your Paris Sesame card is encoded for two days on the RAPD's entire regional Metro and bus transit system to the environs.

The back flap contains the heart of your pass: the validation stamps and the specified number of day-boxes that you date in ink in numerical sequence.

Finally, present your pass for a string of discounts throughout France: in Alsace, Burgundy, Brittany, Champagne-Ardennes, Dauphine, the Loire Valley, Nord-Pas de Calais, and Provence-Riviera. Wherever you go, stop first at the tourist offices to show your France Railpass. An agent there will give you booklets filled with regional coupons. It is surprising what you get: discounts in regional hotels, guided tours, wine tasting, museum passes. . . . They vary from region to region.

Collect your free gift at the Printemps department store. Pay less when you visit the SNCF Railroad Museum at Mulhouse. Travel at half-fare on the Bateaux Parisiens sightseeing cruises on the Seine in Paris and pay half to visit more than a hundred state monuments at sites throughout France, such as the Arc de Triomphe, the tower of Notre Dame, and Mont St. Michel.

You pay 30 percent less for the guided Paris-Vision City Bus Tour, and receive discounts on admission to Paris's Science Museum and for travel on the scenic Chemins de Fer de la Provence (see below). Three Parisian restaurants and the Pullman hotel group offer 15-30 percent off on weekends in July and August.

Two people traveling together (not during the summer season) can buy a nine-day France Saverpass paralleling the Eurail Saverpass for about 25 percent less than the cost of two regular France Railpasses.

## France Rail'N Drive

The France Rail'N Drive program allows you to combine the France Railpass with an Avis car rental. Avis has 450 locations throughout France including more than 200 in train stations. SNCF/Avis's fifteen-day package gives you four days of unlimited train travel in France plus three days of Avis car rental (category A) with unlimited mileage, VAT (value-added tax), and basic insurance included. (Gasoline is extra.) Their one-month package allows you nine days of unlimited SNCF travel and six days of Avis car rental.

Air France offers the Air France Fly, Rail'N Drive package, which gives you air fare, six nights of accommodations at any of more than

150 first-class hotels, four days of train travel, and three days of Avis car rental, all for extremely reasonable U.S. dollar-guaranteed prices.

To sample France's rail speed and adventure to offbeat corners, travel on the TGV Genevois from Paris to Geneva, the Chemins de Fer de la Provence from Nice to Digne, the new TGV Atlantique, and the Metro Basque from Bayonne to St. Jean-Pied-de-Port described here.

## TGV Genevois
## Computer-Age Anachronism

The inquisitive computer inside the Gare de Lyon quizzes you with electronic questions. "Where are you going? First or second class? How many people? Do you accept the supplement?"

You answer, "No supplement," when you are traveling by Eurailpass or France Railpass. The surcharge for the high-tech train to Geneva, the EuroCity TGV Genevois, is covered by your pass.

Still, you must reserve a seat. You may not stand in the aisle. So you feed the chocolate-brown machine a ten-franc coin and then one-franc coins. In about two or three seconds it drops down a reservation ticket, but it seems reluctant to accept "No supplement" for an answer.

The Genevois is one of the select group of trains comprising the EuroCity network. It carries you on one of EC's most fascinating routes, linking Paris with Switzerland's cosmopolitan city through mountainous regions and past villages still anchored in the nineteenth century.

Until the TGV Atlantique's new roadbed opens in fall 1989, your TGV Southeast train is the fastest in the world—but even if it were merely a speedy way of getting from one place to another, you would still find it fun, smooth, and exciting to ride. As it is, you get a scenic eyeful as well.

By using the Paris Metro's Gare de Lyon stop and climbing the escalator to ground level, you reach the the station's TGV platform without ever seeing the light of morning. When you arrive at the platform, you step into the future. Purring, shark-snouted, gray, white, and orange Trains a Grande Vitesse surround you as far as you can see.

The TGVs are screamers. They sound like they are growling as their engines warm for fast getaways. Speeding at 167 mph much of the way, your TGV Genevois cuts your travel time to Geneva by more than 2 hours, to 3 1/2 hours. TGVs conquered air travel and provided excitement for your trip.

TGVs on the Southeast network are single, articulated units of eight

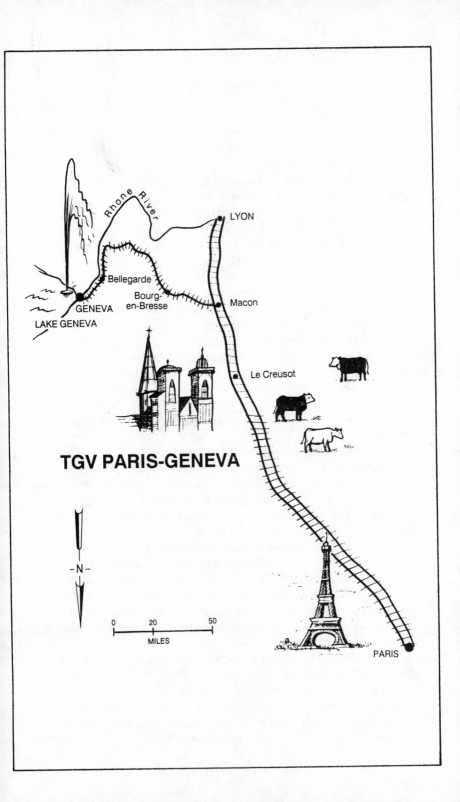

**TGV PARIS-GENEVA**

Rhone River

LYON

Bellegarde

Bourg-en-Bresse

Macon

GENEVA

LAKE GENEVA

Le Creusot

PARIS

– N –

0      20              50

MILES

air-conditioned cars with engines at both ends. At peak travel times, SNCF couples two units together to double the seating to 772 (222 in first class, 550 in second).

You purchase coffee, Parisian croissants, and reading materials in the bar car. In some carriages, you can order a continental breakfast served on the tray in front of you.

The EC TGV Genevois, followed later in the day by the EC Voltaire, the EC Versailles, the EC Henry Dunant, and the EC Jean-Jacques Rousseau, whisks you away promptly at 7:35 A.M. It doesn't immediately leap forward. While toiling through the suburbs of Paris, it vibrates with restrained energy. If you feel some disappointment, it is because you don't feel a jolt when your Genevois enters the high-speed corridor and accelerates to 167 mph. There is no speedometer to fascinate you.

Past the suburbs of the capital, your high-speed trip to Macon is pastoral. You study spotted cows grazing in the fields and ponder the speed of the train. There are no highways paralleling the tracks so you can't accurately gauge your speed, but the buttercups beside the tracks become a mustard-colored blur and you hear no clickety-clack from segmented rails. You know you must be at maximum speed.

You branch from the high-speed line at the new Macon Loche TGV stop, built outdoors in the midst of farmlands. The clickety-clack reminds you that you have returned to old-fashioned—and slower—railbeds.

Past the Bourg-en-Bresse station, two hours from Paris, you enter the Jura region of France. Green woods roll up the impressive heights above the train line. Old villages of monochrome stone houses center around churches that seem to belong on old sepia-tone postcards.

Your attention focuses on the mountains taking shape in the distance. The French word "grandeur" says it all.

You can't escape the anachronism: speeding through ageless Jura mountains and time-forgotten villages in a computer-age bullet.

The passing scenery becomes so eye-catching that French travelers around you fold up the magazines that had interested them before and put away their attache cases still crammed with unfinished business.

Individual farmers tend little fields. Tiny vineyards spot the hillsides. You notice little details that date from quieter times: a river with lily pads, a fisherman in a leaky rowboat, old towns pressed defensively against high mountains, churches of stone, an outcropping with a statue of an unknown hero on its summit.

Finally your Genevois passes the first of many tunnels. You aren't in the tunnel long, but it breaks the scenery. You continue at a brisk pace—no longer at 167 mph, but still very fast.

You finally slow when a broad river, the Rhone, appears on your right. Battlements of once-powerful castles dot the mountainsides overlooking the Rhone. A modern bridge spans the chasm.

At Bellegarde-sur-Valserine, an industrial city at the meeting of the Valserine and Rhone rivers, the only thing level is the huge rail yard. The city trails down the hillside toward the Rhone.

The connecting railcar for the French Lake Geneva resort of Evian-les-Bains stands across the platform below the patina eaves of the weathered train station. "Evian" mineral water is served aboard the TGV Genevois.

From Bellegarde, a long tunnel brings you to a route that twists miraculously through mountain valleys on embankments braced by stone. Mountains tower around the train. You follow the Rhone River below.

Finally your train levels off. TGV chimes sound. Passengers take Swiss bank notes from envelopes and you approach Geneva's Cornavin station along a level route surrounded by endless vineyards.

You arrive at the French/International TGV terminal at Geneva's Cornavin station. Tracks ("Voie") 7 and 8 are separated from Swiss national train traffic by glass doors kept closed except at arrival and departure times.

Deluxe Swiss trains provide excellent connections for Milan and Venice, or you can travel by the EuroCity Catalan Talgo to Barcelona. Geneva's Tourist Office occupies a gleaming suite in the train station.

When you leave Geneva through the SNCF terminal for France or Spain, don't arrive more than a half-hour before departure time. You must linger in the modest waiting room until guards open the doors pneumatically. You show your passport and French visa here when you file past passport control and customs.

## EuroCity TGV Service between Paris and Geneva

| | EC921 Genevois | EC923 Voltaire | EC925 Versailles | EC927 Henry Dunant | EC929 J-Jacques Rousseau |
|---|---|---|---|---|---|
| dep. PARIS (Lyon) | 0735 | 1036 | 1432 | 1740 | 1913 |
| dep. Macon (TGV) | 0917 | .... | 1615 | .... | .... |

| | EC921 Genevois | EC923 Voltaire | EC925 Ver- sailles | EC927 Henry Dunant | EC929 J-Jacques Rousseau |
|---|---|---|---|---|---|
| dep. Bourg-en-Bresse | .... | .... | 1634 | .... | 2111 |
| dep. Culoz | .... | .... | 1723 | .... | .... |
| arr. Bellegarde | 1037 | 1332 | 1746 | 2041 | 2216 |
| arr. GENEVA | 1108 | 1405 | 1816 | 2111 | 2246 |

| | EC920 J-Jacques Rousseau | EC922 Henry Dunant | EC924 Voltaire | EC926 Ver- sailles | EC928 Genevois |
|---|---|---|---|---|---|
| dep. GENEVA | 0709 | 1004 | 1301 | 1650 | 1929 |
| dep. Bellegarde | 0737 | 1032 | 1329 | 1719 | 1957 |
| dep. Culoz | .... | .... | .... | .... | 2024 |
| dep. Bourg-en-Bresse | .... | .... | .... | 1826 | .... |
| dep. Macon (TGV) | .... | .... | 1454 | 1847 | .... |
| arr. PARIS (Lyon) | 1039 | 1336 | 1638 | 2031 | 2309 |

## *Chemins de Fer de la Provence Scenic Gateway to the Riviera*

You climb to your second summit at St. Andre-les-Alpes station overlooking the stone houses of the village and prominent stone church. A fine, long view of snow-covered Alps opens before you to the south. Climbing higher, you see the weirdly scalloped shores of Le Verdon Lake below to the west, with water so calm ducks scarcely bob on the surface.

Riding CP's blue-and-white railcar with self-contained diesel power is so intimate and open that you look over the engineer's shoulder at the rails ahead while your train skirts the edges of deep precipices and climbs steeply over the last range of Alps between the French interior and the Mediterranean.

More rock canyons than you will find in any other part of France, and some as deep as 700 or 900 feet, mark your path. Your railcar teeters precariously on mountain rims and rocks from side to side along a roadbed that chatters your teeth.

You travel down again, past level fields of wheat and mountainsides covered with pine to the Asse River, where you cross into Barreme (pop. 435).

Between Barreme and Digne, the capital of the high country in Provence, you trace the route Napoleon took when returning from Elba in 1815. "The eagle will fly from steeple to steeple until he reaches

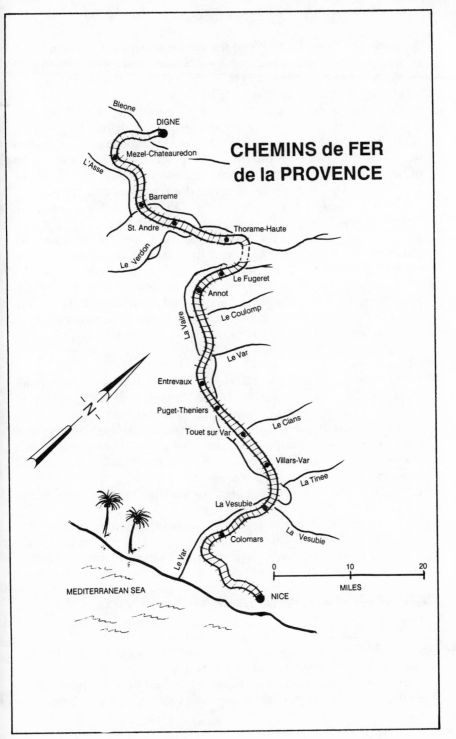

the towers of Notre Dame." Villages boast commemorative plaques and monuments bear the flying eagle symbol inspired by Napoleon's remark. A house near Barreme's town square carries the inscription that Napoleon slept there on March 3, 1815.

Nice, in the Rivera, attracts visitors like a sunny magnet. Adventurers enjoy frolicking along the beaches and feeling the charm of the Riviera while sipping coffee on the busy, four-mile-long Promenade des Anglais bordering the Mediterranean through the capital and delightful Queen of the Riviera. Monte Carlo, a destination adventurers enjoy visiting for its casino and princely flavor, is twenty-four minutes away by train.

The little-known Chemins de Fer de la Provence (CP) narrow-gauge private railroad brings you here from Digne through Cote d'Azur's 103-mile-long back door, a bright, crisp ride through sunshine and mountain air, gorges, pre-Alps, and river valleys. It is a little trip, an off-the-beaten-track secret, and CP accepts your Eurailpass.

By comparison with SNCF's bright and efficient Gare de Ville terminal in Nice, CP's Gare du Sud is a shock. Sud is a four-track station, the oldest in Nice, built in 1892, but the Place de Gaulle outside can be an enchantment. You pass the sidewalk fruit-and-fish market and at the kiosk buy snack items ranging from excellent pizza to extraordinary, odd pastries.

The Gare du Sud at the Place de Gaulle is about a fifteen-minute stroll from SNCF's main station. In the Gare du Sud, ask for a map of your route to Digne at the "Voyageurs" ticket counter.

The driver shifts your railcar's large diesel engine into low gear and accelerates sharply through Nice's city streets. You not only cross traffic intersections, but you have to stop for red lights when you meet them. You pass stop signals and cross boulevards bumper-to-bumper with automobiles before entering a black tunnel that takes you out of the city center.

The conductor takes your Eurailpass to record the number. He returns it with a pink "Billet Gratuit" for your 103-mile journey.

You watch the surroundings through panoramic windows. The driver maneuvers jerkily. The orange seats and maroon leatherette headrests do not recline but are comfortably padded. It is a very wide carriage for a narrow-gauge railcar. The rubber-mat floor still shows mop marks.

Running rockily along the river Le Var, you begin to notice strange secluded hilltop chateaux. At St. Martin-du-Var station house, you see tulips and other flowers blooming under the trees in back.

You are traveling parallel to highway N202 on the east and the river on the west. Orient yourself by the names shown on road signs.

After stopping at La Vesubie, you cross La Vesubie River on a gray steel-girder bridge to run counter to the racing river while the highway continues high on the mountainside. The Vesubie, a tributary of the Var, is fed by Alpine snows. Its valley reachs up to your right through gorges cut into vertical walls, a popular area for French tourists. You are entering the mountains and it becomes more fun. A tunnel takes you to the left bank of the cottonwood-lined Var. As you pass, you see a woman cranking up the red-and-white highway barrier to let road traffic resume.

Past Touet sur Var station house and the Cians Bridge, a small road breaks away to your right for the Cians gorges, some of the finest in the Alps.

Puget-Theniers, the largest village along this route (pop. 2,000), is a southern town at the meeting of the Roudoule and Var rivers. You leave the Maritime Alps district and enter Alps de Haute Provence—at one and the same time the High Mountains and Provence.

You see high chateaux on the hillside before entering Entrevaux, a surprising fortified town (pop. 1,040) surmounted by its citadel. It lies on the west bank of the Var at the foot of a curious rocky spur.

When you leave Entrevaux, rocks take on strange, worn shapes. You first see distant snow at the time you enter your first snow tunnel. Streams in the Var Valley become wilder. Horses—grown mares and brownish-gray yearlings—romp in the fields.

You leave the Var to the east, flowing from the Daluis gorges, and continue up the Coulomp valley below landslide-scarred slopes to the Var's tributary, the Vaire, and then follow the Vaire Valley.

Rising above Annot's church steeple and red-tile roofs surmounting high facades, you gain your first true Alpine sensation. The mountainside is terraced in rock. Above Le Fugeret, your train wanders freely, through tunnels and loops, to gain altitude. Snow remains on the ground until April.

Passengers peer from the windows and take an interest in the jagged rocks to the east and the curious birds flapping as you pass through a jagged gorge. Everything looks greener.

You cross the Vaire River and pass through a black tunnel onto a second bridge across the Verdon River, a tributary of the Durance, which forms magnificent gorges in the limestone of the Haute-Provence. The fresh pine-scented air has a mountainous feeling to it.

You reach the first summit of your mountain railroad. Thorame-Haute's newly built mountain stone church looks handsome beside the flower-decorated station house.

Now you travel downhill through the upper valley of the Verdon in the same direction as the rushing river to the east. The hills are covered with trees of many different shades of green. You receive a hint of the Alps by forests of beech, pine, and larch. The crisp air and bright sky make this a summer tourist destination for the people of Provence.

Geologists recognize the name Barreme for the name "Barremian," given to part of the lower cretaceous layer.

Past Barreme, your train seems to be speeding downhill, but it can't be going too fast, because new Renaults on highway N85 outdistance you with little trouble. Children in the backseats fan the air with their waving at you.

Past the stone Chaudon-Norante station house, you enter the pre-Alps of Digne, climbing through tunnels and along a creek to that capital of the Lavender Alps—a mountain city looking onto Alps nearby.

Lavender is characteristic of Haute-Provence. In the 1930s, farmers began cultivating plantations of this wild-growing mountain flower on higher slopes. Breathe deeply in July, when mauve flowers scent the air.

In Digne, the CP and SNCF stations share the same building and use side-by-side rails. You might expect it would be easy to transfer from one to the other for through connections, but Digne is on a secondary line sadly overlooked as a stop by SNCF. Outside the city, the Digne station offers no hotels, facilities, restaurants, or snack bars. Walking into the city takes fifteen to twenty minutes, but usually a bus waits for your train so you may hurry aboard after your arrival (not covered by pass).

In summer you have a break. At 1:55 P.M. you are met in Digne by SNCF's connecting Alpazur holiday railcar to the mainline Grenoble station. From there you ride TGV 345 miles to Paris or Corail 102 miles to Geneva.

## Chemins de Fer de la Provence

### Summer Service between Nice and Digne

| | | | | | | | | | | |
|---|---|---|---|---|---|---|---|---|---|---|
| 0620 | 0839 | 0935 | 1236 | dep. | NICE (Sud) | arr. | 1406 | 1657 | 1928 | 2045 |
| 0644 | 0901 | 0956 | 1304 | dep. | Colomars | dep. | 1346 | 1636 | 1905 | 2022 |
| 0654 | 0910 | 1005 | 1314 | dep. | St.-Martin-Var | dep. | 1338 | 1629 | 1858 | 2015 |
| 0702 | 0916 | 1011 | 1321 | dep. | La Vesubie | dep. | 1330 | 1621 | 1851 | 2008 |
| 0707 | 0921 | 1016 | 1328 | dep. | La Tinee | dep. | 1323 | 1614 | 1844 | 2001 |
| 0721 | 0936 | 1031 | 1343 | dep. | Villars-Var | dep. | 1304 | 1556 | 1825 | 1943 |

## Summer Service between Nice and Digne

| | | | | | | | | | |
|---|---|---|---|---|---|---|---|---|---|
| 0728 | 0944 | 1039 | 1351 | dep. Touet sur Var | dep. | 1254 | 1547 | 1816 | 1934 |
| 0749 | 1006 | 1101 | 1358 | dep. Puget-Theniers | dep. | 1240 | 1533 | 1801 | 1920 |
| 0753 | 1010 | 1107 | 1304 | dep. Entrevaux | dep. | 1235 | 1528 | 1756 | 1915 |
| 0818 | 1033 | 1129 | 1425 | dep. Annot | dep. | 1216 | 1509 | 1737 | 1855 |
| 0823 | 1038 | 1134 | 1430 | dep. Le Fugeret | dep. | 1209 | 1501 | 1727 | 1845 |
| 0828 | 1044 | 1139 | 1435 | dep. Meailles | dep. | 1202 | 1456 | 1722 | 1840 |
| 0841 | 1056 | 1154 | 1449 | dep. Thorame-Haute | dep. | 1153 | 1448 | 1712 | 1831 |
| 0853 | 1107 | 1206 | 1459 | dep. St. Andre-les-Alpes | dep. | 1137 | 1435 | 1700 | 1810 |
| 0910 | 1116 | 1224 | 1516 | dep. Barreme | dep. | 1122 | 1420 | 1645 | 1759 |
| 0926 | 1136 | 1242 | 1533 | dep. Mezel-Chateauredon | dep. | 1103 | 1402 | 1628 | 1743 |
| 0937 | 1152 | 1255 | 1545 | arr. DIGNE | dep. | 1045 | 1345 | 1611 | 1729 |

## Summer Connections with
## SNCF's Alpazur Holiday Railcar

| | | | | |
|---|---|---|---|---|
| 1355 | dep. | DIGNE | arr. | 1552 |
| 1421 | arr. | St. Auban | dep. | 1528 |
| 1426 | dep. | St. Auban | arr. | 1522 |
| 1532 | arr. | Veynes | dep. | 1415 |
| 1613 | dep. | Veynes | arr. | 1352 |
| 1813 | arr. | GRENOBLE | dep. | 1205 |

## Grenoble Connections
### Corail to Geneva

| | | | | |
|---|---|---|---|---|
| 1822 | dep. | GRENOBLE | arr. | 1143 |
| 2044 | arr. | GENEVA (Cornavin) | dep. | 0942 |

### TGV to Paris

| | | | | |
|---|---|---|---|---|
| 2035 | dep. | GRENOBLE | arr. | 0955 |
| 2145 | arr. | Lyon (Part-Dieu) | dep. | 0848 |
| 2149 | dep. | Lyon (Part-Dieu) | arr. | 0845 |
| 2215 | dep. | Macon (TGV) | dep. | .... |
| 2359 | arr. | PARIS (Lyon) | dep. | 0645 |

# TGV Atlantique
# Life in the Fast Train

Sparks are already sizzling from pantographs, rims are being worn in to spin at the fastest circumferential wheel speed known to man, and francs are changing hands at Paris's Montparnasse station's ticket counters. This new line is no longer in your crystal ball. You can already ride—free on a Eurailpass or France Railpass—three round

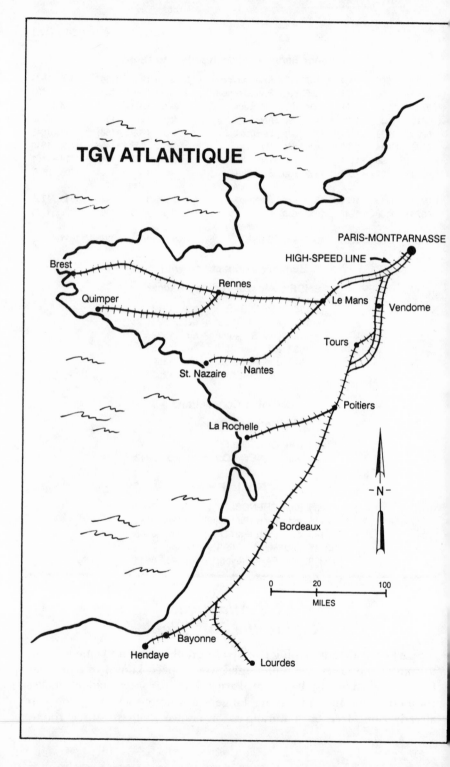

TGV ATLANTIQUE

PARIS-MONTPARNASSE

HIGH-SPEED LINE

Brest

Quimper

Rennes

Le Mans

Vendome

Tours

St. Nazaire

Nantes

Poitiers

La Rochelle

-N-

Bordeaux

0    20    100

MILES

Bayonne

Hendaye

Lourdes

trips daily on the TGV Atlantique between Paris's Montparnasse station and Nantes, but only for 250 miles and "only" at 125 mph where it's possible.

In fall 1989, timed to coincide with the bicentennial year of the French Revolution, you can take full advantage of the TGV Atlantique, the fastest train in the world. At 186 mph to Brittany, you travel fully one-third faster, 60 mph, than its fastest foreign competitor along the first segment of the TGV Atlantique's 219-mile Y-shaped line between Paris and the whole of the Atlantic coast stretching from Brittany to the Pyrenees. But it won't be until June 1990 that you will be able to continue to Tours, Bordeaux, and the Spanish border.

The color scheme of the new ninety-five "Trains a Grande Vitesse," or "High Speed Trains," built by Alsthom-Francorail in Belfort looks strikingly different than the trains you ride in France's southeast. Instead of the orange ribbonlike appearance, the TGV Atlantique's livery is blue, silver, and white. Two locomotives, front and rear, power your train—twelve parts, about 780 feet long and 540 tons heavy.

The TGV Atlantique is a second-generation TGV. It is bigger, faster, and built on experience gained from operating the space-age technology of the milestone 167-mph TGV Southeast network.

While you are flying out of Paris's Montparnasse station at 186 mph, think frogs. You are passing through the wooded distict of Perche, where you may see some of the more than one hundred marshes, ponds, and pools that once domiciled thousands of protected frogs and toads.

Surveyors for the high-speed railroad reported that these prized frogs would be displaced or destroyed by new construction. The Society of French Batrachians (meaning amphibians without tails) demanded: "Move the ponds and the frogs."

Workers spent weeks digging a new pond in the national forest. Rainfall quickly filled it, but the frogs refused to move.

Frogs are creatures of habit. Like salmon, they instinctively go back to the pond where they were born to reproduce.

Someone had to grab the frogs on land in early spring when they came out of hibernation and carry them to their new homesites before they could jump back into their original ponds and lay eggs. Conservationists built secure fences and planted a series of frog traps around the old ponds. They also fenced the frogs' projected new quarters to keep them, once relocated, from packing up and hopping back to their old hangouts.

Unfortunately, hungry herons soon discovered the traps held fast-food frogs. They ate the rare, prized, protected batrachians. Horrified conservationists rushed in devices to frighten away the hungry herons. Their machines worked. In one month, conservationists carried 400 frogs and 1,000 toads from their old pond to their new one. When you realize that a female toad lays about four to five thousand eggs a year, it is reasonable to guess that quite a few naive tadpoles call these waters "home" and return here to reproduce.

Ecologically minded SNCF officials also insisted on running the Atlantique's route through farmland instead of forests and building underpasses below the rails so large mammals could roam back and forth. They built a greenbelt alongside the tracks in Paris to provide a bicycle and hiking path as well as a recreation area.

Leaving from Paris's Montparnasse station, you ride the high-speed railbeds to Le Mans and Tours, but continue on older railbeds at a modest 137 mph. Via Le Mans you reach Nantes, Quimper, and Brest. From Tours you reach La Rochelle, Bordeaux, or Spain.

Engineers worked diligently to guarantee comfortable travel at such speeds. If you wonder at your smooth ride, you can credit the newly designed air-cushion suspension which gives you, at 186 mph, comfort equalling conventional Corail carriages running at 100 mph on InterCity SNCF trains.

The area served by the Atlantique is less rugged than the Paris-Lyon route so you don't have to travel over such steep gradients. Combine this with revolutionary synchronous electric motors pulling you at higher speeds with only four motors instead of the TGV Southeast's six, and you see that it was possible for SNCF engineers to design new trains consisting of ten passenger cars instead of eight, to seat 485—116 seats in first class and 369 seats in second—30 percent more than TGV trains in the southeast. Doubled trains carry up to 970.

Between three unconventionally designed first-class cars and six second-class cars, you will find a new and improved bar car where you can buy drinks and snacks and look at videos. Your bar car is decorated differently to give you a feeling of something special. It gives you a shop, stools at the bar, and a brasserie-type area with tables and fifteen folding seats which you can reserve during peak traffic.

In first class, families will find two special compartments, a playroom for children and a diaper room for infants. Travelers in wheel chairs use specially designed spaces and toilets.

In two of the three first-class cars, you have a choice of sitting in sofa-type seats located on each side of a table in partitioned four-person salons, or across the corridor in single open seats facing one other. Meals are prepared in service nooks and served at your seat.

In the third first-class car, decorated in harmony with the others, you sit in an eight-seat horseshoe-shaped lounge with a table that can be arranged for meetings on board. Three telephone booths are available for domestic and international conversations.

Sixty-five million passengers use Paris's Gare Montparnasse yearly, including twenty-two million TGV riders. Some of those formerly used Paris's Gare d'Austerlitz. Now that they use the Gare Montparnasse, it is Paris's busiest train station, an honor that once belonged to the Gare de Lyon.

## Metro Basque
### Heart and Soul of Basque Country

Local Basque leaders call the railcar that takes you to the heart and soul of French Basque country, "Metro Basque." It runs between Bayonne, the northern limit of the Basque coast in France, and St. Jean-Pied-de-Port, a different world thirty-one miles, 1 1/4 hours, and 515 feet above it. St. Jean-Pied-de-Port, as its name suggests, sits at the foot of the pass of Roncevalles in the Atlantic Pyrenees, the gateway to Spain only five miles above.

Breaking your journey here on a trip between Madrid and Paris is an adventure, a diversion, and a prerequisite when you are interested in Basque culture.

Many Americans of Basque descent return every two or three years to visit their relatives. St. Jean's busy season is July and August, when French, German, English, and American visitors (not counting Spanish Basques, who are not considered tourists) swell the population of St. Jean's 3,000 permanent inhabitants to 12,000 to 15,000. You enjoy the many summer festivities such as jai alai (which is as important to the Basque as the church), folkloric dancing, and serenades of choral groups.

Many young Basques came to the New World because here only the oldest sons inherit their parents' farms and properties. Without property, the younger sons tended to immigrate to the New World to make their fame and fortune. Many did become prosperous. Because Paul Laxhault is of Basque origin, many Basques have a keen interest in American politics and a fondness for American visitors.

Even now the population is not increasing.

Bayonne's station, where you begin your climb, is remodeled, grand, but undistinguished on the outside, and efficient inside. You snack in the modern buffet adjacent. Look for the departure times posted prominently above the information office and ticketing windows.

You see a pair of modern blue railcars built in 1981, by Francorail,

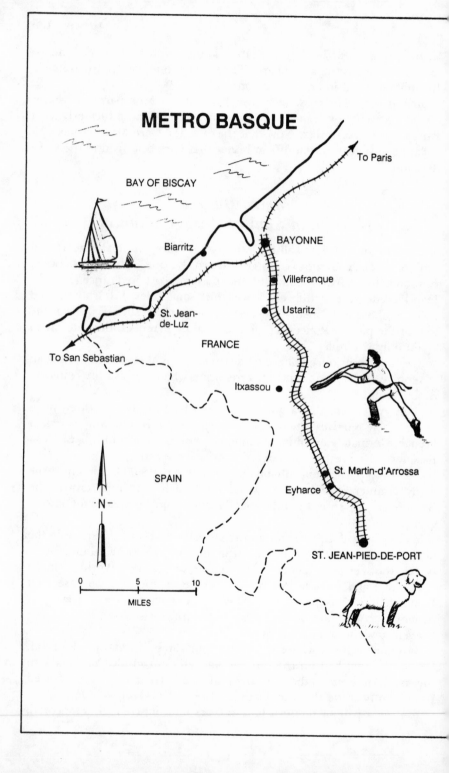

# METRO BASQUE

To Paris

BAY OF BISCAY

Biarritz

BAYONNE

Villefranque

Ustaritz

St. Jean-
de-Luz

FRANCE

To San Sebastian

Itxassou

SPAIN

-N-

St. Martin-d'Arrossa

Eyharce

ST. JEAN-PIED-DE-PORT

0       5       10
MILES

waiting on track No. 1. The first-class section in the rear contains sixteen seats for nonsmokers and eight, through an automatically opening glass door, for "fumeurs."

It's a comfortable, modern, pleasing train, no doubt completed by the same interior designers who won awards for the Corail trains.

Both cars have seats arranged like salons. First class has two-opposite-two maroon bucket-type seats facing each other. Second class, through another glass door that you open with a push on a lever (like Corail), is configured similarly with slightly less distance between brown leatherette seats. There is almost no difference between first and second class except for the blue carpeting in first and nonskid rubber flooring in second. Both are modern, spotless, and decorated with tidy, plaited curtains.

A few minutes late for departure, and concluding his chatting with the driver, the white-capped dispatcher waves his white-and-green paddle. The driver scampers aboard, closes the doors, and starts your electrified railcar on its single track away through a tunnel.

While your conductor checks the tickets and nods at your Eurailpass or France Railpass, you cross the Nive, a broad, brown river, and enter a second, long tunnel. Woods and fruit trees surround your line. Thorny berry thickets flourish on the slopes of the elevated railbed while you pass through flat farm country, with cornstalks thriving in the fields.

Your conductor announces your first stop, Ustaritz, on the speaker system. Ustaritz's station house is brown stucco with brown trim. All stations on this line are clearly marked even when the signs are covered with climbing, green vines.

You still travel on the level, running parallel to the slow-flowing Nive, to your second stop, Cambo-les-Bains, where white postwar homes are roofed with tiles.

Your next stop, Itxassou, is interesting because villagers here still don curious costumes and perform their annual, elaborate Corpus Christi procession.

Now you are beginning to climb modestly past whitewashed farmhouses with sagging tile roofs. Many Basques drive up the parallel two-lane blacktop highway, but still prefer the train occasionally to relish the scenery.

You feel the temperature cool when you slow for the station house serving St. Martin-d'Arrossa and the nearby villages of Eyharce and Osses. This is the junction of two rivers which form the now-raging Nive. You see large white Basque houses with cornerstones and brown or green shutters and trim. A few passengers change here for buses to Saint Etienne de Baigorny.

Finally you see black-faced sheep for the first time, happily munching the long green grass on the slopes. Some sheepherders own them; some rent. You see merinos with long, fine, silky wool, and the Basque sheep, manech, which are black and white with curved horns. But if you visit during the summer, you must go to the peaks of the Pyrenees to find them. The sheep are kept in the cities for six months until May 1, and then they spend six months in the high mountains.

On every side of the wide valley, trim Basque villages nestle amid manicured pasture lands. Each is centered on a church with a clock tower—the local custom is to toll the hour twice. Everything is green, casual, pastoral, the epitome of quiet.

High above the ridges, hawks cry and immense golden vultures soar on the breeze, eyeing the flocks of long-wooled sheep below. Herds of sleek, tan cattle graze beside shaggy dark ponies called "pottoks," which are horses unchanged in appearance since they were portrayed on the walls of the Paleolithic limestone caves not far away.

At last you see St. Jean-Pied-de-Port, the former capital of Lower Navarre, built by Garcia Ximenes in 716. It became a French town as a result of the Treaty of the Pyrenees in 1659. Louis XIV had it fortified by Vauban and you can still see its ramparts, its walls, and its citadel dominating the town and the Pyrenees. When Wellington crossed the Pyrenees in 1813, he entered France via St. Jean-Pied-de-Port.

You are on the pilgrim's route through northern Spain to Santiago de Compostela. (Read this book's section on the Talgo Pendular to Santiago de Compostela.)

Bracken fern, green in spring, reddish brown in the fall, cover the steep slopes of the surrounding mountains which dwarf the wooded hill above the town. Farmers scythe fern into tall, conical stacks for fodder, or simply burn it, turning the air blue with pleasant-smelling smoke.

Disembark at St. Jean-Pied-de-Port and walk from the train station to the city center along steets clearly posted with signs. The Syndicat d'Initiative in the center (on the left as you approach) is located in a modern building.

Inspecting the seven Gothic gates in the wall that used to surround the whole town (which were formerly locked at night) gives you an excellent grasp of the complex angles and divisions of this curiously exciting village.

St. Jean consists of shops and stone houses, each with two or three apartments, scattered along cobblestone streets fronted with steps instead of sidewalks. The crosspieces over the doors proudly proclaim who built them and when. Like all Basque houses, town and country, these are sturdy, half-timbered with stone and whitewashed stucco facades. Green or red-brown shutters are obligatory, for they are the Basque colors, but "Basque red" comes in many shades these days, depending on where the owner buys his or her paint.

The citadel you see brooding over the rooftops is used as a high school in winter and a museum in summer. Sheep graze in its moat.

The church's clock tower set into the city wall contains a small room that served as the city hall in medieval times. From the gate in the base of the tower, you cross a graceful stone bridge arching over the Nive.

Monday is market day all year long, all day long, in St. Jean, as it has been for centuries. You can buy berets (black only) from traveling peddlers, rope-soled canvas Basque slippers, Citroen tractors, Michael Jackson cassettes, fresh-killed wild doves and ripe cheeses. Two thousand lambs are bought here every Monday.

## Summer Metro Basque Service

| | | *(1)* | | | | | |
|---|---|---|---|---|---|---|---|
| BAYONNE | dep. | 0615 | 0925 | 1206 | 1556 | 1809 | 2026 |
| Behereharta | dep. | .... | .... | .... | .... | 1817 | .... |
| Villefranque | dep. | .... | .... | .... | .... | 1822 | .... |
| Ustaritz | dep. | 0630 | 0941 | 1222 | 1611 | 1827 | 2042 |
| Jatxou | dep. | .... | .... | .... | .... | 1830 | .... |
| Halsou-Larressore | dep. | .... | .... | .... | .... | 1834 | .... |
| Cambo-les-Bains | dep. | 0642 | 0951 | 1232 | 1621 | 1842 | 2053 |
| Itxassou | dep. | 0650 | 0959 | 1240 | 1629 | 1850 | 2101 |
| Louhossoa | dep. | .... | 1006 | 1247 | .... | 1857 | .... |
| Pont-Noblia | dep. | 0703 | 1013 | 1254 | 1642 | 1904 | 2114 |
| Osses-St. Mart.-d'Arrossa | arr. | 0713 | 1023 | 1304 | 1652 | 1914 | 2124 |
| Osses-St. Mart.-d'Arrossa | dep. | 0714 | 1024 | 1305 | 1653 | 1915 | 2125 |
| ST. JEAN-PIED-DE-PORT | arr. | 0728 | 1038 | 1319 | 1707 | 1928 | 2139 |

| | | | | | | | *(2)* |
|---|---|---|---|---|---|---|---|
| ST. JEAN-PIED-DE-PORT | dep. | 0552 | 0755 | 1340 | 1532 | 1752 | 2003 |
| Osses-St. Mart.-d'Arrossa | arr. | 0606 | 0809 | 1354 | 1546 | 1806 | 2017 |
| Osses-St. Mart.-d'Arrossa | dep. | 0606 | 0809 | 1355 | 1547 | 1807 | 2018 |
| Pont-Noblia | dep. | 0616 | 0819 | 1405 | 1557 | 1817 | 2028 |
| Louhossoa | dep. | 0625 | .... | .... | 1605 | .... | 2035 |
| Itxassou | dep. | 0632 | 0833 | 1419 | 1612 | 1831 | 2042 |
| Cambo-les-Bains | dep. | 0641 | 0842 | 1427 | 1623 | 1841 | 2053 |
| Halsou-Larressore | dep. | 0646 | .... | .... | .... | .... | .... |
| Jatxou | dep. | 0649 | .... | .... | .... | .... | .... |

| | | | | | | | |
|---|---|---|---|---|---|---|---|
| Ustaritz | dep. | 0652 | 0851 | 1436 | 1633 | 1850 | 210 |
| Villefranque | dep. | 0657 | .... | .... | .... | .... | .... |
| Behereharta | dep. | 0702 | .... | .... | .... | .... | .... |
| BAYONNE | arr. | 0710 | 0907 | 1453 | 1649 | 1906 | 211 |

(1) Mondays only.
(2) Fridays, Saturdays, and Sundays only.

# Iberia

## Vital Tips for the Trains
## of Spain and Portugal

Look for Spain's least conspicuous trains. The low-to-the-ground, gray-and-cream tilting Talgo Pendular units may be the best you will ride in Europe.

Forget old news. The trains of Spain have changed direction. Now you will agree they are innovative, fun to ride, and charged with excitement for the 1992 summer Olympic games.

Sparkling stations such as the one in Vigo, brilliant trains such as the Talgo Pendular, well-managed hubs such as Madrid's Chamartin station, and first-class lounges open free to Eurailpass travelers make Spain a great nation to visit by train if you don't mind the great distances and long travel times.

Renfe, the acronym for the Spanish Railroads, "Red Nacional de los Ferrocarriles Espanoles," requires reservations on most of its long-distance trains, but because of computerization you make them easily at any Renfe office or train station or even up to two months in advance from the U.S., although Madrid's downtown Renfe office at Alcala, 44 (use the Banco de Espana Metro stop) is often more convenient. Renfe accepts bank credit cards for payment, but be sure to flash them in advance to alert the booking agent. Reservations on Talgo Pendulars cost about $2.

The better trains also have supplements payable by point-to-point ticket purchasers, but you are exempt if you hold a Eurailpass or Renfe Tourist Card (see "National Rail Passes" below).

131

In addition to the Talgo Pendular, Renfe operates the former-generation Talgo IIs (which are excellent), InterCity trains, ELTs ("Electrotrens"), and TERs ("Trens Espanol Rapido"), which are heavy, fast diesel railcars. These higher-class trains are all air-conditioned. Choose Talgos whenever you can, but the TERs are well suited to their runs.

Madrid is the hub of the country. You will probably use Chamartin station in the northern part of the city, one of Europe's brightest stations. The smaller "Norte" or "Principe Pio" station is served by trains to Galicia, Gijon, and Santander.

Atocha station's surface train yard in downtown Madrid is closed for rebuilding on the site of the adjacent freight terminal. Until the new Atocha is opened, use the terminal temporarily named "Madrid-Mediodia" for the line toward Chamartin.

Reach Chamartin, Norte, and Atocha stations by underground Metro. (Get a Metro map—"Plano"—upon entering the system.) Trains cost about fifty cents per trip. Some are old and creaky, like boxcars; others are modern with upholstered seating. Alternately, when it is convenient for you to use the Recoletos and Nuevos Ministerios stops, you can board the shuttle trains between Chamartin (track 1) and Atocha Apeadero. They run less often, but they are free with a Eurailpass.

Barcelona also offers three major train terminuses and a subway system to confuse you. The mainline platforms at Termino station are closed for reconstruction until the beginning of 1990. Trains that normally would call here are being diverted to Barcelona's Sants station (also called "Central"), where you can board trains for the Barcelona airport. The smaller, underground Passeig de Gracia station, with a large reception hall, is a good place for you to debark because of its excellent location. It is adjacent to the subway (line 3) and only four blocks north of the Placa de Catalunya.

Seville also has three train stations, but these are not interconnected. The Moorish facade of Eiffel's Plaza de Armas station is breathtaking.

You enter Spain from France, but the catch here is that Spanish trains run on wide-gauge (5 1/2 foot) rails. This means you must change trains at the border or your train has to change gauge at the border. Renfe changes gauge either by physically jacking up the carriage shells and switching undercarriages so delicately that travelers hardly notice it (the couchettes of the Puerta del Sol train and the Sud Express), or by mechanically widening or narrowing the wheels while your train passes over a work pit at the border (the Catalan Talgo).

The three best trains across the French border are EuroCity trains. The EC Catalan Talgo between Barcelona and Geneva is the best day train. The other two are night Talgo trains carrying modern sleeping cars: the EC Barcelona Talgo (Barcelona-Paris) and the EC Paris-Madrid Talgo.

All of Renfe's overnight Talgos carry only sleeping accommodations and white-tablecloth restaurants—no couchettes or sitting coaches. While pricey, they give you the most comfortable overnight travel in Europe.

Renfe's standard domestic overnight trains are called "Estrella," and usually convey first- and second-class sleepers, brown-and-white couchettes (French Corail equipment), and through cars.

If you wish to reach Portugal without visiting Madrid, the most direct way from France is aboard the legendary Sud Express. One of the famous nostalgic trains, the Sud Express carries French couchettes between Lisbon and Paris via Medina del Campo and San Sebastian, Spain, and crosses the famous Eiffel Bridge en route.

A fast Spanish train now connects with French overnight train No. 4415 (carrying first- and second-class French couchettes and through carriages) from Paris at La Tour-de-Carol, France, for Barcelona. This is your gateway for Andorra.

For transiting Spain for Morocco, your best bet is the French second-class couchette departing Paris-Austerlitz at 10:30 P.M. on train No. 404, arriving at Algeciras for the ferry crossing at 7:30 A.M. on the second morning. Riding this couchette obviates the need to change trains at the border or in Madrid. Be sure to reserve in advance.

Renfe's first-class lounges ("Rail Clubs")—like first-class airline lounges—are oases of quiet and exclusivity featuring overstuffed furniture, magazines, and television, with free coffee and soft drinks brought by enthusiastic hostesses. For admission, the hostess checks your first-class reservation coupon ("Billette Plazas Sentadas y Literas") on one of the Spanish EuroCity trains (the Paris-Madrid Talgo, the Barcelona Talgo, or the Catalan Talgo), a sleeping compartment, or on a domestic Spanish Talgo, InterCity, or Electrotren. Because these trains require reservations anyway, all first-class travelers including Eurailpass holders may use this pleasant convenience.

Look for "Rail Clubs" at Madrid-Chamartin station (search carefully for the small brass plaque on the main level by the entrance to track 1), Madrid's new Atocha station, at Barcelona's Sants station (opposite the cafeteria), and in the new Vigo terminal (brightly marked in the center).

There is a secondary train network across the north of Spain, but you won't find it on the Eurailpass train map—the conductors do not accept Eurailpasses. FEVE, "Ferrocarriles de Via Estretcha," claims to be the longest continuous narrow-gauge network in Europe—a claim that is echoed by Switzerland's Rhaetian Railroads.

## Portuguese Railroads

The Portuguese Railroads ("Companha dos Caminhos de Ferro Portugueses," or "CP") suffered for years from Portuguese economic difficulties and political uncertainties. Things are looking brighter. Except for occasional red-and-cream carriages, all CP carriages and railcars have stainless-steel exteriors built in Portugal by Sorefame to Budd Company designs, except for the new Alfa Service equipment built by Sorefame to French Corail specifications. The first-class cars are clearly marked with broad yellow stripes.

CP's trains run on wide-gauge rails, the same as Spanish trains, so you won't be delayed at the border. From Madrid, you enter Portugal on either the Estrella Lusitania overnight train—carrying first-class sleepers, second-class Spanish couchettes (French Corail equipment), and first- and second-class through carriages—or the amiable TER Lisboa Express diesel train with dining. Brusque customs inspections at the border make both crossings unpleasant.

Two other possibilities for crossing the border between Spain and Portugal are more adventurous. Railcars, with first- and second-class seating, take you between Vigo's 1988 station and Porto's Sao Bento station.

In the far south, a ferry large enough for two small autos overhanging the ends and a few passengers clinging to the edges crosses the Guadiana River at Vila Real de Santo Antonio. This connects CP's local service through Portugal's Algarve region to the Damas bus company's eight-times-daily service between Ayamonte and Huelva/Seville (not covered by Eurailpass). Talgo Pendulars and Estrella trains run once daily between Huelva and Madrid. Presumably when the new 2,000-foot suspension bridge across the Guadiana at Ayamonte is completed in 1990, bus service will replace the ferry.

## National Rail Passes

Renfe's national rail pass, the "Renfe Tarjeta Turistica" or Renfe Tourist Card, is available for eight, fifteen, or twenty-two days. It costs about two-thirds of a Eurailpass; a second-class card costs about half of a Eurailpass. It is sold in train stations in Madrid (plus Renfe's Alcala office, window 12, but not at Renfe's Madrid airport office), Barcelona, Irun, Port Bou (border crossings to France), or at Renfe's Paris office, 3, avenue Marceau, 75116 Paris (Tel. 4-723-52-00).

CP has first-class (only) national rail passes available for seven, fourteen, and twenty-one days, but there is little reason to buy them. Portugal's small size limits your train traveling potential. Ask about them at the train information office in Lisbon's Santa Apolonia station.

The four train adventures described in this chapter take you on the Talgo Pendular from Madrid to Santiago de Compostela, the unusual ride along Spain's Costa del Sol, the terrifying trams through Lisbon's Alfama district, and two stretches almost the length of Portugal.

## *Tilting Train Pilgrimage*
## *Lazy Way to Santiago de Compostela*

While you are lounging lazily on Spain's sparkling Talgo Pendular train, waiting for the television to blink on and wondering whether this posh new entry for Europe's greatest-train honors really tilts around curves as designed, you might consider reading Chapter XIII, "Santiago de Compostela," of Michener's *Iberia.*

You are entering the Galicia region from Madrid and are still three hours from Santiago, your destination.

When one traveler made this trip, he came alive with Michener's sentence: "I was fortunate in reaching Compostela at the precise point in the year when I could best witness the significance of the town and its cathedral in Spanish life, for El dia de Santiago (the day of St. James) occurs each year on July 25, and is the occasion for a religious celebration of great dimension." The traveler looked at his watch. It was indeed July 24.

A pilgrimage to Santiago de Compostela is still important not only for the devoted, but for casual students of world history. In 812 A.D., a hermit saw in the heavens a bright star hovering over a vacant field where the body of St. James (Sant Iago), uncorrupted by the passage of time, was unearthed. The apostle, who became known as St. James Matamore, the Slayer of the Moors, was later seen riding a white horse and instilled the spirit for the reconquest of Spain from the infidels. Today Santiago de Compostela's cathedral stands where that vacant field presumably lay.

The pilgrimage aboard the Talgo Pendular, free on a Eurailpass, is the convenient, but lazy, way to visit Europe's number two (after Rome) holy city and the site of one of Christendom's most venerated cathedrals.

During the eight-hour, 420-mile run, you are treated to the scenic contrasts of desiccated Old Castile and the twisting adventure of a mountain railroad into green Galicia.

The train leaves from Madrid's third station, Principe Pio (also

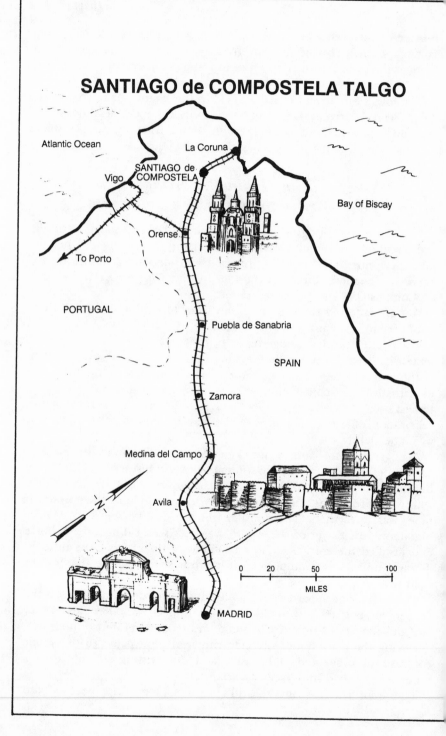

# SANTIAGO de COMPOSTELA TALGO

Atlantic Ocean

La Coruna

SANTIAGO de
COMPOSTELA

Vigo

Bay of Biscay

Orense

To Porto

PORTUGAL

Puebla de Sanabria

SPAIN

Zamora

Medina del Campo

Avila

0    20    50    100

MILES

MADRID

known as "Norte" station). It has the advantage of subway service to and from the platform (use the "Norte" Metro stop). Principe Pio is a boring terminus. The day's major excitement occurs when the slate blue and white Talgo begins boarding. A comely stewardess sporting a chic brown derby, brown skirt, and yellow blouse, struts along the platform. She greets passengers with free copies of Madrid's *El Pais* newspaper.

Talgo Pendulars are among the most comfortable-riding and innovative in Europe. Talgo stands for "Tren Articulado Ligero Goicoechea y Oriol." The last two names are those of the inventors of the system and the first three words mean "lightweight articulated train." Because they are articulated units, the string of shorter, connected, low-profile parlors bends around curves like a rubber snake. The latest generation, called the Pendular, additionally tilts according to ingenious design. The natural rocking of the chassis causes them to round curves so smoothly you'll see scarcely a ripple in your coffee.

You stretch out in oversize, two-opposite-one, deep bucket seats. They have folding tables in their backs, but when you recline, your seat's cushions slide forward so you don't disturb the person behind you. The twenty-one-inch wide seats have a thirty-nine-inch pitch in first class. Each first-class parlor holds twenty-six seats; the second-class parlors, four across, hold thirty-six.

The bar located between the first- and second-class sections is magnificent, circled with an elaborate golden frieze. All is stainless steel behind the serpentine glass counter fitted with thirteen cantilevered stools (three more at a back bar). The adjacent kitchen is equipped with a gas griddle and two rings.

The Virgen del Pilar diesel locomotive pulls away from Madrid at 1:30 P.M., exactly on time, with a rumble like thunder. You see a long, panoramic, industry-free view open back on the city through a forest of encina, or live oak, trees. Spanish children delight in eating these trees' nuts, which are similar to chestnuts and almonds.

Almost instantly the conductor comes through to check your reservation card and ticket or pass.

About halfway to Avila (pop. 40,000), your Talgo enters the summer-parched high plateau known as Old Castile. Outside, the ground is rocky and not very rich, so you are hardly surprised when you come eye-to-eye with a black bull snorting angrily and pawing the yellow leavings of a wheat harvest.

Entering Avila, watch for Europe's most vivid enduring example of medieval fortification. When the station no longer blocks your view, your eyes rivet to the sight and you can trace out the cathedral and the crenulated walls and battlements not far to the south.

Past Avila, the rocks become more hostile and the live oaks juiceless. Your Talgo climbs relentlessly. It is uncompromising country.

Lunch, catered by the Wagons-Lits company, is served aboard the Talgo Pendular between Madrid and Santiago. The four-course menu, served at your seat, costs about $15 and consists of 1) fish, 2) beefsteak or chicken, vegetables, and potatoes, 3) cake, cheese, or yogurt, and 4) choice of fruit. Wine and mineral water cost extra. Dinner is not served, but the bar car is available for snacks.

When your Talgo reaches Medina del Campo (3:40 P.M.), busy agricultural market and major railroad junction, and pulls to a stop next to the Eiffel-designed canopy of the brick train station, you can't but remark how green things are becoming. Sunflowers are tall, pines begin dotting the hills, and farmers are harvesting leafy vegetables.

Your Talgo makes a "V" turn when the Virgen del Pilar shuffles by on an adjacent track and the new Virgen de la Macarena diesel locomotive takes charge of your train and pulls away with passengers facing backwards. You rotate your seat to look forward once more.

At 4:10 P.M., your Talgo passes Toro, the fine-looking village with picture-book profiles of the Romanesque Collegiate and San Lorenzo churches. The Duero below, one of Spain's five major rivers, flows slowly but still looks fresh and blue. Wheat flourishes north of the river, grapes to the south. The light blossoms of almond trees dot the landscape in spring.

Irrigation takes hold outside. There is heavy cultivation. Stalks of corn line the fields, peach and pear trees droop with fruit, tractors ready the slopes for vegetables and, in the distance, sheepherders prod their flocks with crooked staves.

When the Virgen de la Macarena locomotive begins its serious climb into the Leon Mountains, it passes hay deposited in peaked piles. Burros and horses mill about. The land is now dry and soon changes into mountains.

Except for the handsome Romanesque facade of the train station, modernized to look very efficient, historic Zamora (4:29 P.M.) now seems to be composed entirely of tall red-brick and white-brick apartment structures. The return Talgo arrives on the adjacent track. It left from Vigo/La Coruna two hours earlier than you started.

With hardly a warning, the video lights up on four television sets suspended from the ceiling so that every passenger can see them easily without craning their necks. The train manager passes down the aisle renting out blue-and-yellow earphones that plug into the outlet in your armrest (about $2). If you don't appear to speak Spanish he will pass you by. The audio is all in Spanish. *Jaws* and *The Mouse that Roared* are evergreens with Renfe.

At about 5:30 P.M., you first glimpse the mountain lake of Sanabria (3,280 feet), spotted with vacationers kayaking and windsurfers maneuvering their bright sails.

The mountain village of Puebla de Sanabria is a postcard-perfect picture of houses with granite roofs and white walls. It lies at the foot of the Sanabria valley, which is alive with streams rushing through its undergrowth. The black slate-covered station house with white lawn chairs overlooking the lake could be a model for a miniature railroad display.

You see the train is entering different countryside, wet and green and chock-full of granite. This is the isolated, rainy region at the northwestern corner of the Iberian peninsula called Galicia. There are no seductive Carmens or flamenco dancers here. Myrtles and camellias bloom. Beaches are empty and churches full. General Franco came from here.

Galicia is one of Spain's least affluent regions and also one of its most independent. Its language is half-Portuguese. Its wealth of granite sets it apart from the rest of Spain just as its culture and Celtic heritage. Bagpipes are the native instrument.

Builders have turned their abundance of the gray-and-white stone into barns, corncribs, garages, homes, terraces, and fences that range across the countryside in elaborate mazes only goats understand.

By the time your Talgo reaches La Gudina (6:18 P.M.), thoughts of dried Old Castile are replaced by the view to the north beckoning with charisma. An occasional flock of sheep meanders to the train line.

The Virgen de la Macarena curves in and out of tunnels. This is the true mark of a mountain railroad. Fields look like patchworks. Ferns flourish on embankments beside the windows. Pastoral fields of corn and vineyards spread below. The majestic Cantabrian Cordillera Mountains rise before you, almost blue in the distance, crisscrossed with brown firebreaks.

This corner of Spain is on the western fringe of the Middle European Time Zone. In summer, the sun is high even at 7:15 P.M.

At Orense (pop. 87,000), your carriage for Santiago dawdles while workers split the train. Passengers lug their suitcases up and down the aisle to get into the correct half. Some continue to the spanking new terminal at Vigo (pop. 265,000) overlooking its busy, beautiful, natural harbor on the Atlantic coast north of Portugal. The segment taking you to Santiago continues farther to La Coruna (pop. 250,000), Galicia's principal port and city.

It is getting late. You are restless to arrive, but the vistas are some of the most idyllic in Spain. You see tiny, cone-shaped haystacks and grapevines trained on wooden trellises. The hills roll as far as the horizon.

The Virgen pulls steadily on a long, steady climb until finally, a few minutes late, it snakes through the crisscrossing pattern of rails to arrive at track No. 1 in Santiago de Compostela (pop. 100,000).

The station is across town from the cathedral, but still it is the popular destination for throngs of modern-day pilgrims and students. The guardrails are lined with silver-painted, cast-iron cockleshells. This symbol honors those who came, beginning in the eleventh century, not by tilting train, but by wearing out countless pairs of stout sandals.

Across from the cathedral you should inspect Santiago's five-star Hostal de los Reyes Catolicos, which is part of Spain's National System of Paradors. This national monument, an inn for pilgrims dating from the sixteenth century, is the most desirable hotel in Galicia.

## Talgo Pendular Service
## Madrid to Santiago de Compostela

| | | | | |
|---|---|---|---|---|
| 1330 | dep. | MADRID (P. Pio) | arr. | 1929 |
| 1445 | arr. | Avila | dep. | 1815 |
| 1446 | dep. | Avila | arr. | 1814 |
| 1540 | arr. | Medina del Campo | arr. | 1734 |
| 1629 | arr. | Zamora | dep. | 1630 |
| 1632 | dep. | Zamora | arr. | 1626 |
| 1743 | arr. | Puebla de Sanabria | dep. | 1517 |
| 1818 | arr. | La Gudina | dep. | 1440 |
| 1921 | arr. | Orense-Empalme | dep. | 1338 |
| 1926 | dep. | Orense-Empalme | arr. | 1318 |
| 1950 | arr. | Carballino | dep. | 1255 |
| .... | arr. | Lalin | dep. | .... |
| 2110 | arr. | SANTIAGO DE COMPOSTELA | dep. | 1133 |
| 2112 | dep. | Santiago de Compostela | arr. | 1131 |
| 2203 | arr. | La Coruna-San Cristobal | dep. | 1040 |

## The Welcome Train
### Secret of the Costa del Sol

Jet lag is merciless. When the glass doors of Malaga's "Gateway to the Costa del Sol" airport snap shut behind you, you are newly arrived, glazed with jet lag, and too groggy to glance up to the tiny overhead sign pointing to the train: "Ferrocarril."

Lined-up taxis and standing buses offer you transportation to your beach apartment, condo, or hotel, but your best ride is the Costa del Sol train.

At first you may be chagrined at the tackiness and disrepair of the Costa del Sol, but after you get to know the convenience of the Costa del Sol train and the Portillo bus system you move around easily and discover a fascinating and very enjoyable experience.

The train runs twenty miles along the most popular stretch of Spain's sunny strand, from Malaga (pop. 505,000) to Fuengirola. The arrow at the airport points out a paved path (perfect for luggage with wheels) that leads for two minutes through the parking lot to the elevated train stop.

Renfe's Costa del Sol train is kept the best secret in the south of Spain because it loses money. The national railroad makes no pesetas on this cheap service with a view that gives you a clever budget way to orient yourself to the fascinating jumble grown up along the warmwater beaches.

An excursion on this cunning train shows off the many sights of the coast stretching west from Malaga. From the windows you get marvelous views of the quaint village of Mijas snuggled in the mountains, the blue Mediterranean lapping at the sand, rows of olive trees and eucalyptus groves, snow-covered Sierra Nevada mountains in the distance, artichokes, horses, and truck farming. Of course, you also see the endless houses, condos, and hotels embracing starkly modern, traditional Spanish, and elaborate Moorish styles, all distinguished by the identical color: blinding white.

Designers have modified the no-frills, yellow-striped, blue train carriage for airport service. They created floor space for suitcases at the entry doors and built special overhead racks broad enough to support piles of luggage. The two-opposite-two maroon leatherette seats are in good condition despite heavy use, but the linoleum floor is scuffed from the dragging of countless suitcases.

The efficient, self-propelled, electric train set, a "Unidad Electrica" railcar with attached carriage, is the workhorse of local and regional

Mijas •

FUENGIROLA

Benalmedena

COSTA DEL SOL
RAILROAD

TORREMOLINOS

Mediterranean Sea

To Cordoba

MALAGA

0        2        5
MILES

transportation throughout Spain. Each unit seats 260 (700 standing) at a maximum speed of 87 mph. They have run reliably since 1974, so Renfe is continuously adding new units.

Carriages pass half-hourly between Malaga-Guadalmedina and Fuengirola. Show your Eurailpass or your Renfe Tourist Card or buy a ticket on board. Only at the bigger, fully staffed stations do personnel in ticket booths at the entrance sell tickets.

A ticket from the airport to Torremolinos (trains are second class only) costs 50 pesetas (about forty-five cents). Riding the entire stretch, twenty miles, costs 150 pesetas (about $1.35). Round-trip fares are less.

Most of the line is above ground, but in Malaga, Torremolinos, and Fuengirola the stations are subterranean. The entrances to the underground Torremolinos and Fuengirola stations are difficult to see—even when you are standing next to them. Escalators take you to street level, but descend by stairs. There are nineteen stops between Malaga and Fuengirola. Making the complete run takes fifty-one minutes.

This line gives you easy access to a series of communities, none far from the line, but most passengers board at Malaga-Renfe, Malaga airports (National and International), and Torremolinos. Note that there are two airport stops. The one closer to Torremolinos, which used to be called "Vuelos Charter," is for the International terminal. The one closer to Malaga, "Aeropuerto," is for the National terminal. This is probably the one you will use, but be sure to check in advance.

The underground Torremolinos station entering on the square between Avenida Santos Rein and Calle de Emilio Estaban is the most complete of the line. Decorated with blue, green, red, and yellow tiles and blue benches, there is a magazine stand, a few lockers, a ticket kiosk, and a public telephone.

A tunnel connects the Malaga-Renfe stop to the separate mainline Malaga train terminus, where rays of red and yellow gleam through Moorish colored-glass windows. Luggage lockers are on the far side (125 pesetas). A second exit leads directly to the parking lot and taxi stand, the post office in back, and the bright snack bar/cafeteria and bank across the street.

A Talgo Pendular leaves from the mainline station in the afternoon for Madrid by way of Cordoba. Four overnight trains run the same route: the Talgo "Costa del Sol" sleeper to Madrid, an express to Madrid only with first- and second-class coaches, a first-class sleeper, and a second-class couchette train. The Estrella Picasso continues through Madrid to Bilbao three times a week and the Estrella Gibralfaro goes via Cordoba to Barcelona. Branch lines lead to Seville, Granada, and Algeciras.

Spaced along the Costa del Sol's main arterial highway, parallel to the railroad, you will see Portillo bus stops. After you have stored your luggage, the Portillo bus company is an easy way to get around. Riding their relay system of long-distance, middle-distance, and local buses stretching from Malaga to Algeciras (for an excursion to Gibraltar) is actually more convenient than renting a car and finding a place to park it.

The Costa del Sol is now a string of "urbanizations" (real estate developments) rambling end-to-end along blue Mediterranean shores like suburbia overflowing—not entirely admirable, but agreeable and comfortable for everyone. After the initial surprise of the clutter, it becomes fascinating to discover its hidden pleasures.

You will soon find that this area is not typically Spanish. It is a unique international settlement that takes on a flavor of its own when all the Norwegian restaurants, Danish bakeries, Swedish smorgasbords, Irish pubs, and Finnish coffeehouses merge with German Bierstuben, English teahouses, Canadian beer bars and American hamburger cafes, shopping malls, golf courses, yacht harbors, and beaches.

The marvelous result of this conglomeration is that it works. The English tongue is the common denominator. Nationals of all ages from everywhere in Europe, America, and the British Commonwealth coexist in harmony and shared enthusiasm.

It is said that the Costa del Sol is not for everybody, but when it's a good place for gray-haired folks (tearooms, short distances, warm weather), swinging singles (bars close at 6 A.M.), and families with children (activities, beach), you wonder exactly who wouldn't enjoy an inexpensive, warm-weather visit here.

## Welcome Train Timetable

| Distance in Miles | Station | Time in Minutes |
|---|---|---|
| 0 | Malaga-Guadalmedina | 0 |
| 1 | Malaga-Renfe | 3 |
| 2 | San Andres | 6 |
| 3 | Los Prados | 8 |
| 5 | Vuelos Nacionales (Aeropuerto) | 11 |
| 6 | Vuelos Internacionales (Charter) | 15 |
| 7 | San Julian | 18 |

| Distance in Miles | Station | Time in Minutes |
|---|---|---|
| 8 | Campo del Golf-Campamento | 20* |
| 9 | Los Alamos | 21 |
| 9 | La Colina | 23 |
| 11 | Torremolinos | 29 |
| 11 | Montemar-Alto | 32 |
| 12 | El Pinello | 33 |
| 13 | Arroyo de la Miel | 36 |
| 16 | Torremuelle-Benalmedena | 40 |
| 17 | Carvajal | 45 |
| 18 | Torreblanca | 46 |
| 19 | Los Boliches | 48 |
| 20 | Fuengirola | 51 |

*Service three times daily.

## Terror Trams of Alfama
### Adventure Cheap and Easy

You swoop and rise through hills and drops that measure a good 500 feet. You clutch, white-knuckled, at the grips of the advertisement-pasted cars while rows of pastel houses whiz beside you and glimpses of churches flash at you from cobblestone alleyways.

You look up and see stairways leading toward blue skies. Automobile horns honk on streets above your head. On your train's grinding struggle to the summit, your trolley wheezes, jerks, creaks, and chatters so loudly that many passengers standing elbow-to-elbow wonder, "Can this wreck take it one more time or is its axle going to snap and take me with it?"

Circling through Alfama, Lisbon's Moorish neighborhood that survived the murderous earthquake of 1755, you ride the most infamous stretch of rail adventure in Europe. Portugal's capital city of 812,000 can easily claim to have the most thrilling streetcar network built. Their tram system is widely held to be the most terrifying in the world.

Riding through Alfama on one of the rickety, two-axle trolley cars is an adventure that ages you prematurely, like a ride on a killer roller coaster. Part of the excitement comes from riding on cars that groan from neglect and seem to go back to shortly after Ulysses founded Lisbon. They climb the hills with the reckless drive of San Francisco's cable cars—but vehicles in Lisbon advertising blue jeans, beer, and vacations in Paris have no strong cables to save them from breaking away and skidding into the Tagus River below.

Most of the little trams (not covered by Eurailpass) are only large enough for fourteen sitting on the green leatherette seats and twenty hanging on the cracking leather straps or clutching at the chromium-plated poles. The floors are made of brown, abused wooden slats with dust accumulated in their crevices.

Riding downwards, fascinating side scenes plunge past you and the rows of houses you glimpsed ahead seem to twirl around and fly past you on the opposite side.

Lisboans on the trams gaze calmly at the passing sights. Mothers cradle their babies and hum lullabies while young boys stretch and rap the church windows alongside and smudge fingertips against the stuccoed walls sweeping past. Some alleys are so narrow that the streetcars fill the few feet separating houses. Pedestrians dodge nimbly into doorways to avoid the pushy, onrushing trams. Stop-and-go signals are essential on the narrowest curves to regulate traffic and reduce the number of head-on collisions.

Instead of the automatic, electric signal lights you expect to see, you are amazed to find casually dressed guards still assigned to blind corners, directing traffic by hand with a signal baton and rickety box to sit on, coping with streetcars plummeting down the wrong direction of one-way streets and mad auto drivers sneaking behind them.

The most daring of the lines climbing the Alfama hills is renegade line No. 28. It is your ultimate test. It runs the wrong way—against auto traffic. Visiting Lisbon and not riding a No. 28 streetcar is like visiting San Francisco and not riding a cable car or visiting a theme park and not riding a roller coaster.

So that the trams could maneuver through the claustrophobic maze of streets, engineers laid the tracks narrow-gauge (only 23.6 inches) with only one pair of thin rails. Luckily, just when an approaching tram seems ready to crash into another and panicky tourists realize the emergency brakes might not be working, the tracks part at the last instant and the cars veer sideways as if testing the riders' nerves and sanity.

Double trolley carriages are out of the question. It would be an indictable murder offense to try to pull passive passenger trailers around the curves.

In such a hodgepodge, the safe use of vehicles secured by tracks embedded in cobblestones is essential. Their limited freedom prevents reckless or annoyed tram drivers from nicking or scraping the already peeling whitewash on the house walls (or the advertising on the trams, for that matter).

The Lisbon streetcar system is one of the largest and one of the creakiest in the world. It has thirty struggling lines. The youngest is older than most of today's straphangers. Although the network was consolidated in 1974 with the opening of the Lisbon subway, the last extension of the tram system was in 1958.

In all fairness, in a city offering magnificent surprises to walkers, the trams are convenient, if unnerving, and inexpensive. Considering the hilly terrain and capricious nature of the streets, it is surprising the trams do as well as they do.

You find your way by use of a free map from the tourist office. Schedules pinpointing the zigzagging routes of trams and buses throughout the city are posted on the walls of glassed-in bus stops in the business district. A thorough guide to the public transportation system of Lisbon and its environs (including an official map of bus and tram lines) is sold in the booth at the foot of the Santa Justa elevator ("Eiffel elevator").

To sample the dashing of the remarkable trams through Alfama, take Nos. 10, 11, or 28 to the Graca terminal, which is more of a four by eight-foot orange-and-white kiosk than a terminal. Riders leap onto the trams whenever they can—anytime one slows enough to make leaping reasonably safe. They enter the back and pay on board to the conductor—not the driver.

The conductor will be dressed in civvies but you will spot him easily by his shoulder strap, his leather pouch, his paper punch, and especially his interest in collecting the fare from you. Don't worry if you don't find him at first. He'll find you. Fares vary depending on your destination. To exit, divide the glass doors to the front behind the driver and climb off through the driver's compartment.

Along your route you will find the excellent Miradouro (meaning "belvedere") Santa Luzia, where you will see a splendid panorama of Lisbon and shipping on the Tagus River.

The Belvedere of Santa Luzia is an oasis of trellises, benches, and blue-and-white-tiled murals. Under the vines' shade, local men play cards and checkers. There are bathrooms and a tourist office here, too. This is the perfect place to begin a walking tour of Alfama. Bus line No. 37 loops right at the portals of the Castelo da Sao Jorge.

Happy to be back to steady terra firma, you nod to your fellow passengers to say, "Well, we made it—this time at least."

Convenient and reasonably priced special tourist transportation tickets allowing travel on all of Lisbon's subways, trams, and funiculars cost about $6.25 for four days, or $8.60 for a week. They are sold Mondays through Fridays from 8 A.M. to 8 P.M. at Carris kiosks throughout

Lisbon. You will find them outside the Santa Apolonia station, in the so-called "Eiffel elevator," and at the foot of the Park Eduardo VII near the Praca Marques Pombal.

## Subways and Double-Decker Buses

Lisbon has a limited but inexpensive subway system. The main station, "RS" for Rossio, is at the apex of the V-shaped system in the downtown area. The subway entrances on the Avenida da Liberdade are indicated by large red *M* (for "Metropolitano") signs on the street. The metro stations are impressive and are elegantly adorned with azulejos (glazed colored tiles).

To use the metro, obtain a pocket map at a tourist office or check in any subway station the maps of the system at the foot of stairs leading from the street. Save money by buying your tickets from the orange-colored ticketing machines (directions are printed in three languages, including English) for 35$ (about twenty-five cents). Tickets sold by agents (in some stations only) cost 40$ (about thirty cents), but books of ten cost 320$ ($2.35). You board the train in the direction of the last station shown on the branch you wish to use.

To complete Lisbon's public transportation system, Carris purchased venerable, green, double-decker buses directly from London. Sitting in the front seats on the top level of these jolly green giants is a treat, but standing on the platform in the back of a jammed bus at rush hour is a giant green terror. You will need both hands to hang on and a foot to hold your packages.

## *Portugal Up Close*
## *Algarve, Alfa, and Choice of Commuters*

"Under no circumstances should you take the train from the Algarve to Lisbon." Algarvian Senhor Jaoa Lima, graduate of the University of Wisconsin, was very adamant. He waved his arms like a sea gull. "If you must, take a bus. They have videos."

"We didn't come all the way from California to the Algarve to watch a video in Portuguese. We want to see Portugal up close, the people, and how you live."

Lima looked discouraged. "The videos merely have Portuguese subtitles."

"We complain continuously to the government for better train service to our region," he confided. "If you want to ride an excellent train, take the train from Lisbon to Porto."

Contrary to Lima's expectations, the Rapido train taking you from Portugal's Algarve region is spacious and clean, often arrives in Lisbon

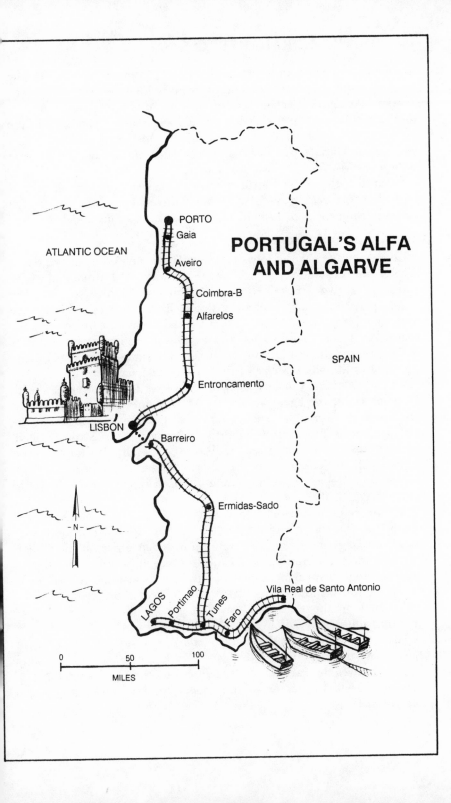

ATLANTIC OCEAN

PORTO
Gaia

Aveiro

Coimbra-B

Alfarelos

Entroncamento

LISBON

Barreiro

Ermidas-Sado

LAGOS

Portimao

Tunes

Faro

Vila Real de Santo Antonio

**PORTUGAL'S ALFA AND ALGARVE**

SPAIN

-N-

0      50      100
MILES

seven minutes early, and is as quiet as a dormitory—except for the raucous noises you hear resounding from the bar two carriages away.

Many Portuguese are critical of their country's facilities, but even their secondary trains are decent, their food is never bad even in the bistros, and Lisbon's subway is convenient. On the other hand, when you say the facade of their magnificent neo-Manuelino Rossio train station is dirty, they say it is "discolored."

Because of the network structure in Portugal, you are virtually locked into using Lisbon as your base for train travel. There are no through trains passing through Lisbon. Lisbon has five stations and five lines.

## Santa Apolonia Station

Conveniently near the foot of Alfama is the dark-rose-colored Santa Apolonia train station, your gateway to the trains of Europe and where you may have your Eurailpass first validated at window No. 11.

Santa Apolonia faces out on a taxi loop and a modern sculpture honoring immigrants to Portugal. Buses and trams pass by on the main roads. You reach Santa Apolonia easily by walking from the city center or by streetcar Nos. 3, 16, or 24. It is a tidy station, but small. Santa Apolonia is literally the end of the line for international traffic.

When you enter, you find the ticket windows 1 to 11 straight ahead. On your right, the agent at window 11 sells international tickets and reservations. Although usually a formality, because except for the Lisboa Express TER train to Madrid the trains are rarely totally filled, CP requires you to make seat reservations for all CP's Rapidos and name trains to Spain even if only shortly before departure—and then only at your departure station. Computerized reservations have yet to come to Portugal.

On the right hand wall is a booth where you can change money (open 9 A.M. to noon and 2 to 6:30 P.M.). On the left is a kiosk with magazines, cigarettes, etc. The train information office on the far left (look for the i sign) functions as a tourist office after international train arrivals. English-speaking ladies give train information and will book hotels for you without charge. Along the left corridor, train schedules are posted on the walls and you find a post office and a baggage checking counter.

Through the middle is the train gallery. You must show your ticket or Eurailpass to pass through the gate. Track No. 3, where the "Sud Express" leaves for Paris, is on the left and on the right is track No. 5. You must walk farther down the gallery to find track No. 1, Alfa Service to Porto.

## Alfa Service

Alfa Service is the name CP gives its proud seven-times-a-day fleet of 1985 Corail carriages between Portugal's two major cities, Lisbon and Porto.

Because the trains are Rapidos (train Nos. 9 and 12 are termed "InterCity"), you will need reservations. Book in advance at Santa Apolonia station (about $2) or—when the train is not filled—buy them at the special day counter beside track No. 1.

The exteriors have been fabricated in Portugal of stainless steel but the interiors duplicate snappy French Corail materials and design. The only difference is the language of the newspapers the passengers read.

The bar car features "Corail Servico Alfa" with sandwiches, cakes, coffee, and bottles of liquor. Hostesses wearing red bandannas and chic, striped aprons take orders from your seat. You may order meals on the 11 A.M. and 8:15 P.M. departures from both the Lisbon and Porto terminals.

The highlight of your trip to Porto comes after your train stops for clearance in Vila Nova da Gaia and you inch across the Douro River on the bridge designed entirely of metal in 1877 by the French engineer Eiffel. The best general panorama of the old stone city of Porto (pop. 330,000) spreads on the right bank before you. You see the old town, topped by the towers of the cathedral and the Clerigos belfry, rising in tiers from the Douro. Overlapping series of hillside alleys are lined with architecturally dazzling houses decorated with corbels and (occasionally) tiled facades.

Sadly, you leave this view when your train enters the tunnel and comes to a stop in Campanha station, but this gives you a chance to board one of the many connecting trains and continue to the downtown Sao Bento station to see the great display of artistic tiles covering the walls of the reception hall, the pride of CP. Although in need of a good cleaning, they're a feast for the eyes. Painted in 1930 by Jorge Colaco, these tile pictures include a full-color frieze of everyday life in Portugal and feature historic panoramas in blue: Joao's entry into Porto (top right) and his capture of Cueta (bottom right).

## Algarve Service

The best train to the Algarve, the "Portuguese Riviera" stretching along Portugal's sunny southern shores, is the crack InterCity Rapido Sotovento ("South Wind"). Like its sister evening InterCity Rapido, it runs daily, whisking you in 4 1/4 hours from Lisbon's waterfront Terreiro do Paco station to Faro.

The Terreiro do Paco station, decorated with tiles depicting Algarvian city crests, lies adjacent to the finest square in Lisbon, the Praca do Comercio, known to all as Terreiro do Paco, the "Palace Terrace." Here you board, through separate first- and second-class entrances, CP's half-hourly blue-and-white ferries across the Tagus River to the Barreiro station. Eurailpasses are accepted aboard.

Allow time at Terreiro do Paco to obtain reservations for the Rapidos (about fifty cents). You can only make them in this station. Similarly, you can only make your return reservation at your Algarvian destination.

After your ferry crossing to Barreiro, follow the crowd down a ramp past kiosks, shops, and a waiting room through a ticket-checking station onto your waiting, stainless-steel train.

Running 155 miles in three hours (52 mph) to Tunes, the junction for connecting trains to Lagos, your Rapido is not fast, but comfortable and gives you just the right pace to distinguish the harvest years painted on the cork trees. You see sights you never see from the colorless, commercial highway. You absorb the feeling of the region as you observe casual cowherds with staff and cap and brown bulls with wicked-looking horns drinking from streams. You see olive trees, or- ange groves, pine and eucalyptus forests, and many small farms.

You will cross what seems like an invisible line across Portugal. South of the line the villages consist of boxy, flat-roofed houses. North of it, they are all peaked with tile roofs.

## The Sintra Commuter

A trip to Sintra to see its palace begins at Lisbon's Rossio station. Rossio station is the busy commuter station located in the heart of Lisbon across from the Teatro National (National Theater) on Rossio Square. CP accepts Eurailpasses on this line. You enter the station through one of the most astonishing facades of the European railroads. It is in the neo-Manuelino style of the nineteenth century (connected to the adjacent hotel so royalty could proceed directly), but terribly dirty/discolored by the traffic exhaust from Rossio Square across the street.

On the ground floor there is an information counter (English spok- en), but follow the stairs and several flights of escalators all the way past various shops to "Gare," where you get tickets—or enter the side door on the top level (with taxi access) if you want to use the steps ("calcada") leading down from the crest of the hill above.

Electric signboards display coming train departures and their track numbers. At the head of each track (5, for Sintra), another electric sign shows the next departure time and the current time. Schedules are posted in an alcove beyond track 10.

The two-class stainless-steel trains depart through a long tunnel into Campolide station. Lisbon appears to be a hodgepodge of suburbs along the railroad line to Sintra. Finally, you see to the left the Royal Palace atop the moutainside above the Portela de Sintra station.

Outside the end-of-the-line peeling-paint Sintra station, taxis stand offering to take you to the palace.

## The Cascais Commuter

Your trip to Cascais on the coast is an excursion along the Tagus River, also covered by Eurailpass. You easily reach (and find) the Cais do Sodre station because it is the end of the line for many streetcar and bus lines (buses No. 45 and 35 from Santa Apolonia station), which therefore carry "Cais do Sodre" on their signboards.

With a Eurailpass you walk through Cais do Sodre station's gates to the boarding area, where videos will inform you of your track number (according to destination) and departure time. Departures of the simple, one-class stainless-steel trains are shown on videos between track Nos. 2 and 3.

After the Alcantara station, your Cascais Commuter passes under the Ponte 25 de Abril suspension bridge—Portugal's "Golden Gate." You run a block from the Tagus until you reach the Henry the Navigator Memorial, where you begin to travel alongside the sailboats and Tagus promenade. Your best view of the bridge is looking back immediately before you reach the Belem station—a superb view.

The Belem station is a convenient place to debark to view the Belem Tower, the great Jeronimos Monastery across the highway, and the Henry the Navigator Memorial.

Past the Alges stop, your train travels closer to the Tagus and you have a better view of the shipping, the breakwaters, and then the beaches. All along the stretch from Alges to Cruz Quebrada to Caxias, looking back toward Lisbon gives you a fine long view of the graceful suspension bridge.

You don't appreciate the splendor of the coast—the blue water and frothy waves breaking on the white sand—until just before your stop at S. Pedro station, where you see a nice panorama of things to come.

Estoril is your glamor stop, in front of the Casino. The tourist office is across the street. Past Estoril to Cascais, you pass beaches and luxury hotels. The beach for which Cascais is famous begins just before its unsheltered end-of-the-line train station.

There are departures for Estoril and Cascais about every half-hour until 2:30 A.M. Departures for Belem leave Lisbon about every fifteen minutes.

## Alfa Service, Lisbon to Porto

| Train No. | 1 | 3 | 5 | 7 | 9 | 11 | 13 |
|---|---|---|---|---|---|---|---|
| dep. LISBON (Apolonia) | 0715 | 0815 | 1100 | 1430 | 1620 | 1700 | 2015 |
| arr. Entroncamento | .... | .... | .... | 1532 | 1724 | .... | .... |
| arr. Alfarelos | .... | .... | .... | .... | 1817 | .... | .... |
| arr. Coimbra-B | .... | 1029 | .... | 1636 | 1831 | 1904 | 2219 |
| arr. Aveiro | .... | 1103 | .... | 1710 | 1908 | 1938 | 2253 |
| arr. Espinho | .... | .... | .... | 1737 | 1942 | .... | .... |
| arr. Vila Nova de Gaia | 1006 | 1145 | 1352 | 1749 | 1955 | 2020 | 2335 |
| arr. PORTO (Campanha) | 1015 | 1155 | 1400 | 1800 | 2007 | 2030 | 2345 |

## Alfa Service, Porto to Lisbon

| Train No. | 2 | 4 | 6 | 8 | 10 | 12 | 14 |
|---|---|---|---|---|---|---|---|
| dep. PORTO (Campanha) | 0715 | 0825 | 1100 | 1440 | 1700 | 1725 | 2015 |
| arr. Vila Nova de Gaia | 0723 | 0834 | 1108 | 1449 | 1709 | 1735 | 2024 |
| arr. Espinho | .... | .... | .... | 1502 | .... | 1752 | .... |
| arr. Aveiro | .... | 0910 | .... | 1528 | 1745 | 1819 | 2100 |
| arr. Coimbra-B | .... | 0943 | .... | 1602 | 1818 | 1853 | 2133 |
| arr. Entroncamento | .... | .... | .... | 1706 | .... | 2001 | .... |
| arr. LISBON (Apolonia) | l015 | 1155 | 1400 | 1810 | 2030 | 2110 | 2345 |

## Rapido Service, Lisbon to the Algarve

| IC9003 | IC9005 | | | IC9002 | IC9004 |
|---|---|---|---|---|---|
| 1410 | 1805 | dep. LISBON (T. do Paco) | arr. | 1235 | 1830 |
| 1440 | 1835 | arr. Barreiro | dep. | 1205 | 1800 |
| 1452 | 1847 | dep. Barreiro | arr. | 1156 | 1748 |
| 1748 | 2144 | arr. Tunes | dep. | 0855 | 1450 |
| 1750 | 2147 | dep. Tunes | arr. | 0848 | 1447 |
| 1758 | 2155 | dep. Albufeira | dep. | 0843 | 1442 |
| 1812 | 2209 | dep. Loule | dep. | 0827 | 1428 |
| 1825 | 2223 | arr. FARO | dep. | *0812 | *1415 |
| *1838 | 2228 | dep. Faro | arr. | 0757 | 1349 |

| IC9003 | IC9005 | | | | IC9002 | IC9004 |
|---|---|---|---|---|---|---|
| 1851 | 2239 | arr. | Olhao | dep. | 0748 | 1336 |
| 1923 | 2303 | arr. | Tavira | dep. | 0717 | 1306 |
| 1955 | 2327 | arr. | Vila Real de | dep. | 0643 | 1231 |
| | | | Santo Antonio | | | |
| 1958 | 2330 | arr. | (Guadiana) | dep. | 0640 | 1228 |

*Change trains.

# Scandinavia
# and Finland

## Vital Tips for the Trains
## of Scandinavia and Finland

Hans Christian Andersen traveled by mail coach and sailing ship on his first trip from his home, Odense, on the island of Funen, to the Danish royal capital of Copenhagen in September 1819. You can make that trip now in three hours by a Danish "Lightning" train.

The great Scandinavian writer was the consummate adventurer: "To travel is to live." He believed travel meant meeting new people, visiting new surroundings, absorbing new impressions, discovering new joys in nature, and feeling vibrantly alive.

Scandinavia offers the 1,250-mile network of the Danish State Railroads (DSB), the 2,650 miles of the Norwegian State Railroads (NSB), the 7,000 miles of the Swedish State Railroads (SJ). The 3,650 miles of the Finnish State Railroads (VR) complete your Nordic adventuring. You can ride these from the storks nesting in the chimneys of Denmark to the blue fjords and stark glaciers of Norway to the Land of the Midnight Sun and Lapland above the Arctic Circle in Sweden and Finland.

Scandinavia's best trains are NSB's "Tomorrow Trains" taking you on the Express Special routes from Oslo north to Trondheim and south to Stavanger. SJ's are comfortable; DSB's are efficient. VR's white-and-red, 1989, 100-mph InterCity trains have redesigned interiors and exteriors, entrances, and passageways. First class offers stereo earphones.

Your most likely gateway to Scandinavia is the mainline from Germany via alternating DSB and GermanRail ferries from Puttgarden to Rodby (named for the migratory flight path of birds) and on to Copenhagen.

From here, you travel up Sweden's West Coast through Gothenburg to Oslo or across Sweden to Stockholm. All major through trains—the InterCities and the EuroCities—take the ferry.

You remain in your carriage while it is being shunted aboard, then have the run of the ferry and return to your compartment upon docking. Aboard the ferry, cigarettes and liquor are available in the twenty-four-hour duty-free shops, even at prices higher than at home. No matter what they cost compared to home, cigarettes and liquor are bargains here—something made obvious by the long lines of Swedish shoppers struggling with bulging red plastic shopping baskets.

Don't miss your chance to enjoy an open-faced sandwich, Danish pastry (especially aboard a DSB ferry), and Danish beer in the cafeteria. Be sure to do enough duty-free shopping to last your entire stay in Scandinavia.

EuroCity service to Scandinavia is carried aboard the EC Alfred Nobel, a GermanRail night train with only first- and second-class sleeping cars and second-class couchettes. It skirts Copenhagen to take you between Hamburg and Stockholm, Gothenburg, or Oslo.

You also reach Norway by several ferries from Denmark or by train via Storlien, Sweden, to Trondheim. You can't travel by train north of the Gulf of Bothnia between Sweden and Finland. VR closed the line from Kemi to the Swedish border in 1988.

## Stations and Subways

Plan to use the centrally located train stations in all of Scandinavia's capital cities as your bases. Copenhagen H. (for "Hovedbanegard," or "head train station") has been refurbished with a new post office and shops. Oslo Sentral is sparkling new—christened by King Olav V in February 1987. Stockholm Central is a multilevel complex with all services. Helsinki's station has a busy shopping center and subway station connected underground.

In Copenhagen, the suburban transit S-train system is a convenience for everyone. When you book a hotel room at the hotel reservations counter in the station, it is a good idea to ask whether your chosen hotel is near an S-Bahn station. It saves you time and struggling with luggage.

In Oslo, twice-an-hour local train service tunnels through the heart of the city. Use stops such as "National Theater" to get around. Subways ("T-Bane") take you throughout the Oslo area. Similarly, Stockholm's Central station and Helsinki's station are well connected to their regions with subways. Look for a *T* ("Tunnelbana") in Stockholm and an *M* for "Metroon/Metron" in Helsinki.

## Reservations

You are required to make advance seat reservations (costing up to $2.50) on most of the fast trains of the Nordic networks. DSB requires reservations on all trains crossing the Great Belt waterway—specifically the cardinal-red InterCity and 100-mph "Lightning" (Lyntogen) trains running hourly. SJ specifies reservations on their crack trains—the InterCities and long-distance express trains. NSB requires reservations on all Express Special ("ET") trains between Oslo and Stavanger, Bergen, and Trondheim. You pay NSB's mandatory fee even when you board your train at the last minute and find an empty seat. VR asks for reservations on its "EP" Special Fast and "EXP" Express trains from Helsinki.

You don't need reservations on the GermanRail EuroCity trains, Merkur, Hansa, or Skandinavien, taking you between Copenhagen and Germany.

## Midnight Sun Travel

The long distances you travel, especially in Norway and Sweden, and the long summer daylight hours make you want to seriously consider traveling around the clock.

All the Nordic railroads own their domestic couchettes and sleeping cars. Prices for three-bedded sleeping cars compare favorably with those of six-bunk couchettes in the south. Reserve them as early as possible when you are in Scandinavia. Incompatible computer interfaces don't allow you to book them outside the area except by mail.

DSB's "Project Night Train," using BritRail Mark III carriages with superior Danish interiors and painted blue with golden moon and stars, produced a renaissance in overnight travel between Copenhagen and Frederikshavn, Arhus, Esbjerg, and Fredericia. First-class compartments have one bed and second-class ones have two. Couchettes sleep five per compartment.

You ride NSB's 1987 red-and-black (to match NSB's "Tomorrow Train" carriages) pairs of WLAB-2 sleeping cars between Oslo and Bergen, Trondheim, or Stavanger. One car is made up for first-class travel, one for second. They are the longest and quietest in Norway and the widest in Western Europe (which means the corridor accommodates jump seats and tables, and still has room for refreshment trolleys to pass).

You also ride NSB's single sleeping cars between Oslo and Flam or Andalsnes. These are older but excellent for sleeping.

You ride SJ's couchettes and sleeping cars on their routes between Narvik, Stockholm, Malmo, Helsingborg, Copenhagen, Gothenburg, and Oslo. VR has no couchettes, but has very inexpensive double-bedded sleeping cars in first class, and three-bedded ones in second class—eight from Helsinki and four from Turku.

## Using Eurailpass Bonuses

In Denmark, Eurailpasses or regular train tickets include passage aboard the MF *Kronprins Frederik* or her six sister super ships which take you—in your train—across the Great Belt waterway separating Copenhagen's island of Funen from the Jutland peninsula. When your train reaches one of the embarkation ports, Nyborg or Korsor, your conductor locks its doors. After your train is shuttled onto the ferry, its doors are unlocked and you are free to roam the ship. Color-coded sections guide you. Both the red and the blue sections have their own restaurant, cafeteria, and fast-food kiosk.

You cross the fifteen-mile Great Belt in an hour, the better part of your travel time to Odense. The train ferries are steamlined: your train comes off the same end it was onloaded, meaning your seat will be facing the opposite direction when you continue your trip.

Your Eurailpass-covered steamer crossing between Frederikshavn (Denmark) and Gothenburg, Sweden's second city, is operated by Stena Sessan (a private steamship company) and is a good way to reach Gothenburg, but not if you plan to continue onward. The steamer landing is far from the train station and to get there you must carry your luggage through crowded public transportation or take a taxi.

The Fred Olsen Lines KDS gives Eurailpass holders a 30 percent reduction on the trip between Hirtshals near the northern tip of the Jutland peninsula and Kristiansand in Norway. To reach Hirtshals, change at Hjorring from DSB's Frederikshavn mainline to a twelve-mile-long private railroad. In Kristiansand, board the Sorlands main-line between Oslo and Stavanger.

TT Saga line gives Eurailpass holders a 50 percent reduction on normal fares for the ferry crossings between Trelleborg, Sweden, and Lubeck-Travemunde, Germany.

The Danish navigation company, Oresund, gives you a 50 percent reduction for travel on the hydrofoil between Copenhagen and Malmo, Sweden. This is the only fare you pay for a "Round the Sound" trip—one of the most interesting one-day excursions from Copenhagen. Board the hydrofoil at Havngade in Copenhagen for the half-hour trip across the Oresund to Malmo. In the brick station house adjacent to the the landing in Malmo, change to SJ's local train for the forty-mile run through Skane, Sweden's chateau country. Break your trip to enjoy historical sights and the pastoral scenery. On return, board a DSB or SJ ferry from Helsingborg to Helsingor and then continue by DSB train to Copenhagen H.

Also use your Eurailpass to make several other excellent one-day excursions. Make a round trip via the Great Belt to Odense to see the house where Hans Christian Andersen grew up (historians agree that no one knows the house where he was born) and the 1988-remodeled Railroad Museum, to Roskilde to see the Viking Ship Museum, to Hillerod to see Frederiksborg Castle, and to Humlebaek to visit the Louisiana Art Museum.

You receive free transportation from Stockholm to Finland (Helsinki or Turku) on Silja Line's great blue-and-white ferries, but must pay full fare for cabin space (see the "Crossing the Bothnia" adventure).

Finally, you may ride free the ferries crossing the Samso Belt via Kalundborg between Copenhagen and Aarhus, and train ferries between Kundshoved and Halskov or Bojden and Fynshav (for Sonderborg Castle on the island of Als). You receive a 20 percent reduction on the normal fares of the Scandinavian Seaways Co. between Esbjerg (there are inexpensive couchettes connecting here from Copenhagen) and Harwich or Newcastle, England, or the Faroe Islands. Similarly, a Eurailpass earns you a 20 percent discount on the Scandinavian Seaways sailings between Copenhagen and Oslo.

## Nordic Tourist Card

Denmark, Norway, Sweden, and Finland together offer a Nordic Tourist Card ("Nordturist Med Tog") for unlimited travel for twenty-one days in the four Nordic countries, but the first-class version is no bargain compared to the cost of a Eurailpass. Buying the second-class tourist card, however, saves you one-third.

You receive more perks with a Nordic Tourist Card (available at train stations in all Nordic countries) than a Eurailpass, but lose half of the free Silja Line crossing to Helsinki, an adventure described in this chapter. On the plus side, you travel free on the private train between Hirtshals and Hjorring in Denmark and the Fred Olsen Lines KDS crossing between Hirtshals and Kristiansand. Further, you receive a 50 percent discount on the Larvik Line between Larvik, Norway, and Frederikshavn, Denmark, and a 50 percent discount on the Scandinavian crossings between Copenhagen and Oslo. You still receive a free ride on the Silja Line crossing to Turku, but must pay half between Stockholm and Helsinki.

The Nordic Tourist Card also gives you free entry to the train museums in Gavle, Hamar, Hyvinkaa, and Odense plus 15 to 40 percent off the normal rates at more than a hundred Sara, Inter Nor, Danway, and Arctia hotels.

## National Rail Passes

Denmark is so small that with the transportation bargains available, getting around is a steal. It will make you feel like you are robbing a bank when you buy a Danish Rail Pass for a month's first-class unlimited travel for about two-thirds of the cost of a Eurailpass, or for a month's travel, second-class, for about two-thirds of the cost of a Eurail Youthpass (but open to all ages). They are valid on Denmark's domestic ferries as well. Children four to twelve pay half; under four ride free.

Danish Rail Passes are available at any train station in Denmark, as are half-price tickets for travelers over sixty-five and groups of three or more traveling together.

A Norwegian Bargain Rail Pass is a one-way, second-class ticket valid Monday to Thursday for seven days. The price is about $45. NSB automatically gives 50 percent off to travelers over sixty-seven. Buy passes and tickets at any train station in Norway.

Unlimited-travel Finnrailpasses are available at VR's major stations for first- or second-class travel for eight, fifteen, or twenty-two days at about 70 percent of the cost of Eurailpasses.

Also look for capital-city travel cards to save you money on local trains, buses, subways, and sometimes ferries. Buy them at train stations, tourist offices, and kiosks in the areas.

The Copenhagen Card is available for one, two, or three days. You can also buy regional tickets covering areas from Copenhagen to Helsingor, Frederikssund, Roskilde, and Koge.

Oslo Cards for twenty-four, forty-eight, and seventy-two hours provide you free travel, free car parking, and more. The seventy-two-hour ticket gives you half off one round-trip train journey to Oslo from points in Norway.

Stockholm Cards for twenty-four, forty-eight, seventy-two, and ninety-six hours also provide free travel on the "Tourist Line" city tour, free car parking, and admission to a number of museums, palaces, and other attractions. The less expensive "SL Tourist Card" gives twenty-four or seventy-two hours unlimited travel by suburban train, subway, and bus in the county of Stockholm (except the SAS airport bus) and on Djurgarden ferries. A nine-trip strip card saves you 30 percent.

Helsinki Cards for one, two, or three days include free travel, a city sightseeing bus tour, boat trips, and admission to more than fifty sights and museums. For one-third off, you can buy a "Tourist Ticket," a one-day pass limited to subway trains, trams, and buses or a ten-trip ticket giving one-sixth off the single fare price.

Ready yourself for fresh clean air and sparkling fjords as you travel through Lapland and the land of the Midnight Sun on the following adventures: Norway's Bergen and Flam line, a trip into the Arctic Circle, Norway's Rauma Train, and a crossing by deluxe ferry from Stockholm to Finland.

## Bergen and Flam Trains
## Travel with the Trolls

The plateau is a vast stretch of mountaintop, uninhabited, treeless, flat. You see no spiked Matterhorns here, just featureless mountains with tops swept away by glaciers—a frozen, crystalline surface, polished by howling wind. It is Arctic, remote, lonely, and it is only your brick-red train that keeps you from feeling stranded on the top of the world.

You have passed Taugevatn, the highest point of this Norwegian line (4,267 feet), well above the timber line so far north. Now you run along the stark, clear-aired, snow-pocked edge of the Hardanger Plateau.

It is so white that any speck of color seems to be out of place. Just before you stop at Myrdal, you look to your right and see the browns and greens of the mountain walls of a grand canyon of a rift. Peering through openings in the north wall of the snow tunnel, you gasp at the sight so many hundred feet down of the temperate Flam valley.

The Oslo-Bergen route—free on a Eurailpass—is NSB's important flagship route. Without it, Norway's second city would be isolated by land from the rest of the country. Behind Bergen, the wall of the Hardanger Plateau forms a dead end.

When you look at a topographic map of Norway, you can appreciate that this route is an engineering triumph. Engineers successfully designed the line to climb and descend safely from sea level to 4,267 feet in inaccessible, hostile Arctic country.

Your Pernille Express Special train hurried out of Oslo Sentral station punctually at 7:35 A.M. through built-up Oslo and past the suburbs. Climbing alongside a broad river, your long, brick-red, electric train first passes flowery meadows and placid lakes. Then you hear the whine of sawmills at work and see tractors idling beside red farmhouses in patchwork fields close by the rails.

You cross through meager and noticeably thinning farmland, past natural, untouched emerald valleys, and finally out of pine groves and woods of ringed silver birch trees, away from the temperate environment of the Oslo fjord and up into the mountains. You see the waters run faster. The trees thin. Patches of snow appear. The country is mantled in white by the time you arrive in Geilo. At 2,650 feet, you are only miles short of the timber line.

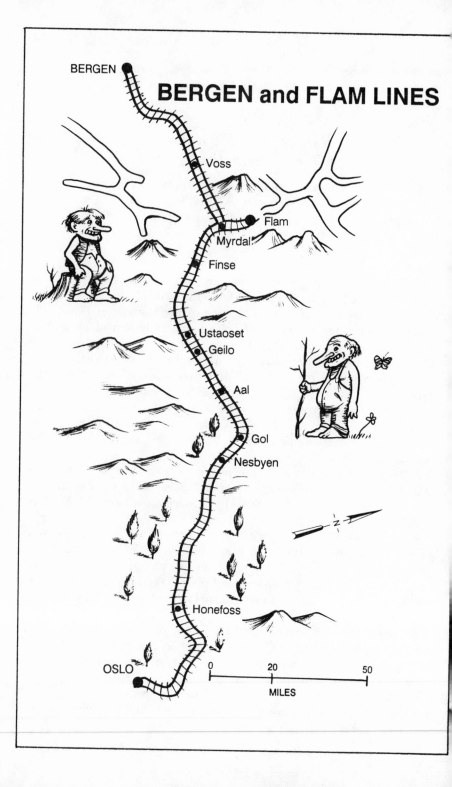

Skiers clunk off down the platform, even in midsummer. They tilt their skis proudly over their shoulders, eager for a good afternoon's sport. Geilo is the St. Moritz of Norway.

As you continue to climb, the scenery changes from ski resort to glacier. You leave the last of the trees at Ustaoset.

At Finse, thirty minutes later, the landscape glares whitely. It is dominated by the frigid Hardanger glacier looming in the south higher by 2,000 feet than Finse (4,010 feet). George Lucas filmed here the bitterly cold opening sequences of *The Empire Strikes Back*.

Finse is the highest station on the line—the entire NSB network, in fact. If you are riding a local train, you might have time to tramp into the snowbanks to take spectacular photos of the glacier, or peek at the old steam-powered snowplow. It is the lonely headquarters for the Bergen line's thirty- to forty-worker crew against nature. They clear snow from the tracks during nine snowy months and repair snowsheds splintered by the power of the snow during what should be their vacation.

Now at Myrdal station, dominated by a mountain with icy whiskers of frozen waterfalls, you don your parka and bundle onto the waiting coaches of the Flam train, each seating thirty-nine on maroon, leatherette-covered benches for two and three, accented with brass studs and hand fixtures. The scuffed brown linoleum floor has seen much service and the heavy-duty overhead racks have carried many backpacks.

You leave behind a high, bleak, and contrary glacial plateau for the green and serene beauty of one of Norway's most pleasant fjords. Your trip doesn't take long—less than an hour—but minute for minute, as your train inches down Europe's steepest route and turns surprising corners, you are rewarded by one of the most breathtaking of Norway's adventurous trains. The conductors also make it Norway's friendliest.

The Flam valley you see is an immense opening through the mountains, similar to the Grand Canyon in the sheer inclination of its mountain walls. You board the Flam line—free on a Eurailpass—at its upper railhead, Myrdal, 2,845 feet above sea level. The lower terminus, Flam, near the ferry landing on the Aurlandsfjord, is fifty minutes (forty-one, going up) and twelve miles down the valley. This section is the steepest of any NSB line. In one stretch you drop one foot for every eighteen you travel, quite brave for an adhesion train without cog-wheels. The five braking systems give your cautious engineer more sureness than a Norwegian mountain goat. Any one system is enough to halt the train safely.

This line was not built for passenger traffic. Perhaps that is why it is so unspoiled. It was built in the wilds, connecting fjord and glacier, to carry construction materials and heavy machinery for completing the central section of the Oslo-Bergen line. They were ferried up the fjord to Flam and then carted by horses up to Myrdal. You see the surviving horse trail of 1895-96 still paralleling the line.

You follow a tortuous path of twenty-one hairpin curves, in and out of tunnels. On the most scenic sections, your engineer thoughtfully slows or stops, so you can linger and absorb the impact of views more dazzling than you have imagined. You see sturdy wild mountain goats peering curiously at the train from granite boulders only a few feet from your window.

At first descent, your Flam train moves roughly parallel to the Bergen line, between snow fences, but after your halt in Vatnahalsen, a stop with a fine hotel and superb view over the steep slopes below, splendid panoramas quickly begin to unfold. You soon reach the highlight of your trip. Your train trudges across a sturdy embankment and the engineer stops politely.

Beside the line, so close you can feel the pressure of the roaring action filling cameras' viewfinders, a fury of foam plunges over a cliff, raging down at you in a smoking torrent. It is not so much a waterfall as rapids out of nowhere. Just before you it vanishes safely into a natural tunnel beneath the trestle supporting your train. This is Kjosfoss, "foss" meaning "waterfall."

You appreciate the announcements, in English, over the loudspeaker by the conductor. These men take a sincere interest in the well-being and pleasure of adventurers who come to visit their proud little valley.

If they feel a certain affinity for Americans, it is because more than a third of the population left this valley during the hard years of 1845-65 to settle in the New World, mostly in the Midwest. More than 1,000 emigrated. More than a century later, 2,000 live here, mostly making their living from farming, and English is widely spoken.

The conductors actually encourage passengers to scatter off the train onto the wooden-plank platform and soggy turf at Kjosfoss, to gawk and admire and pose for photographs before the powerful, raging waterfall/rapids less than a stone's toss away. Its fury easily drowns out the accumulated sounds of shutters clicking.

Farther down, you cross lesser wild rivers without benefit of bridges. (There are no bridges on this line.) Here again, the viaducts were blasted out of the mountains just as the construction engineers blasted the looping tunnels. When you enter the longest tunnel, Nali (1,476 yards), you look back and see the extraordinary sight of the railbed cutting four ledges of the mountainside, one almost above the other.

When you leave the tunnel, you have a brief glimpse of the highest

Flam valley farm, where 3,000 goats are kept to produce orange-colored Norwegian goat cheese. Another waterfall, Fjoandfoss, drops 400 feet down the mountainside in the afternoon shade.

At Hareina (158 feet), a timid little village beside the prospering Flam River where anglers make their catches at the break of day, your views from between tunnels and cuttings disappear, the valley widens, and you see the panorama of the highest toylike farms below. The fields here seem more vividly green than possible because your eyes are still adjusting from the white glare above. Looking ahead, you see the 300-year-old Flam Church, flowering fruit orchards, the blue of the fjord coming near, and the brown of the mountains behind.

The wooden Flam train station is the center of activity for the village. The black-topped platform extends to the landing of the ferries for Balestrand and Gudvangen and the hydrofoils for Bergen. The tourist information office stands nearby. Local buses depart from the kiosk in the parking lot behind the station to the shore of the fjord.

With an adjoining cafeteria open until 8 P.M., the Hotel Fretheim Touristhotell is white with wooden lace and seems more like a romantic summer cottage or guesthouse than a dignified vacation hotel with mostly British visitors. You know before you enter that everything will be spotless, the waitresses will wear dirndls, and all guests will be snoring by 10:30 P.M. but will be up at the crow of the cock and the glimmer of dawn—except that in summer, day breaks at 2 A.M. and roosters crow all night.

Returning to Myrdal and continuing west toward Bergen, leaden-looking, chilling, and forbidding lakes surround you. Reindeer race between boulders and leap over patches of snow. Afternoon sun on granite boulders seems to shiver against icy, rushing rivers. Tattered tunnels burrow like snow snakes. You catch glimpses of brown, purple, and flaky yellow mosses through gapes in the drifts.

Then you suddenly realize the snow is melting and the water is running west instead of east, and you know your train is descending to Bergen and the North Sea's warm Gulf Stream.

You pass giant waterfalls, leaving bleak and wind-scoured snowland and entering valleys with dazzling, purple rhododendrons blooming all around you. No sooner do you clear your ears from the increasing air pressure than you are rolling along the shores of Sorfjorden and then through the five-mile Ulriken tunnel into Bergen's end-of-the-line train terminal.

You still see evidence of Bergen's former isolation. Hansa merchants came to Bergen in the Middle Ages, making it their trade center for dried fish. Even now new buildings are patterned after Hanseatic architecture. Houses have a red- and black-brick look similar to northern Germany's Hansa cities. But this architecture is deceiving, because the Bergenese soon reveal the city is fiercely Norwegian.

You have plenty of time to seek out a hotel and orient yourself to Norway's second city before nightfall. The tourist office is a healthy walk down Kaigatan past the lake for Torgalmenningen, if you neglected to book a hotel in advance.

The Bergenese are particularly friendly to Americans, sophisticated, and many speak English. Bergen is a vital city, a major gateway opening on the West, a devoted cultural city, the former home of Edvard Grieg, the center of an international music festival, and has reputedly the finest youth hostel in the North.

For a fine overview and orientation of Bergen and its harbor setting, make your first project the five-minute funicular ride to the top of Mount Floien.

## Bergen Line Service

| Per-nille | Bergen Express | | | | Henrik | Bergen Express |
|---|---|---|---|---|---|---|
| 0735 | 1545 | dep. | OSLO (Sentral) | arr. | 1400 | 2200 |
| 0850 | 1701 | arr. | Honefoss | dep. | 1243 | 2042 |
| 0851 | 1703 | dep. | Honefoss | arr. | 1241 | 2040 |
| 1003 | 1820 | dep. | Nesbyen | dep. | 1127 | 1925 |
| 1015 | 1833 | dep. | Gol | dep. | 1115 | 1912 |
| 1034 | 1853 | arr. | Aal | dep. | 1056 | 1852 |
| 1036 | 1854 | dep. | Aal | arr. | 1055 | 1850 |
| 1055 | 1916 | dep. | Geilo | dep. | 1034 | 1828 |
| 1106 | 1927 | dep. | Ustaoset | dep. | 1023 | 1815 |
| 1138 | 1959 | dep. | Finse | dep. | 0951 | 1740 |
| 1209 | .... | arr. | MYRDAL | dep. | .... | 1707 |
| 1210 | .... | dep. | MYRDAL | arr. | .... | 1705 |
| 1250 | 2110 | arr. | Voss | dep. | 0839 | 1625 |
| 1251 | 2112 | dep. | Voss | arr. | 0838 | 1623 |
| .... | 2142 | dep. | Dale | arr. | .... | .... |
| 1351 | 2213 | dep. | Arna | dep. | 0738 | 1523 |
| 1358 | 2220 | arr. | BERGEN | dep. | 0730 | 1515 |

### Connecting Flam Line Service

| 1215 | 1625 | 1710 | dep. | MYRDAL | arr. | 1141 | 1541 | 1610 |
|---|---|---|---|---|---|---|---|---|
| 1219 | 1629 | 1714 | dep. | Vatnahalsen | dep. | 1138 | 1538 | 1607 |
| 1313 | 1708 | 1800 | arr. | FLAM | dep. | 1100 | 1500 | 1525 |

**Overnight Sleeping Car Service
between Oslo and Flam**

| | | | | |
|---|---|---|---|---|
| 2250 | dep. | OSLO (Sentral) | arr. | 0701 |
| 0442 | arr. | Myrdal | dep. | 0106 |
| 0500 | dep. | Myrdal | arr. | 0046 |
| 0504 | arr. | Vatnahalsen | dep. | 0043 |
| 0550 | arr. | FLAM | dep. | 0005 |

## *Lapland Arrow*
## *Midnight Sun to Narvik*

Your steep descent into Narvik on the northernmost train in Western Europe is heady stuff. Each bend of your Ofot train opens up the quintessence of Norwegian adventure. You see new vistas of unspoiled mountain, sea, and sky. While your Iron-Ore Railroad train passes through stands of spruce, wild reindeer leap between snowbanks. You lean forward to better watch—on your right—your climactic, precipitous descent down to the Ofot fjord.

The direct descent from the summit is twenty-seven miles, but your zigzagging descent on this stretch of the Lapland Arrow takes nearly a full hour.

First you see pleasing, long views of the waves of the Norwegian Sea breaking on the shores. Then you begin to make out Narvik's wooden houses. Brick shops form a patchwork pattern of color against black conveyer belts and iron-ore loading facilities.

When you adventure by train beyond the Arctic Circle, there is only you, your chugging, solitary locomotive, moonlit freshwater lakes, wild moose, reindeer, cackling birds, and the rich, sweet smells of pine forest and mossy brook.

It's a long thirty-hour trip north from Denmark through Sweden to Norway—an experience for the intrepid, romantic adventurer who admires the green and blue (and white) outdoors. Sweden has the most lakes of all nations.

Setting off in Copenhagen, you travel through the heart of the Scandinavian peninsula to Narvik, Norway's end-of-the-line train station on the Ofot fjord. You see it all while it is light in the domain of the Midnight Sun.

Copenhagen's red-brick train station is a comfortable, busy antique dating from 1911. Metal beams arch over the cheery island of shops

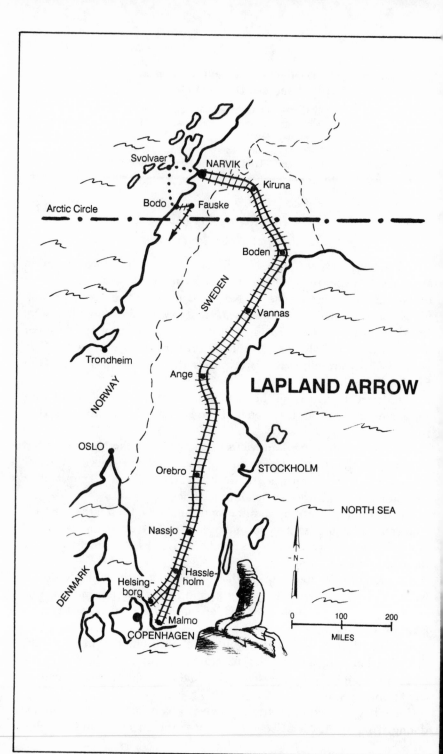

and stalls populating the central hall. You validate your Eurailpass or buy a Nordic Tourist Card in the train information office through the international ticketing ("Billetter udland") room. Young adventurers visit the Inter Rail Center, a haven for those holding Eurail Youthpasses or their equivalent.

One of your highlights comes early in your trip. Your ferry crossing from Helsingor, Denmark, to Helsingborg, Sweden, takes you so close to Kronberg Castle that you can study its emplaced cannons pointing toward Sweden. Shakespeare set *Hamlet* here. No one drawn to this place by the Bard's tragedy has a more photographic view than you from your deck on the train ferry.

You are crossing the most heavily traveled international ferry route in the world. Twenty-two million passengers cross from Denmark to Sweden every year. There is a ferry crossing every seven minutes, 4 train ferries an hour, 400 train carriages a day. Each crossing takes twenty minutes. There are 8 train ferries, 7 car ferries, and 3 passenger ferries. Every ferry makes a round trip in an hour.

Duty-free shopping is limited by customs inspections to a pack of cigarettes, but you have time aboard for a quick snack. After landing in Helsingborg's Ferry train station, a polite, English-speaking SJ conductor inspects your ticket or pass. He wants to make sure you are in the correct carriage for your destination because your Lapland Arrow is the epitome of an omnibus train. It takes carriages to and from dozens of destinations in Sweden.

Even if you stocked up with provisions before you left, you will probably use the one-class cafeteria car (open 6 A.M. to 10 P.M.) during your long journey. Coffee refills are free on SJ.

Your Lapland Arrow bypasses Stockholm while traveling north to Narvik, through fir forests and lakes mirroring the serene beauty of the sturdy, rounded mountains. The lonesome clickety-clack of your train tattoos over and over because of spaces between the northern rails.

In the eerie midnight glow, you inhale the sweet scent of pine in the air and gaze at foggy mists in the rocky terrain and in the birches leafless until early summer. Clouds in the silvery sky reflect in the remote, silent lakes. And then a shimmering orange globe rises in the northeast. It seems like it should be on the eastern horizon, but it is the wee hours and your train is entering the domain of the Midnight Sun. Birds chirp at this unlikely hour. Then the red of sunrise spreads across the peaceful lakes and creates a fragile, glassy pink, beginning your second day north.

In Boden you find a pretty frontier city set along a blue lake. While carriages from Lulea on the Gulf of Bothnia are attached to the head of your train and a new locomotive is added, you have twenty minutes to get off and buy provisions at the kiosk beside the train station.

About 1 1/4 hours out of Boden, your train slows for photographs. Have your camera cocked for the large, neat sign on your left: "Arctic Circle."

From here you pass through barren and remote tundra, climb past scraggly trees and then scrubby bushes, until you reach Kiruna (pop. 27,000), pre-eminent iron-ore mining city and most northerly town in Sweden. You see on the hill the colorful wooden houses painted rust-red, green, brown, and yellow with copper and tile roofs, but you can only imagine the huge, labyrinthine tunnels of the world's largest underground mine.

You thread your way northwest from the mines of Kiruna through green spruce and clean earth damp with melting snow. White stripes of birch trunks pattern the blanket of deep, green grass. Lovers of the outdoors and mountaineers leave your train at primitive outposts. This is one big national park north of the Arctic Circle.

You are traveling along the route of the Iron-Ore Railroad built specifically to carry ore from Kiruna in Sweden to Narvik, Norway, the all-year port kept free of ice by the Gulf Stream. Swedish politicians would have preferred to use a port in Sweden for export of their ore, but the freezing up of the Gulf of Bothnia in winter left them no choice.

Although your line actually crosses Norway, Swedish train experts insist this line carrying twenty million tons of ore annually is the most exciting piece of track in the SJ system. When conditions allow, you can see the complete disk of the sun at midnight from May 26 to July 19.

At last you approach Narvik, following that thrilling plunge described at the beginning of this adventure. Narvik (pop. 20,000) is a pup among cities. In 1880, there were but one or two isolated farms and a few not-so-contented cows grazing here. Narvik was dedicated on May 29, 1901.

The low but constant angle of the sun on the horizon causes very little temperature change between day and night. It is already warm when you awake and still pleasant late into the evening.

The cableway ten minutes from the city center, at the head of Kongensgate ("King's Street"), lifts you 2,000 feet to the very top of Mount Fagernesfjell in only thirteen minutes. When you rise in the gondola above the city, your perspective adjusts. First you see the iron-ore loading facilities open up and then the fjords systematically surround and then dwarf the village while snow-covered mountains appear to rise in the distance.

From the top of the lift, the sun warms the terrace of the restaurant and you see the "Sleeping Queen," a panorama resembling Queen Victoria reposed, 5,191-feet high. The official name of Narvik at the turn of the century was "Victoriahamn," meaning "Victoria's Harbor."

Across from the prizewinning city hall, a small, thought-provoking museum records Narvik's place in history. In May 1940, the British sank ten Nazi destroyers in Narvik fjord and temporarily recaptured the city, the first Allied victory of World War II.

You can return by train directly to Stockholm, take the Nord-Norge buses north to Kirkenes near the Russian border, or take the long and tedious Nord-Norge bus trip south across fjords to Fauske Station for connections with NSB's mainline trains. (Tickets are sold aboard the buses, but Eurailpasses are not honored.)

A more adventurous way south from Narvik, and worth the additional cost, is to take the steamers operated by the Ofotens S. S. Co. to connect with coastal steamers north and south. You can sit snugly in the cafeteria of the thirty-knot m.v. *Skogoy*, built in 1985, or go on deck to watch the landings and deliveries of cargo at the tiny hamlets along the way. You reach the codfish city of Svolvaer for a change to the much larger cruise ships of the Coastal Express Service. This gives you a few hours in Svolvaer to explore the interesting codfishing harbor.

## Summer Lapland Arrow Service

| | | | | |
|------|------|-----------|------|------|
| 0545 | dep. | NARVIK | arr. | 2140 |
| 0640 | arr. | Vassijaure | dep. | 2045 |
| 0647 | dep. | Vassijaure | arr. | 2040 |
| 0726 | dep. | Abisko O. | dep. | 2000 |
| 0838 | arr. | Kiruna C. | dep. | 1840 |
| 0900 | dep. | Kiruna C. | arr. | 1816 |
| 1015 | arr. | Gallivare | dep. | 1705 |
| 1024 | dep. | Gallivare | arr. | 1658 |
| 1256 | arr. | Boden C. | dep. | 1440 |
| 1322 | dep. | Boden C. | arr. | 1420 |
| 1358 | dep. | Alvsbyn | arr. | 1338 |
| 1500 | dep. | Jorn | dep. | 1238 |
| 1531 | dep. | Bastutrask | arr. | 1210 |
| 1705 | dep. | Vannas | dep. | 1050 |
| 1848 | dep. | Mellansel | arr. | 0905 |

| | | | | |
|---|---|---|---|---|
| 2005 | arr. | Langsele | dep. | 0747 |
| 2218 | arr. | Ange | arr. | 0540 |
| 2307 | arr. | Ljusdal | dep. | .... |
| 0040 | arr. | Bollnas | arr. | 0241 |
| 0231 | arr. | Avestra Krylbo | dep. | 0040 |
| 0412 | arr. | Orebro C. | arr. | 2258 |
| 0432 | arr. | Hallsberg | dep. | 2228 |
| 0538 | arr. | Motala | arr. | 2128 |
| 0557 | arr. | Mjolby | dep. | 2109 |
| 0653 | arr. | Nassjo | arr. | 2010 |
| 0750 | arr. | Alvesta | dep. | 1913 |
| 0858 | arr. | HASSLEHOLM | arr. | 1812 |
| 1005 | arr. | MALMO C. | dep. | 1706 |

## Lapland Arrow Connections to and from Copenhagen

| | | | | | |
|---|---|---|---|---|---|
| 0910 | dep. | HASSLEHOLM | arr. | 1756 | 1656 |
| 0928 | arr. | Perstorp | dep. | 1741 | 1640 |
| 0939 | arr. | Klippan | dep. | 1731 | 1629 |
| 0946 | arr. | Astorp | dep. | 1720 | 1618 |
| 1006 | arr. | Helsingborg F. | dep. | 1700 | 1558 |
| 1109 | arr. | Helsingor | dep. | .... | 1450 |
| 1152 | arr. | COPENHAGEN H. | dep. | .... | 1417 |

## Nord-Norge Bus Service
## between Narvik and Fauske Station

| | | | | | | |
|---|---|---|---|---|---|---|
| 0730 | 1715 | dep. | Bodo | arr. | 1120 | 2255 |
| 0845 | 1835 | arr. | FAUSKE station | dep. | 1010 | 2125 |
| 0920 | 1900 | dep. | FAUSKE station | arr. | 1000 | 2105 |
| 1440 | 0010 | arr. | NARVIK | dep. | 0500 | 1540 |

## *The Rauma Train*
## *Marvels per Minute*

You look down the valley and see three railroad lines. You are twisting along one, there's another farther on, on the edge of a cliff, and still farther, below a cascading waterfall on the other side of the valley, you see a third. All three belong to the Rauma Line, carrying

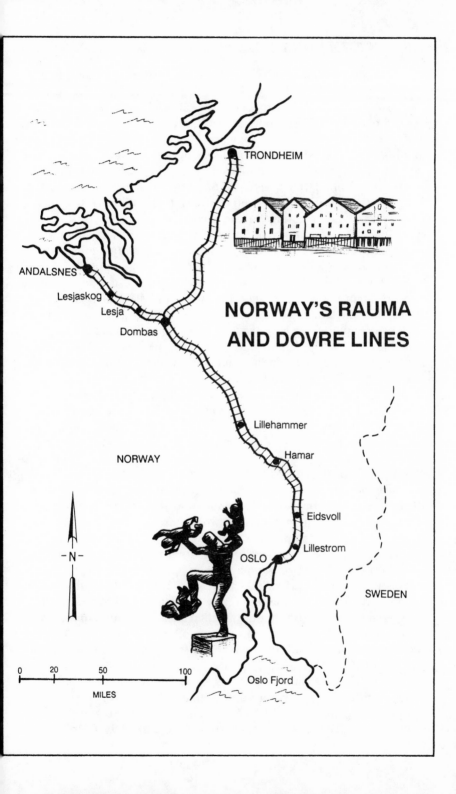

TRONDHEIM

ANDALSNES
Lesjaskog
Lesja
Dombas

**NORWAY'S RAUMA
AND DOVRE LINES**

Lillehammer

Hamar

NORWAY

Eidsvoll

Lillestrom

OSLO

SWEDEN

Oslo Fjord

0    20    50    100
MILES

-N-you in a huge double spiral to reach the valley floor through two circular tunnels in the Norwegian mountainsides.

Halfway down the seventy-one-mile Rauma Line to Andalsnes, you are still nearly 1,700-feet above sea level, the best scenery is yet to come, and you have to get down somehow. Your train must circle to lose altitude. You pass wild mountains, soaring peaks, and crashing water-falls and then you enter mountains cored by internal twists and spirals.

The first tunnel you enter, the Stavem, is 4,650 feet long. In the heart of the mountain, you retrace your path. When you return to daylight, you are running on the second segment, opposite to your direction a few minutes ago. You are several levels farther down the valley and see the Vermafoss falls straight ahead plummeting in misty cascades about 1,250 feet down the mountain ridge opposite.

The Rauma River below you dashes with all the gusto of a Norwegian hare, tumbling down over steep precipices and slabs of rock.

Entering the Kylling tunnel, you sweep through the mountain and under the highway in a long shallow curve, 1,500 feet long and so gentle you don't feel it. Back into daylight, you cross Kylling Bridge over a narrow gorge and see again the Rauma River, now frothing and foaming untamed only 200 feet below. As though to make itself most beautiful, the river snakes around pebbly white islets and sandbars of white granite powder and jumps across rapids, trailing glorious white bubbly wakes.

You have reached the third and lowest track and finally you can look back on this ingeniously engineered line from below. The complex double curve made the Rauma Line about five miles longer, but allowed you to descend 330 feet safely.

While the Rauma River gradually tires and meanders more calmly through wide gentle bends, the mountain scenery by contrast turns starker and more rugged and you are entering a new episode in the adventure of the Rauma Line. You are now traveling at the foot of towering rocky precipices and looking up at triple-divided, monstrous waterfalls crashing down at you.

This is what makes train travel exciting. You have passed from one spectacular phase into one differently wondrous. Passengers run from side to side on the train, putting their heads through pulled-down windows, pointing and shouting to each other with delight. One rider, her hair blowing wildly, shouts above the wind, "This is the most beautiful ride in the world."

This 1 1/2-hour jaunt (weekdays only), unfolding rich detail and color, justifies you making a single memorable trip to Norway, and is, happily, completely covered by Eurailpass, like all NSB travel.

When your Dovre Arrow train from Oslo arrives in Dombas, your diesel-train connection for down the Romsdal ("dal" means "valley") consists of three lined-up second-class cars waiting on an adjacent track. As soon as you board this Rauma Line train here, you leave Dombas through the Gudbrandsdal and Romsdal toward Andalsnes, your terminus on the Ice fjord.

This adventure begins in the morning in Oslo's Sentral station, where the precision-fitted, curved doors automatically slide open sideways and you step aboard the "Dovre Sprinten" ("Dovre Arrow"), one of Norway's smooth Morgandagens Toget, or "Tomorrow Trains." Your fresh-smelling carriage, maroon with black detailing, sparkles with good space, high-quality materials, and unexcelled ambience. You enjoy its appealing shapes, colors, and textures; drinking fresh water from stainless-steel water fountains; and rinsing your hands with spraying heated water.

The "B7" carriages have smooth aerodynamic profiles, making them look different from other European trains. Longitudinal aluminum sections make them five to six tons lighter than steel cars, dynamic undercarriages let them go around curves 10 percent faster, and air-filled rubber cushions dampen track noises and vibration.

Their panoramic windows, almost twice as wide as high, are safer and give you even broader views ahead. The interior decor is in earth tones—not your conventional train appearance.

Your nearly six-hour trip north from Oslo takes you through rich farmlands and then up the eastern shore of Lake Mjosa, Norway's largest. You see red-and-brown wooden summer cottages, the *White Swan of Lake Mjosa* (Norway's oldest paddle-wheeler), and wild flowers dancing like yellow fire—dandelions, buttercups, mustard, and rape-seed (for monounsaturated oil).

Your second stop is in the important hub of Hamar, at the widest point of Lake Mjosa. Inhale deeply here—the air at Hamar and at your third stop, the vacation center of Lillehammer, is fresh and pure, reputedly the most healthful in Scandinavia.

Past Lillehammer, your Dovre Arrow enters the Gudbrandsdal, the "Valley of Valleys." Farmers here still maintain the old building styles. You pass lined-up farmhouses climbing the mountainsides like soldiers.

In Dombas you change to the Rauma Line.

Now, looking forward as you wind down toward Andalsnes on the Ice fjord, the sheer face of unscalable Trollveggen, meaning Troll Wall, stands in front of you. You must crane your neck to see the summits of the huge mountains soaring heavenwards on either side, one after another. From a terrible height, famous waterfalls drop from the mountainside like countless silver fingers.

When you approach Marstein, where the mountains stand so high the stationmaster only sees the sun seven months of the year, your ride has settled down to merely splendid (although you will eventually reach the Trollveggen). You watch capricious mists of cloud dancing midway up sturdy cliffs nearly barren of trees.

You wind around the wedge-shaped, 4,250-foot high Mongegjura Mountain and the weird range of peaks resembling a row of trolls squatting menacingly over the valley. Its gray walls, scarred and stained, rise sheer from the valley floor to 6,000 feet.

An encampment of trolls reputedly established themselves here to gain an advantage over their enemies, gnomes on the valley floor. In one battle, they hid until the gnomes appeared at the foot of the mountains and then hurled down a terrible avalanche to bury them in rock and stone. But the gnomes triumphed in the end, for they had tricked the trolls, who are permitted to roam only at night. For their foolish midday attack, the trolls fossilized into these jagged blue-gray mountain massifs, so steep the snow will not lie on their slopes nor will any vegetation grow.

The valley is almost entirely surrounded by the peaks above you. You cannot see the top of the Romsdalshorn. Finally, you look up at the 6,300-foot Trollveggen, the highest vertical rock face in northern Europe.

Now you descend. You have always been dropping, of course, but now you sense it by the multiplication of the flowering wild plants and the passing of the terrible, high mountains.

You see the river joining the fjord and rows of pleasant homes along ordered streets. This is the tidy township of Andalsnes, where you come to a halt.

Andalsnes (pop. 2,500) is one of the loveliest settings along the coast of Norway. Situated on the Ice fjord, the head of the Romsdalsfjord, at the foot of the Romsdal, it is framed by the Setnefjell mountain on the west and Mount Nesaksla on the east.

You won't find much in Andalsnes but scenery, but that is more than enough. Molde, the stopping place for the coastal steamers, is a superb 2 1/2-hour mail boat trip across the fjord.

To ensure connections by train at Dombas you must leave, weekdays only, on the 7:55 A.M. Dovre Arrow from Oslo, or the 8:40 A.M. Dovre Express from Trondheim. The bus ride back to Dombas from Andalsnes is comparatively boring (and not covered by Eurailpass). Traveling in the overnight sleeping car between Andalsnes and Oslo that is coupled automatically in Dombas saves you these practical problems.

Your Dovre train from Oslo continues from Dombas to Trondheim,

Norway's third city. About twenty-five minutes north of Dombas, you pass the highest point of the line, about 3,360 feet, and see the snow-capped, highest mountain in Norway (7,500 feet) to the west. You arrive in good time to orient yourself. Trondheim (pop. 135,000) is a busy, colorful port. Norway's kings are crowned here in Nidaros Cathedral, a national shrine.

## Dovre Line Service

| Dovre Arrow | Dovre Express | | | | Dovre Express | Dovre Arrow |
|---|---|---|---|---|---|---|
| 0755 | 1515 | dep. | OSLO (Sentral) | arr. | 1525 | 2217 |
| 0813 | 1535 | dep. | Lillestrom | arr. | 1503 | 2158 |
| 0921 | 1643 | arr. | Hamar | dep. | 1355 | 2049 |
| 0923 | 1645 | dep. | Hamar | arr. | 1353 | 2047 |
| 1004 | 1730 | arr. | Lillehammer | dep. | 1310 | 2005 |
| 1006 | 1732 | dep. | Lillehammer | arr. | 1308 | 2003 |
| 1049 | 1815 | dep. | Ringebu | dep. | 1227 | 1923 |
| 1107 | 1834 | dep. | Vinstra | dep. | 1210 | 1906 |
| 1127 | 1900 | arr. | Otta | dep. | 1149 | 1845 |
| 1129 | 1902 | dep. | Otta | arr. | 1147 | 1843 |
| 1203 | 1932 | arr. | DOMBAS | dep. | 1117 | 1815 |
| 1205 | 1934 | dep. | DOMBAS | arr. | 1115 | 1813 |
| 1259 | 2030 | arr. | Oppdal | dep. | 1015 | 1718 |
| 1301 | 2032 | dep. | Oppdal | arr. | 1013 | 1716 |
| 1350 | 2122 | arr. | Storen | dep. | 0922 | 1625 |
| 1435 | 2205 | arr. | TRONDHEIM | dep. | 0840 | 1545 |

## Rauma Line Service

| Train* | Bus | | | | Train* | Bus |
|---|---|---|---|---|---|---|
| 1213 | 1935 | dep. | DOMBAS | arr. | 1110 | 1800 |
| .... | .... | dep. | Lesja | dep. | .... | .... |
| .... | .... | dep. | Lesjaverk | dep. | .... | .... |
| 1256 | .... | dep. | Bjorli | arr. | 1030 | .... |
| .... | .... | dep. | Verma | arr. | .... | .... |
| 1343 | 2135 | arr. | ANDALSNES | dep. | 0945 | 1600 |

*Weekdays only.

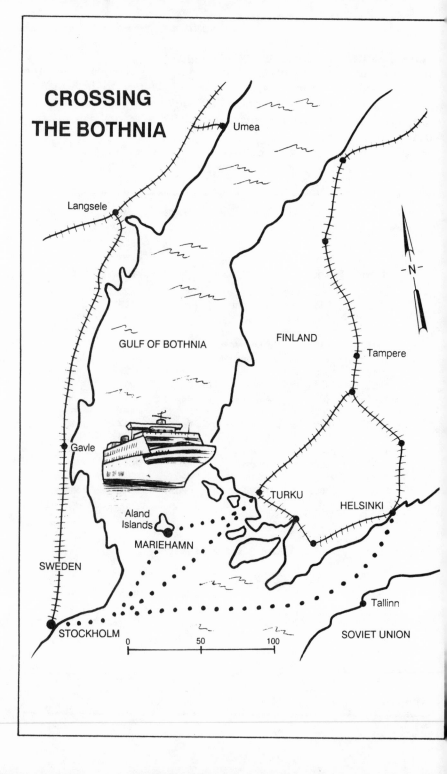

## *Crossing the Bothnia*
## *Free Deck to Finland*

"Tervetuloa. Welcome aboard the Finlandia." The veteran captain of the Silja Line speaks from the bridge of your ship crossing from Stockholm to Helsinki—a vantage point some one hundred feet and twelve stories above the water.

You watch fir trees gliding by your deck chair. Your entry to Finland across the Gulf of Bothnia is not absent of scenery as you might expect. You sail through a never-ending archipelago of thousands of islands and islets that are tree-covered remnants of the glacier era.

Almost everything is fresh aboard ship—and well kept up. Passengers are doing whatever pleases them. Their natural mobility aboard ship allows them to gather into compatible groups. Everyone seems friendly. You hear that Finnish is the predominate language on board, but everyone speaks English to you. All announcements are in Swedish, Finnish, and English.

Most of the travelers seem to be in their twenties, although active elders are gathering on the deck chairs. You can also hear a few infants, and dogs trot down the decks on midnight walks led by their masters and mistresses.

Nordic children seem to be having the best of it. Northern countries know how to look after their offspring. Children frolic in a glassed playroom filled with colored plastic bubbles. You can see that they are returning from a family excursion to the "big city" of Stockholm.

Several cruise lines, including the beautiful red-and-white ships of the Viking Line, carry passengers across the Gulf of Bothnia from Stockholm to Turku or Helsinki, but Eurailpass holders are particularly interested in the Silja Line. They can board free.

You depart from Silja Line's Stockholm pier in the port of Vartan—in the northwestern part of town. Silja Line's information and ticketing offices are located there and you can also make use of a self-service cafe, children's playroom, souvenir kiosk, tourist information (for arrivals), waiting room, telephones, rest rooms, lockers, and check-in counter which opens two hours before sailing. A mailbox is outside.

Pickup is free by a white Silja Line bus from the Klarabergsviadukten bridge across from the highest level of Stockholm's Central train station. Look for the Silja Line pickup sign on the bridge. Ask for details at the Central station's Tourist Information Office on the bottom level.

You can also take a Tunnelbana (subway) train to Ropsten, the end-of-the-line station, or Gardet, next to the end of the line. From

Ropsten there is Silja Line bus pickup every ten minutes. From Gardet you walk—a relatively easy, ten-minute hike. Signs to Vartahamnen, Silja Line's port, are posted in the subway.

Silja Line's two twenty-two-knot luxury liners sailing nonstop to Helsinki, the m.s. *Finlandia* and m.s. *Silvia Regina*, built in 1981, carry up to 2,000 passengers on their daily voyages year-round (except for Christmas eve). Three restaurants, located on deck 7, seat 1,100 diners and include a dance floor with live music. A smorgasbord cafeteria is part of the ship's facilities as well. A stairway from this deck takes you to the Sky-Bar, seating 200. This area gives you a view of the Baltic Sea and archipelago through sweeping panoramic windows.

These large passenger ferries (25,600 tons) take you in a rich style at no charge. Their two sister ships, the m.s. *Svea* and m.s. *Wellamo* to Turku (put into service in 1985 and 1986), are even larger (33,830 tons). They offer a hairdresser, a disco, a casino, conference facilities, duty-free shops, and a purser's office for changing money.

Silja Line's ships were designed for service between Finland and Sweden, but they also comply with rules of construction for long international voyages and meet the requirements for ice-navigation without the help of icebreakers. Due to dense traffic and narrow routes in the archipelagoes, the bottoms of the hulls are designed for minimal wave generation and minimal response to heavy seas.

You board free with a Eurailpass. How you sleep is up to you. The Helsinki-Stockholm ferries sell 647 cabins, 70 couchette bunk beds, and 240 reclining Pullman chairs for deck passengers. The bunk beds in the "Sleep-in" compartments are allocated for passengers purchasing basic transportation on a first-come, first-served basis. When some are left over, Eurailpass travelers may use them. Pullman chairs ("Sittsalong") are not uncomfortable. Washrooms are handy. You stow your small bags in nearby lockers. Leave your large luggage in the luggage room.

The cabins are a good value when you are not paying for a ticket. You buy a bunk in a four-person cabin for about the same price as a second-class couchette on a train. The ships' cabins give you many comforts: shower, bunk beds, mirror, toilet, wash basin, and open closet. (Advance reservations: Silja Line, 505 Fifth Avenue, New York, NY 10017. Tel. 212-986-2711.)

Choose between two daily departures from Stockholm to Turku (morning and evening) and one only at 6 P.M. to Helsinki. Note that the time in Finland is an hour earlier than in Sweden. Steamers departing from Turku and Stockholm in the morning call at Mariehamn in the Aland Islands—an interesting stop for postage stamp collectors.

When you notice the channel narrowing and private marinas appearing along the shore, the captain announces the ship will be landing in Helsinki in a half-hour. On debarking in Helsinki, pass through the customs hall and you will see an office to change money and a tourist office where you can book a hotel room in the city for a small service charge. Tram Nos. 3T and 3B from the Olympiakajen stop in back of the terminus give you a grand trip into the city.

In Turku, the Harbor train station is separate from the main Turku station. Slate-gray and cream-colored coaches with bright apricot-colored plush upholstery wait at the Harbor station to take you onto the VR network with diesel trains to Helsinki and Joensuu. These carry cafeteria cars with snacks and coffee.

## Service between Stockholm and Turku or Helsinki
### by Silja Line, Train, and Bus

| | | | | | | | |
|---|---|---|---|---|---|---|---|
| 0815 | 1800 | 2115 | dep. STOCKHOLM (Vartahamn.) arr. | 2015 | 0900 | 0700 |
| 1445 | .... | .... | dep. Mariehamn (Vastrahmn.) dep. | 1540 | .... | .... |
| 2015 | .... | 0800 | arr. TURKU (Harbor) dep. | 1000 | .... | 2130 |
| 2048t | .... | 0815b | dep. Turku (Harbor) arr. | 0950b | .... | 2042t |
| 2332t | 0900 | 1055b | arr. Helsinki (Etelasatama) dep. | 0730b | 1800 | 2031t |

b—bus connection to/from Helsinki bus station.
t—train connection to/from Helsinki train station.

# Germany

## *Vital Tips for the Trains of Germany*

On the fast, efficient trains of the German Federal Railroads ("DB—Deutsche Bundesbahn"), you can travel to the Alps, North Sea beaches, the Rhine River, and the Black Forest. This system covers 15,000 miles of train tracks and passes through 6,000 train stations in a country the size of Oregon. Many conductors and staff speak English.

DB's unmatched network of 150 InterCity trains serves all of Germany's big cities. DB's EuroCity trains take you by day into neighboring western countries. DB also operates the EC Alfred Noble, the overnight train to Oslo and Stockholm, and DB sleepers and couchettes within Germany and across its frontiers.

You receive an onboard timetable called "Ihr Zug-Begleiter" ("Your Train Companion") on every high-speed IC, EC, and even D train showing not only arrival and departure times at every stop along your way, but—more useful—telling you where to change for your ultimate destination.

It is possible for you to board randomly at any of the sixty IC-network cities and, by following the on-board timetable, arrive with all speed in any other station you choose by making one split-second across-the-platform change or two at most. DB's platforms are designed to simplify connections. You find your carriage by consulting the "Wagenstandanzeiger" train-composition boards on the platforms or the digital signs overhead which show where the first- and second-class sections come to rest. When you make your connection to another IC train, it is likely that a corresponding car, first- or second-class, will be waiting for you just twenty feet across the platform.

DB's standard livery makes it easy for you to see at a glance which carriages are first class and which are second. The red-and-cream carriages are first class, the blue-green-and-cream ones are second class. DB's IC, EC, and even D trains use the same carriages. Don't look for yellow stripes to indicate first class on these carriages. Look to the color of the body.

Most of DB's IC and EC trains carry one or two salon carriages, the rest of the train consisting of compartment carriages. A dining car is located between the first- and second-class sections.

DB's reservations fees for their fast trains are included in their surcharge, which Eurailpass holders don't pay. However, if you insist on a reservation, pay the surcharge.

Planners, technicians and timetable experts have red-lined the year 1991. A new 60-mile segment between Mannheim and Stuttgart will be opened at the same time the completed 230-mile stretch between Hanover and Wurzburg will be christened. The era of the 155-mph InterCity Express (ICE) will be upon you. Eventually ICE's 1,200-mile high-speed network will take you throughout Germany twice as fast as an auto and at least half as fast as a jet.

Where needed, most DB stations have been modernized with escalators to the platforms (Dusseldorf, Hamburg, Hanover, Heidelberg, Mannheim); one has an automatic conveyer belt for your luggage (Offenburg). Most of them provide free luggage carts, but at Munich Hauptbahnhof you must have a one-Mark coin to release a cart. This annoying release mechanism refunds your Mark when you lock up your cart.

DB does not accept credit cards, but train conductors accept travelers checks—in U.S. dollars, Deutsche Marks, and English pounds sterling only.

## InterCity Trains

A funny thing happens in your InterCity train north from Wurzburg. Your train pauses and the rear vestibule fills up with Germans peering out the exposed rear window.

Then your IC pulls up a ramp built especially for two parallel pairs of strong rails and concrete sleepers onto an overpass and into the Rossberg tunnel.

New fences and newly planted seedlings surround you. You are already flying at 125 mph over the first stretch which will eventually carry the ICE at 155 mph.

It doesn't seem like you are going so fast—there are no roads or houses and very few cows to stare at you—until you pass another train flying in the opposite direction. It disappears into a speck before you can comment on it.

This segment cut a half hour off the travel time between Munich and Hamburg and set the note for DB's 1,200-mile high-speed network.

It seems like you shoot from tunnel to tunnel—from the Rossberg to the Muhlberg to the Landrucken, DB's longest (6.7 miles). Above the tunnels, the gracious thick forests do not appear to mind the velocity beneath. In the tunnels, you just see lights flying through the blackness.

This tunneling changed DB's plans. Depressurization of their experimental high-speed trains in the tunnels caused complaints. (Engineers recognize the Bernoulli effect at work.) DB's new trains had to be made pressure tight. It was a blow, especially because the Landrucken tunnel lies on the line chosen for the train's inaugural run. It meant not only sealing the windows, doors, and ventilation, but redesigning the closed toilet systems.

Even as you make your travel plans, the DB network is being improved. Mile by mile and mph by mph the system is accelerating. As new segments of high-speed line are opened, precise timings of InterCity/ EuroCity lines are adjusted.

## Regional Railcar

DB's sea-green, smooth-riding regional railcar, VT 628, is the cornerstone of its secondary-line concept. You won't be asked for a ticket on these railcars. They run without a conductor. They are pleasing to ride, comfortable, and Spartan, with two tablelike forms in first class which give you space below for suitcases.

The second-class section behind the driver has jump seats to provide room for baby buggies and bicycles. These riders watch over the driver's shoulder as he accelerates to a maximum speed of 75 mph.

## S-Bahn Trains

DB's rapid-transit, frequent-service "S-Bahn" trains run in regions of intense train travel in and around Frankfurt, Hamburg, Munich, Nuremberg, Rhine-Ruhr/Dusseldorf, and Stuttgart. You will especially appreciate them in Munich, where S-Bahn trains parallel Munich's subways and use the same underground station entrances along the Hauptbahnhof-Marienplatz-Ostbahnhof corridor. Look for the green-and-white *S* signs marking station entrances, but remember that a Eurailpass is valid only on the S-Bahn trains, and not on the U-Bahn trains.

## Airport Trains

The Frankfurt Airport is Europe's model for excellent train/plane connections. S-Bahn trains leave five or six times an hour eastward to Frankfurt, stopping at Frankfurt's main train station and three other city stops, or westward to Mainz and Wiesbaden. Lufthansa's Airport Express carries airline-ticketed passengers up the Rhine River route as far as Dusseldorf.

The feature making Frankfurt's airport stop so useful is DB's big trains. DB's InterCity and EuroCity trains take you directly between the airport and Vienna, Copenhagen, Munich, Paris, Amsterdam, Milan, Geneva, Hamburg, Basel, Hanover, and Berchtesgaden. All of these, except the Lufthansa train (you must have a flight coupon), are covered by Eurailpass.

Frankfurt Airport is intimidating with its size and complexity. The agent at the DB counter on the arrivals level of Terminal C (transatlantic arrivals) reserves trains for you throughout Europe, but you must tell him the train numbers because his office's facilities are limited. You may also validate your Eurailpass and buy (and validate) GermanRail Tourist Cards here (see below). Don't go to the DER travel agency counter next door.

To board your train, simply follow the blue-and-white signs illustrating a DB locomotive. Push your luggage on the airport's escalator-friendly carts right to the doors of your train at the train station below.

Dusseldorf's airport is connected to Dusseldorf's main train station by S-Bahn trains you reach by escalator right from the airport's main hall. When Munich's airport in Erding is completed in 1991, you will also be able to use Munich's S-Bahn to get there and back.

## Holiday Trains

In summer you have the option of riding special holiday ("Fern Express") trains without change to small holiday villages. These holiday trains, identified as "FD" trains in DB's timetable and on the digital platform signboards, are DB's answer to driver's fatigue and competition of automobiles.

FD trains leave early in the morning, use modern carriages, carry a cafeteria or Quick-Pick self-service cafeteria, make few stops, and arrive directly in their small holiday destinations while it is still light.

## Using Eurailpass Bonuses

Eurailpass gives you free two of the most popular excursions in Europe: Romantic Highway and Castle Road Europabus (Lines 189 and 190) trips, and the famous Rhine Cruise.

In addition, you receive free Moselle River cruises and free use of a broad range of regional bus transportation giving you train and bus access to practically every hamlet in the Federal Republic.

Your free Moselle River cruise is provided by the KD German Rhine Line between Koblenz and Cochem. Regional transportation is provided by the following bus companies: AutoKraft GmbH, Kiel; Kraftverkehr GmbH—KVG Stade and KVG Luneburg; Regionalverkehr Hanover, Cologne, Oberbayern and Schwaben-Allgau.

Eurail Youthpass holders ride the express steamers by paying a surcharge, while all Eurailpass holders must pay extra to travel by hydrofoil ("Tragflugelboot"). Specifically not included are the tourist cruise ships making multiple stops between Basel and Rotterdam and between Trier and Koblenz.

Fringe benefits include half off the normal fares for the ferry crossing between Lubeck-Travemunde and Trelleborg, Sweden, on the TT Line; half off the fares on the regular steamer services on Lake Constance; reduced fares on the highly recommended cogwheel train up the Zugspitze from Garmish-Partenkirchen; half off the Freiburg (Breisgau)/Schauinsland Railroad; and 10 percent off Oberbayern GmbH Munich sightseeing tours and 20 percent off some half- and full-day excursions out of Munich. Students with a valid student ID get 25 percent off the bus between Berlin and Braunschweig operated by Bayern Express and P. Kuhn Berlin.

## GermanRail Tourist Card

You buy GermanRail Tourist Cards from travel agents and at DB and DER offices (see Appendix under "GermanRail") for four, nine, or sixteen days either first or second class. Adventurers under twenty-six may buy a Junior GermanRail Tourist Card for nine or sixteen days of second-class travel. Buy either one in Germany at German prices.

First-class GermanRail Tourist Cards cost about 25 percent less than Eurailpasses. Second-class gives you an additional one-third savings. The Junior GermanRail Tourist Cards are so cheap that adventurers under twenty-six consider devising various combinations with other passes and using them end-to-end.

GermanRail Tourist Cards give you all the national travel benefits of a Eurailpass, but in addition you travel free on the Main River from Mainz to Frankfurt, purchase reduced-fare train travel to West Berlin, and receive a special low price for bicycle rental at almost three hundred train stations.

Anyone under twenty-three and students under twenty-seven can buy in Germany a one-month "Tramper" ticket for only slightly more than the sixteen-day Junior Tourist Card.

One-year passes allowing travel at half-fare are sold to young people. All between eighteen and twenty-two, and students under twenty-seven, are eligible for the "Junior-Pass." All between twelve and seventeen may buy the "Pocket-Money-Pass" for even less.

Adventurers in Germany cruise up the Rhine, travel through East Germany to West Berlin, ride through the Black Forest, and travel by Europabus through well-preserved medieval towns.

## *Rollin' on the Rhine*
## *Lured by a Siren's Song*

The Rhine River is squeezed down to one-third its width. The Lorelei towers 430 feet above you. You feel the rock's magnetism and almost hear the beautiful Lorelei's singing attracting fishermen and causing their deaths on those rocks and cliffs close to the prow of your white steamer.

The quiet of your waterway's west bank is constantly pierced by shrieks of racing ICs, ECs, and other fast trains blurred along DB's mainline below castles and above barges. DB's line along the east bank rumbles with freight trains and passenger trains to the wine villages dotting that shore.

Traveling by train along the Rhine in one of DB's comfortable ICs or ECs, studying the scenery from above the river, epitomizes relaxing train travel at its finest. Every once in a while a hilltop jewel sparkles into your eye.

Your cruise from Koblenz to Mainz gives you time to savor the beauty of this river. Vater Rhein, Europe's busiest waterway, carries a constant stream of barges and passenger ships, including the KD German Rhine Line steamer you are riding without charge courtesy of Eurailpass.

You are participating in Eurailpass's most beloved bonus.

Eurailpass holders ride free on the KD German Rhine Line (Koln-Dusseldorfer Deutsche Rheinschiffahrt) making regular runs between Cologne and Frankfurt/M, but Eurail Youthpass holders must pay an extra charge for riding express steamers.

Dusseldorf and Mainz are the end stations, but your best compromise is a 5-hour trip upstream (or 3 1/2 hours downstream) from Koblenz to Rudesheim. You sail past the Lorelei, the Rhine gorge, dozens of world-famous castles, and through the Rhine's most scenic region.

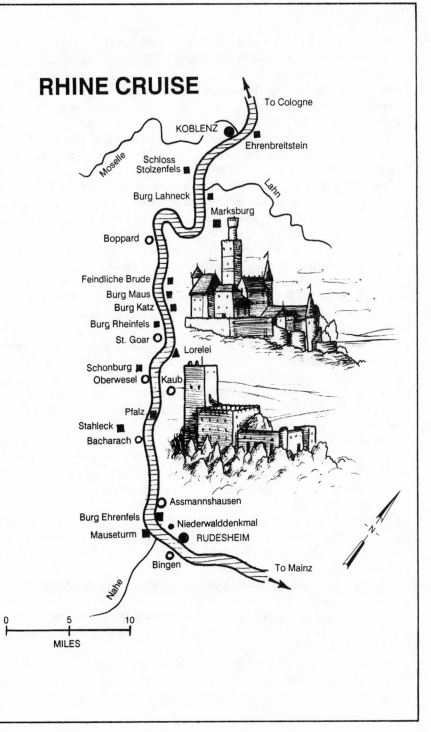

# RHINE CRUISE

To Cologne

KOBLENZ

Ehrenbreitstein

Moselle

Schloss Stolzenfels

Lahn

Burg Lahneck

Marksburg

Boppard

Feindliche Brude

Burg Maus

Burg Katz

Burg Rheinfels

St. Goar

Lorelei

Schonburg

Oberwesel · Kaub

Pfalz

Stahleck

Bacharach

Assmannshausen

Burg Ehrenfels

Niederwalddenkmal

Mauseturm

RUDESHEIM

Bingen

To Mainz

Nahe

N

0    5    10

MILES

You have little trouble making train connections on either end.

It is best to make the cruise on a sunny day. In the morning the west bank presents portraits for your camera and in the afternoon the east bank puts its historic castles in the right light.

When you commence this stretch filled with castles, it is useful to remember that the English word "castle" has two equivalents in the German language. You pass both "Burg," a fortified castle built for defensive purposes, and "Schloss," a palace which may or may not have been fortified and was usually the seat of royalty.

If you begin your trip in Koblenz, where the Moselle (Mosel) River flows into the Rhine, check first in the office of the KD German Rhine Line in the Koblenz Hauptbahnhof. Either take bus line No. 1, marked "Rhein," which runs to the landing every twenty minutes from across the street in front of the station (the round Tourist Office side), or—only when you are sailing upstream ("Rheinaufwarts")—walk ten to fifteen minutes directly east down the Markenbildchenweg to the "Rheinanlagen," KD's second landing on the Rhine. Ships sailing upstream call here five minutes after casting off from KD's main Koblenz landing.

Seamen release the ropes and your ship bound upstream steams against the current of the Rhine. Passengers scramble for chairs.

Huge Festung Ehrenbreitstein, atop the hill overlooking your vessel, is one of the strongest fortresses in Europe. The French captured it in 1799 only by starving out its defenders. The neoclassical architecture that you see today was added between 1817 and 1828.

Below the railroad bridge, you see orange-brown Schloss Stolzenfels with crenelated turrets and walls high on the west bank. Once a customs point for the city of Trier, Friedrich Wilhelm IV of Prussia had it reconstructed in 1825-45 for a summer residence.

At the confluence of the Lahn and the Rhine, you dock in Oberlahnstein, formerly a rich and important center because of its toll station and local silver mining. Burg Lahneck was built to protect it. Over the centuries this castle has collapsed into ruin, thus becoming an inspiration for Rhine Romanticists.

The best-kept castle on the Rhine, high above Oberlahnstein, is the Marksburg on a steep slate cliff 490 feet over the Rhine. It contains cannons, weapons, chastity belts, and a good castle inn. Nowhere else on the Rhine are the Middle Ages so well preserved as in the Marksburg. Now it is the seat of the German Castles Association and houses the largest collection of castle-related literature in Europe.

All high castles have one aspect in common: a lovely view. Long sight lines on the river were necessary to supervise the collection of tolls from passing ships and an overview of the surrounding lands and forests was necessary for protection from enemies.

A big curve in the Rhine takes you past Osterspay which is famous due to Schloss Liebeneck, high above on the east bank, erected around 1700 as a hunting and summer castle. You still see the original baroque forms despite the numerous subsequent alterations.

The barren hills are interrupted by lovely Boppard, a popular stop-off.

The yellow-and-gray Lufthansa Express streaks down the western shore. This airport train is the only one with a flight number.

On top of the hills sit the castles of the Feindliche Brude. Legend has it that two arguing brothers erected ramparts between their castles. Since then the castles have been referred to as "The Hostile Brothers."

Passing Bad Salzig on the west bank in springtime is unforgettable because of its flowering cherry orchards. You sail back to the west bank below Burg Maus ("Mouse Castle"), one of the technically outstanding structures of its time. It was built in 1356 by the Archbishop of Trier. In 1806, it was partially destroyed and rebuilt between 1900 and 1909.

St. Goarshausen, with partly intact city walls, on the east bank, is hemmed tightly below Burg Katz on a jutting cliff. The castle was built in 1393, by the Counts of Katzeneinbogen, one of the richest families in medieval Germany.

St. Goar back on the west bank is a pilgrim's center for the grave of St. Goar, who died in 611, below the Rheinfels ruins.

Burg Rheinfels is so close it seems you could reach up and rub the dust off the walls of its rambling terraces. This mighty ruin used to be the greatest castle on the Rhine. It was destroyed by the French in 1797.

Now you are below the Lorelei rock. When you pass the cliff, your captain plays a tape of Heinrich Heine's poem about the Lorelei virgin combing her golden hair and singing to lure sailors to the rocks. Now the song of the beautiful Lorelei is the best-known folk song of the Rhine. This is the narrowest spot of the river. In the water you see the rocks of the "Sieben Jungfrauen" (Seven Virgins) turned to stone.

In Oberwesel, on the west bank, you pass the homes of fishermen and Rhine sailors. It is a tiny and romantic place dominated by its fourteenth-century, red-brick Gothic Liebfrauenkirche (church), narrow and steep like a ship.

Schonburg castle is situated above Oberwesel. It was built in the twelfth century. At one time it served as an imperial castle. Today parts of it are used as an international youth hostel.

The five-sided customs fortress in the center of the Rhine upstream from Kaub, the "Pfalz," was completed in its current form in the seventeenth and eighteenth centuries. Its many pinnacles and little towers contain a naval museum. From water level it looks like a stone barge on the swirling Rhine. Following its restoration it was repainted in the old Gothic colors.

Above Kaub on the east bank, a friendly city profiting from slate quarrying, you see Burg Gutenfels (1200), one of the most important examples of defensive and living structures in the period of the Hohenstaufer. It is now used as a hotel.

Crossing again to the west bank you arrive in Bacharach, a village with sixteen watchtowers and black-slate-roofed Burg Stahleck above. Burg Stahleck, built in 1134, was destroyed in 1689. Beautifully rebuilt between 1925 and 1967, it serves as a youth hostel.

Eleventh-century Burg Nollig was erected upstream of Lorch as part of Lorchhausen's main fortifications. Ships which had to avoid the Bingerloch, the whirlpool on the Rhine, docked here for reloading of their cargoes onto smaller ships or for transportation overland.

You sail past the Mauseturm ("Mice Tower") on an island near the west bank. Since the rise of Rhine Romanticism, Mice Tower on a rock in the Rhine has become Bingen's emblem although it actually once was a customs house belonging to Burg Ehrenfels, the magnificent tower on the opposite bank. Later Mice Tower served as a signal tower for this once perilous stretch of the Rhine. Now that the danger of the Bingerloch, the whirlpool, has been alleviated, the tower merely serves to remind you of the story that Bishop Hatto, who fled here after burning starving farmers' barns, was eaten alive by thousands of rats who swam the Rhine and scaled the tower's walls to reach him. Since its renovation in 1972, you again see the Mauseturm in its medieval hues.

Where the Nahe River flows from the west into the Rhine, you stop in the wine village of Bingen, below Burg Klopp. Bingen's train station is on the mainline west of the Rhine, but is not large enough for InterCity or EuroCity trains to stop, so you must take a local train to Mainz or Koblenz for connections.

Famous Rudesheim is an excellent village to stop over or to conclude your trip on the Rhine with a glass of wine on the famous Drosselgasse, a street only about 10 feet wide and 200 yards long, but resounding with the constant percussion of bands playing traditional oompah to modern music. Enjoy a free wine-tasting session at a celebrated winery. You will feel the Rhineland's "Frohsinn," gaiety, everywhere.

Be sure to top off your trip with a gondola ride up over Rudesheim's vineyards to the colossal Niederwalddenkmal, the neoclassical memorial on an outlook plateau 980 feet above the city, commemorating the unification of the German Empire after the 1870 defeat of the French. Born of national enthusiasm in an era fond of monuments, the proportions of the lady are equally optimistic. She is about 125 feet tall and weighs some 700 pounds. From her feet you see one of the top ten panoramas in Germany.

Rudesheim's train station is well situated below the village near the east bank of the Rhine. From here you make connections on the secondary line running along the east bank of the Rhine and into Mainz.

Mainz is an excellent place to stay overnight. It is only eighteen minutes to the Frankfurt airport, it lies on mainlines served by InterCity and EuroCity trains, and you push your luggage carts to the hotels across the Bahnhofplatz from the station with no stairs to climb.

KD German Rhine Line sails frequently during July and August, less often in the spring and fall, and not at all between late October and late March.

---

## KD German Rhine Line Summer Service

### Upstream, Cologne to Mainz

| | | | | | | | | | |
|---|---|---|---|---|---|---|---|---|---|
| COLOGNE | dep. | .... | .... | .... | .... | .... | .... | 0915 | 1100 |
| Bonn | dep. | .... | .... | .... | .... | .... | 0915 | 1145 | 1345 |
| Bad Godesberg | dep. | .... | .... | .... | .... | .... | 0945 | 1210 | 1420 |
| Konigswinter | dep. | .... | .... | .... | .... | .... | 1000 | 1230 | 1435 |
| Bad Honnef | dep. | .... | .... | .... | .... | .... | 1017 | 1250 | 1455 |
| Remagen | dep. | .... | .... | .... | .... | .... | 1050 | 1320 | 1531 |
| Linz | dep. | .... | .... | .... | .... | .... | 1105 | 1340 | 1552 |
| Bad Breisig | dep. | .... | .... | .... | .... | 0845 | 1130 | 1410 | 1620 |
| Andernach | dep. | .... | .... | .... | .... | 0935 | 1215 | 1500 | .... |
| Neuwied | dep. | .... | .... | .... | .... | 0955 | 1235 | 1520 | .... |
| KOBLENZ | arr. | .... | .... | .... | .... | 1115 | 1350 | 1650 | .... |
| KOBLENZ | dep. | .... | 0900 | .... | .... | 1130 | 1400 | .... | 1800 |
| Niederlahnstein | dep. | .... | 0924 | .... | .... | 1155 | .... | .... | 1825 |
| Braubach | dep. | .... | 0958 | .... | .... | 1225 | 1445 | .... | 1855 |
| Boppard | dep. | 0900 | 1040 | .... | 1210 | 1315 | 1525 | .... | 1935 |
| St. Goarshausen | dep. | 1010 | 1150 | .... | 1330 | 1430 | 1630 | .... | .... |
| St. Goar | dep. | 1015 | 1155 | .... | 1340 | 1440 | 1640 | .... | .... |
| Bacharach | dep. | 1120 | 1255 | .... | 1445 | 1545 | 1745 | .... | .... |
| Assmannshausen | dep. | 1225 | 1350 | .... | 1540 | 1640 | 1840 | .... | .... |
| Bingen | dep. | 1255 | 1420 | .... | 1605 | 1705 | 1905 | .... | .... |
| RUDESHEIM | arr. | 1310 | 1430 | 1435 | 1620 | 1720 | 1930 | .... | .... |

### Upstream, Cologne to Mainz

| | | | | | | | | | |
|---|---|---|---|---|---|---|---|---|---|
| Eltville | dep. | .... | .... | 1535 | 1725 | 1825 | .... | .... | .... |
| Wiesbaden-Biebrich | arr. | .... | .... | 1620 | 1810 | 1910 | .... | .... | .... |
| MAINZ | arr. | .... | .... | 1645 | 1830 | 1930 | .... | .... | .... |

### Downstream, Mainz to Cologne

| | | | | | | | | | |
|---|---|---|---|---|---|---|---|---|---|
| MAINZ | dep. | .... | 0845 | .... | 1015 | 1215 | .... | .... |
| Wiesbaden-Biebrich | dep. | .... | 0905 | .... | 1035 | 1235 | .... | .... |
| Eltville | dep. | .... | 0925 | .... | 1055 | 1255 | .... | .... |
| RUDESHEIM | dep. | 0920 | 1015 | .... | 1200 | 1345 | 1400 | 1620 |
| Bingen | dep. | 0935 | 1030 | .... | 1215 | .... | 1415 | 1635 |
| Assmannshausen | dep. | 0948 | 1045 | .... | 1230 | .... | 1430 | 1648 |
| Bacharach | dep. | 1020 | 1115 | .... | 1305 | .... | 1505 | 1720 |
| St. Goar | dep. | 1100 | 1200 | .... | 1350 | .... | 1550 | 1800 |
| St. Goarshausen | dep. | 1110 | 1210 | .... | 1400 | .... | 1600 | 1810 |
| Boppard | dep. | 1155 | 1255 | .... | 1445 | .... | 1645 | 1850 |
| Braubach | dep. | .... | 1325 | .... | 1515 | .... | 1715 | 1920 |
| Niederlahnstein | dep. | .... | .... | .... | 1537 | .... | 1737 | 1942 |
| KOBLENZ | arr. | .... | 1350 | .... | 1600 | .... | 1755 | 2000 |
| KOBLENZ | dep. | .... | 1410 | .... | 1605 | .... | 1805 | .... |
| Neuwied | dep. | .... | 1450 | .... | 1650 | .... | 1850 | .... |
| Andernach | dep. | .... | 1510 | .... | 1705 | .... | 1905 | .... |
| Bad Breisig | dep. | .... | 1535 | 1635 | 1735 | .... | 1935 | .... |
| Linz | dep. | .... | 1550 | 1650 | 1750 | .... | .... | .... |
| Remagen | dep. | .... | 1605 | 1705 | 1805 | .... | .... | .... |
| Bad Honnef | dep. | .... | 1630 | 1730 | 1830 | .... | .... | .... |
| Konigswinter | dep. | .... | 1650 | 1750 | 1850 | .... | .... | .... |
| Bad Godesberg | dep. | .... | 1700 | 1800 | 1855 | .... | .... | .... |
| Bonn | arr. | .... | 1720 | 1820 | 1915 | .... | .... | .... |
| COLOGNE | arr. | .... | 1850 | 1950 | .... | .... | .... | .... |

## The Paranoia Express
## Armed Guards and Police Dogs

You know your train is long, but you never know exactly how long. You dare not get out and walk along the platform for fear guard dogs will take pieces out of you.

Your train from West Germany, the Federal Republic, to West Berlin passes through 112 miles of ominous countryside known as the German Democratic Republic. Armed guards and vicious-looking police dogs patrol the platform. Barbed-wire fences surround your train. Everyone inside is jittery.

BERLIN

Friedrichstrasse

ZOO

Wannsee

Potsdam

BERLIN TRANSIT

GERMAN
DEMOCRATIC
REPUBLIC

Magdeburg

Marienborn

Helmstedt

GERMAN
FEDERAL
REPUBLIC

Braunschweig

N

0    10    20                    50

MILES

HANOVER

Your train, known to passengers as the "Paranoia Express," gives you possibly the most dramatic perspective of the world today—as well as giving you entree to Berlin, the busy center of ancient and modern history, Germany's cultural headquarters, and popular stage of nonstop night life.

As soon as you leave Helmstedt, passport inspectors, customs officials, and ticket supervisors come through your carriage in waves (Eurailpass holders must pay full fare through East Germany). They imprint black "DDR" ("Deutsche Demokratische Republic") stamps on your passports and give you separate transit visas for no charge.

East German scenery is disappointing after this dramatic crossing. The landscape you see is dull, flat as a breadboard. Occasionally you glimpse a village in the distance or confront a casern up close. Thinly camouflaged tanks stand side by side. Sometimes you see peasants in rows in the fields, planting or picking by hand.

Few passengers go to the restaurant car for lunch. You know it must be expensive by the way almost everyone else is unpacking their sandwiches, soft drinks, and bottles of beer. It is a Mitropa dining car, meaning owned and staffed by the East German Reichsbahn. What traces of decoration remain reflect the style of the 1930s. You select from sandwiches, soft drinks, cake, coffee, beer, and vodka. The sandwiches are open-faced. The Magdeburg cheese has a nice taste, but the bread is yesterday's. Waiters take your West German currency and give you back West German change.

By now your train has crossed the plain and come upon Potsdam. Your only pleasant view of the trip extends over a lake to a collection of high-rise buildings. By themselves, the buildings are nondescript, but the lake reflects attractively their yellow-brown striping.

When your train immediately passes the great dome of the Nikolai Church dominating Potsdam, your view is spoiled by the pedestrian Inter Hotel placed in front of it.

It isn't long before you realize you are suddenly back in civilization. And civilization must mean Berlin. Your train stops at the Berlin Wannsee train station in West Berlin. This is the first of several West Berlin stops. Travelers gather together their luggage, carry-ons, and overcoats for the mass exodus at the Berlin Zoo train station in the center of West Berlin.

When you disembark at the Zoo station and watch your train departing for East Berlin, it is empty.

West Berlin's Zoo train station was remodeled for Berlin's anniversary celebrations in 1987. It is a burst of light compared with your trip through East Germany.

A short walk out of the front of the station leads you to the West Berlin tourist office in the Europa-Center complex. The route is so well marked that managers of other West German city tourist offices must be envious.

The Europa-Center on the Kurfurstendamm is a city within a city. It is the focus of twenty-four-hour modern Berlin. You find beautiful restaurants and an outdoor cafe, countless boutiques, a gambling casino, nightclubs, a quizzical fountain in the shape of a ball representing the planet Earth, and a multistory water clock which attracts passers-by for its gurgling change of the hours.

The GermanRail Tourist Card for unlimited train travel in West Germany comes with an attached Berlin coupon allowing you to travel to and from the isolated city for about two-thirds of the normal fare. You must make a round trip and complete it before expiration of your tourist card, so unless you return almost immediately, much of the usefulness of your pass will expire.

Also attached to the GermanRail Tourist Card is a coupon for a free two-hour Berlin tour. The tours have a substantial retail value, but even if you must pay for them they are a good value considering that they are some of the best organized, best narrated, and most interesting city tours in Europe.

Your city tour passes a succession of high points and historically interesting sights, including a stop at Potsdamer Platz where everyone climbs a wooden platform to look across the Berlin Wall. The bus visits the neoclassical Brandenburg Gate, copied from Athens; Checkpoint Charlie, made famous during the Berlin Airlift; and the Reichstag, which Hitler ordered burned.

You continue to Charlottenburg Palace with its green patina dome; the 1936 Olympic Games' stadium with its five rings; Schoneburg's town hall where President Kennedy delivered his "Ich bin ein Berliner" speech; the huge International Congress Center; and on the Kurfurstendamm, where you start, the Kaiser Wilhelm Memorial Church and the Europa-Center.

After you have seen the remodeled Zoo station, visit the delightful jewel-box Wittenbergplatz subway station, Germany's first and finest. It has been brightly restored in Jugendstil as a historical monument.

Returning from East Germany via Leipzig—through Weimar to the border crossing at Bebra—is a surprisingly different adventure. The compartments are sprinkled with gray-haired ladies on their way to visit brothers or nieces and nephews in the West. Only retired workers are granted visas and they are not allowed to take valuables or currency.

A woman comes past, wearing a lapel pin saying, "Bank." You are required to change your East German marks into West German ones, one for one. The catch is you must have your original money-conversion receipts. When you change your money, the East Germans look on jealously, for they are forbidden to do so.

Passport control officers carefully check visas, compare passport photos with your likeness, and look under the seats for stowaways.

The East German passengers speak guardedly, choosing their words for political correctness, fearing someone will tap them on the shoulder and tell them their permission has been rescinded. Yet when they finally see the West German policemen in Bebra, where there are no border formalities, they rush to the windows, look back and forth, realize there is no possibility of their train turning back, and break into smiles.

The last stretch before Bebra, past Erfurt, is by far the prettiest you see in East Germany. There are rolling, forested hills, village houses with tiled roofs, and half-timbered farmhouses. Beside the tracks, yellow-flowering bushes and blue larkspur seem to shout, "Hurrah!"

The most dramatic impression of the difference between East and West Germany comes after your train enters the West and you see the beauty of farms well tended instead of fields lying fallow, and homes well kept instead of houses crying for repair.

Beside the haystacks you see new children's bicycles, and in driveways you see highly polished new automobiles. One picture is worth 10,000 words.

The usual jumping-off place for West Berlin is Hanover's Hauptbahnhof because it offers InterCity and EuroCity (the EC Helvetia) connections from all over northern Europe. Escalators take you up and down to the platforms, there are many luggage carts, an InterCity hotel is integrated into the station, and DB ticketing counters 14, 15, and 16 are specifically set aside for Berlin ticketing and discounts.

## Train Service between Hanover and Berlin

| 0612 | 0853 | 1039 | 1312 | dep. | Cologne | arr. | 1545 | 1828 | 2041 | 2332 |
| 1019 | 1304 | 1503 | 1703 | dep. | HANOVER | arr. | 1204 | 1401 | 1635 | 1919 |
| 1116 | 1421 | 1601 | 1800 | arr. | Helmstedt | dep. | 1102 | 1303 | 1537 | 1820 |
| 1126 | 1432 | 1613 | 1810 | dep. | Helmstedt | arr. | 1052 | 1249 | 1527 | 1810 |

| 1135 | 1441 | 1622 | 1819 | arr. | Marienborn | dep. | 1044 | 1241 | 1519 | 1801 |
| 1140 | 1446 | 1627 | 1824 | dep. | Marienborn | arr. | 1039 | 1236 | 1514 | 1756 |
| 1400 | 1724 | 1848 | 2044 | arr. | Berlin (Wannsee) | dep. | 0811 | 1008 | 1242 | 1529 |
| 1415 | 1740 | 1902 | 2059 | arr. | BERLIN (Zoo) | dep. | 0757 | 0955 | 1229 | 1514 |
| 1434 | 1801 | 1920 | 2119 | arr. | Berlin (Fried.) | dep. | 0740 | 0936 | 1130 | 1439 |
| 1504 | .... | .... | 2149 | arr. | Berlin (Hbf.) | dep. | 0710 | .... | .... | 1409 |

## Through the Valley of Hell
## Cuckoo Clocks and Characteristic Houses

Your ride through Hell's Valley ("Hollental") is romantic enough for an archduchess on her way to her wedding. Marie Antoinette's advisors planned her carriage trip through this scenic valley in 1770, on her way from Vienna to Paris to marry the future King Louis XVI. She was 14 1/2 years old at the time. She was beheaded 23 years later.

When you travel on the Black Forest Railroad, you see the famous Black Forest houses, onion-dome churches, and even occasional cuckoo clocks. Its sixty-two miles from Offenburg to Donaueschingen take you over the crest of the Black Forest in an unusual series of loops. In the heart of the Black Forest you change to your connecting Hell's Valley ("Hollental") train, which justifies its name in only a few spots. Both are covered by Eurailpass.

When German railroad construction from Paris reached Freiburg, now the western terminus of the Hell's Valley train, dreamers talked of linking Paris to Vienna by train through Hell's Valley. On May 23, 1887, the Hell's Valley Railroad was opened—the first German State railroad with mixed cogwheel and adhesion traction.

It remained that way until 1933 when the cogwheels were taken out and special locomotives put into service on the steep stretch. The line was electrified in 1936 on a trial basis and patched into DB's grid in 1960. Now you ride in an undistinguished railcar, but the landscape remains more romantic than on most other stretches.

Setting out from Offenburg (522 feet), the first stretch of the Black Forest Railroad takes you past vineyards, fruit trees, wheat, hops, corn, and below a striking Romanesque hilltop castle.

While you pass along a pretty stream with fishermen in green jackets and hats on the right of your train, the hillsides grow steeper and more wooded and the first houses with red geraniums in window boxes appear. This is a sure sign the Black Forest is not far away.

The eye-catching gilded minute and hour hands and numerals on

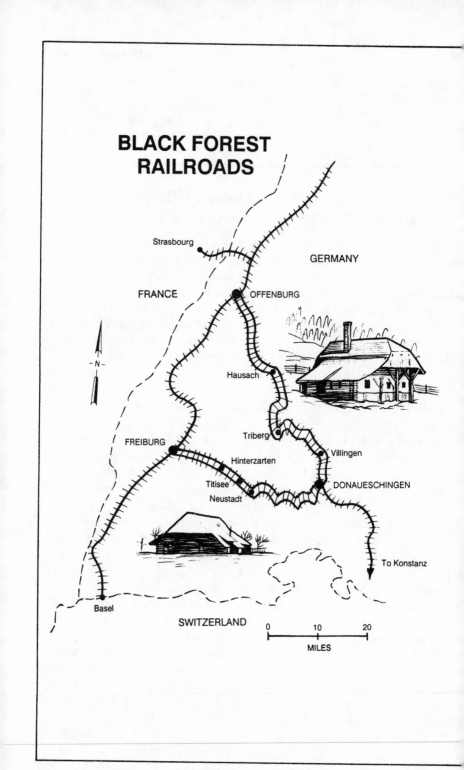

# BLACK FOREST RAILROADS

Strasbourg

GERMANY

FRANCE

OFFENBURG

Hausach

Triberg

FREIBURG

Villingen

Hinterzarten

Titisee

DONAUESCHINGEN

Neustadt

To Konstanz

Basel

SWITZERLAND

–N–

0   10   20

MILES

the brown-and-tan clock tower give Gengenbach a Black Forest feeling. The newer houses tend to have long sloping roofs.

When you stop at Hausach (790 feet), the Black Forest store across from the station is decorated with multicolored baskets on a rope. From Hausach, you begin one of the most rugged and picturesque stretches in Germany.

The valley is more romantic with black-and-white cows in the fields and houses with gigantic roofs. They have eaves on four sides and balconies of hand-carved wood, front and back, but not the sides where the tentlike roofs overhang nearly to the ground.

Soon you see thatched, wooden Black Forest houses to your right—just like in the tourist literature—and an onion-shaped church belfry, also on your right. Some houses offer rooms to let: "Zimmer Frei."

The farms get bigger, the trees get bigger, and the climb gets steeper. You are traveling across the pages of a picture book of the Black Forest. It is pleasant to see all these textbook examples from the comfort of a train.

At Hornberg (1,260 feet), you come to a stop at a site overlooking the village and looking up at a castle on a hill, flying a small black, red, and yellow German flag.

Across the valley you see a cuckoo clock factory. Hikers wearing leather shorts and green knee-socks and carrying walking sticks tramp through forests down the mountainsides.

Now it gets wilder suddenly. You pass through tunnel after tunnel—every one punctuated by screeches from the train's whistle. Read their conveniently placed names as you enter. Between tunnels, you have picture-postcard views of farms and forests.

Triburg (2,020 feet), the watch- and clockmaking center, is the highlight of this stretch, in the heart of the Black Forest. This is a good place to break your trip. Walk directly to the Black Forest Museum to enjoy quietly (except for the blasting mechanical organ) old local costumes, watch- and clockmaking exhibits, and a working model of your Black Forest Railroad.

Back on your train, you continue to climb. You emerge from a long tunnel into a thick forest.

The Black Forest is more attractive than other woods not because the trees grow close together, but because they are evenly spaced, not wild. They are uniform, almost tailored, so they don't allow much light to fall except for a few spots of sunlight on the flooring of pine needles.

After you cross the summit you pick up speed. Although you aren't rushing, your pace seems breakneck compared to your slow ascent.

Past Sommerau (2,729 feet), the hills below you still have their wild look. Exiting the tunnel before St. Georgen brings a whole new experience. The surroundings are mundane, more developed, and modestly industrialized. The excitement and enchantment is over. By the time you reach the large brown-brick, tile-roofed Villingen station house (2,309 feet), industry has sadly triumphed over the Black Forest.

In Donaueschingen (2,221 feet), change from your Black Forest train, which continues to Lake Constance, for the Hell's Valley train.

DB's sea-green railcar takes you west again. You reenter the Black Forest. The trees grow stonger and stronger and surround your slick railcar as you glide downhill toward Hufingen (2,220 feet) in Hell's Valley. You are making a charming if not spectacular journey through forests, fields, and meadows in a second section of the Black Forest.

Titisee (2,814 feet) is your major stop on the Hell's Valley line. Titisee ("See" means "lake," although it's not visible from here), the premiere resort of the Black Forest. It is a hiker's and vacationer's paradise. On your right stand vacation homes; on your left forests trail down to the valley.

The segment between Hollsteig and Hinterzarten takes you up at a gradient of one foot for every eighteen you pass. This is the third steepest segment in Germany using adhesion traction.

Hinterzarten (2,903 feet), a stylish mountain resort, is the highest point of the Hell's Valley Railroad, higher even than the summit of the Black Forest Railroad. You are surrounded by trees of every sort, leaves rustling in the breezes, hiking trails, and timbered houses. The air feels woodsy.

Downhill you travel through the thick of the Black Forest. It must be idyllic if Marie Antoinette passed here. You see trees, mountains, and many autos. Then you see nothing. You are passing through a tunnel. The conductor checks your Eurailpass. You enter two tunnels and pass Posthalde station without stopping. Then you reach another tunnel.

There are supposed to be nine tunnels between Posthalde and Freiburg, but it seems you pass at least a dozen. Many are very short and are possibly counted as underpasses. In DB's list the shortest tunnel is 157 feet long, by Ravennaviadukt. Maybe 150 or 125 feet is too short to be counted as a tunnel.

By the time you reach Himmelreich (1,493 feet), you have left behind most of the heavy forest.

When you stop in Kirchzarten (1,286 feet), across from Gasthaus Alte Post, the kilometer markers show you have 11 km (6.8 miles) left to travel.

You travel through a broad valley, mountains surround you, rye and corn flourish, and you near Freiburg-Littenweller stop (1,040 feet) on the outskirts of Freiburg. Still in the Black Forest, you see red-tile roofs, gardens for pensioners, picnic grounds, and a sports stadium on your right.

Now you have 5.6 km to the main train station. But that didn't used to be true because the train ran through the middle of Freiburg. In 1934, the track was moved and the line rerouted in a loop around the city, thus adding another 1.4 kilometers to your trip. This meant all kilometer markers had to be changed, but the administration skimped. They changed only the markers near their offices in Freiburg. When you reach Freiburg-Wiehre's green station house (918 feet), you come to kilometer marker "0."

When you arrive in Freiburg's Hauptbahnhof you have entered the "Twilight Zone." You have traveled on a line with a negative length. Look for the enameled, black-on-white kilometer marker: "-1.4," with numbers arranged vertically.

Freiburg (pop. 200,000), which is more completely known as "Freiburg im Breisgau" to locate it specifically, is a jewel of southern Germany. It was founded in the twelfth century by the Dukes of Zahringer. Its Gothic cathedral, octagonal tower, and dazzling market square make your visit here unforgettable.

It was in Freiburg on May 4-5, 1770, that Archduchess Marie Antoinette said goodbye to Austria and entered France at Strasbourg.

## Black Forest Railroad Service

| E | D | | | | D | E |
|---|---|---|---|---|---|---|
| 0741 | 0835 | dep. | OFFENBURG | arr. | 0822 | 0918 |
| 0748 | .... | dep. | Gengenbach | dep. | .... | 0910 |
| 0755 | .... | dep. | Biberach | dep. | .... | 0903 |
| 0801 | .... | dep. | Haslach | dep. | .... | 0857 |
| 0807 | 0854 | arr. | HAUSACH | dep. | 0802 | 0851 |
| 0808 | 0855 | dep. | HAUSACH | arr. | 0801 | 0849 |
| 0816 | 0903 | arr. | HORNBERG | dep. | 0753 | 0842 |
| 0817 | 0904 | dep. | HORNBERG | arr. | 0752 | 0841 |
| 0830 | 0918 | dep. | TRIBERG | dep. | 0740 | 0828 |
| 0841 | 0932 | arr. | ST. GEORGEN | dep. | 0724 | 0813 |
| 0845 | 0933 | dep. | ST. GEORGEN | arr. | 0723 | 0812 |
| 0855 | 0944 | arr. | VILLINGEN | dep. | 0714 | 0804 |
| 0858 | 0946 | dep. | VILLINGEN | arr. | 0712 | 0751 |
| .... | .... | dep. | Klengen | dep. | .... | 0747 |
| 0907 | 0954 | arr. | DONAUESCHINGEN | dep. | 0703 | 0741 |

*E* trains and *D* trains alternate departures every two hours on the minute until 7 P.M.

**Hell's Valley Railroad Service**

| E | | | | E |
|---|---|---|---|---|
| 0714 | dep. | DONAUESCHINGEN | arr. | 0842 |
| 0727 | dep. | Doggingen | dep. | 0833 |
| 0740 | dep. | Loffingen | dep. | 0816 |
| 0746 | dep. | Rotenbach | dep. | 0811 |
| 0756 | arr. | NEUSTADT | dep. | 0800 |
| 0801 | dep. | NEUSTADT | arr. | 0754 |
| 0807 | arr. | TITISEE | dep. | 0748 |
| 0808 | dep. | TITISEE | arr. | 0747 |
| 0815 | dep. | Hinterzarten | dep. | 0743 |
| 0831 | dep. | Himmelreich | dep. | 0724 |
| 0834 | dep. | Kirchzarten | dep. | 0718 |
| 0839 | dep. | Freiburg-Littenweller | dep. | 0713 |
| 0843 | dep. | Freiburg-Wiehre | dep. | 0709 |
| 0847 | arr. | FREIBURG (Breisgau) | dep. | 0703 |

*E* trains depart hourly on the minute until 7 P.M.

## Medieval Germany by Europabus
## Castles, Romance, and Rococo

In the 1890s the city fathers decided never to build a train station. They expected iron horses to corrupt the ambience of their fair city. They wanted Rothenburg ob der Tauber (on the Tauber River) to remain the finest surviving medieval town.

This city, by law, remains as it was in the seventeenth century, after the Thirty Years War. The city council regulates progress so carefully that even house colors are set out in official government rule books. The housewife with the prettiest window-box flower display wins a cash prize.

Adventurers with even the slightest curiosity in seeing old gabled houses, Gothic roofs, oriel windows, fortress walls, fairy-tale watchtowers, cobbled streets, and graceful, flowing fountains make visiting here top priority.

Take a local train to a small secondary station outside the city walls, or better, travel to Rothenburg aboard a sea-green Europabus along the Romantic Highway and Castle Road. It is the cheapest way when you hold a Eurailpass. You ride free.

Romantic Highway and Castle Road Europabuses converge on Rothenburg after passing along the most scenic coach routes in Germany. Because they are operated by a subsidiary of DB, you ride them free with a Eurailpass or GermanRail Tourist Card.

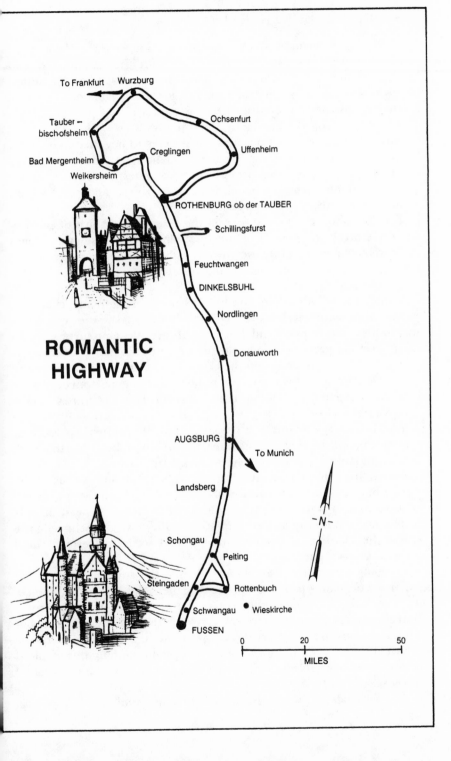

ROMANTIC HIGHWAY

To Frankfurt  Wurzburg

Tauberbischofsheim

Ochsenfurt

Bad Mergentheim

Creglingen  Uffenheim

Weikersheim

ROTHENBURG ob der TAUBER

Schillingsfurst

Feuchtwangen

DINKELSBUHL

Nordlingen

Donauworth

AUGSBURG

To Munich

Landsberg

Schongau

Peiting

Steingaden

Rottenbuch

Schwangau  Wieskirche

FUSSEN

~ N ~

0          20          50

MILES

Europabus is the network of long-distance motor coaches throughout most of Europe operated in association with the national railroad administrations. Their vehicles are usually luxury coaches with continuous windows and ample luggage space below. Passengers on the scenic routes are assisted by English-speaking guides giving personal directions and showing the highlights along the way.

Sorry, "Romantic" does not necessarily refer to boy meets girl.

Instead, you feel a special Romance—a nostalgic pleaure in half-timbered houses, restored ramparts, town gates, baroque cherubs, palace gardens, arching stone bridges over rivers, and royal castles implanted on steep, rocky slopes.

The Romantic Highway gives you the essence and spirit of picture-book Germany. It seems like the founders of the medieval villages deliberately lined up all the worthwhile sights of the region in order to show you everything without making you detour. They could not have done it better.

Your big, smooth-riding coach takes you through one charming village after another. Discovering Dinkelsbuhl makes the whole trip memorable. Nordlingen and Donauworth are pleasant surprises with their carefully preserved and colorfully painted Romantic structures.

The Romantic Highway and the Castle Road crisscross at Rothenburg ob der Tauber, giving you the option there of changing from one to the other and starting or ending at eight worthwhile terminuses on the octopus network.

You board southbound Europabuses in Frankfurt, Wurzburg, Mannheim, and Heidelberg, or connect from Nuremberg. Northbound, you travel from Fussen, Munich, or Augsburg.

Depending on your connection, you have about two hours in Rothenburg to climb the Town Hall belfry, dating from the fourteenth century, and to walk along the wide city wall—but first head directly from your stop on the Schrannenplatz straight down the Schmiedgasse to see the Plonlein, the most photographed scene in Germany (and every photo is a gem).

Traveling south from Rothenburg during the summer, you choose either a Europabus to Fussen in the Allgauer Alps or one to Munich, the beer-hall city and bright spot of Bavaria. Both buses pause in Dinkelsbuhl. On a good day you arrive at the Scheweinemarkt, but alternate stops are often used. Ask your guide for directions to the Deutsches Haus. You do not want to miss photographing this admired fifteenth-century gabled building which you see on the "Visit Germany" travel posters.

Your Europabus driver to Munich pulls onto the Autobahn at Augsburg, bringing you into Munich's Starnberger station next to Munich's Hauptbahnhof, but if you plan to change to a train, save time by getting off at the Augsburg train station.

The driver of the second Europabus south from Rothenburg continues through Bavaria to Fussen with distant views of King Ludwig's fantasy Neuschwanstein Castle. You bypass the astonishing church in the Wies going south, but stop there northbound. Its breathtaking rococo interior makes it often mentioned as Germany's finest church.

On Sundays only you connect with the EC Schweizerland to Munich. On other days Fussen is the end of your line. Its only welcome is a nearby youth hostel.

The Castle Road between Rothenburg and Heidelberg is so-called because it connects red-sandstone Heidelberg Castle, heart of Romanticism, on one end, with the gray-granite Neuschwanstein Castle on the other, and features castles, large and small, around every curve of the Neckar valley (Heidelberg to Rothenburg). Board either in Mannheim or in the "Student-Prince" university town, spend your lunch hour in Rothenburg, and then join a Romantic Highway bus to Fussen or Munich.

Make reservations at a Europabus office in Germany or by postcard (to arrive at least three days before departure) to Deutsche Touring GmbH, Am Romerhof 17, 6000 Frankfurt/Main 90, Tel. 069-7903240. Indicate date, route, and number of seats you require. Seat reservations are free of charge.

Europabuses from Frankfurt to Munich operate daily the year round, but additional buses run during the summer from Wurzburg to Fussen and from Mannheim/Heidelberg to Fussen beginning early in June until late in September.

You must pay a nominal registration and baggage checking fee for luggage. It includes insurance up to about $1,200.

When you want to tempt the rage of Rothenburg's city fathers, use the small, local railroad that is, in fact, outside of Rothenburg's city walls. Rothenburg's train station is served via Steinach, seven miles away, on the mainline between Wurzburg and Nurnberg. Connections are poor and bus service is sometimes substituted (covered by Eurailpass), especially on weekends. Be sure you check the timetable for the day you will be traveling. Bus connections are usually a few minutes different from train connections.

## Romantic Highway Summer Europabus Service

### between Frankfurt and Wurzburg
### and Augsburg, Munich, and Fussen

| | | | | | | |
|---|---|---|---|---|---|---|
| .... | 0815 | dep. | FRANKFURT/M (Hbf./Sud) | arr. | 1955 | .... |
| .... | .... | arr. | Wurzburg (Omnibusbf.) | dep. | 1810 | .... |
| 0900 | 1015 | dep. | WURZBURG (Omnibusbf.) | arr. | .... | 1920 |
| .... | 1035 | dep. | Ochsenfurt (Mainbrucke) | dep. | 1745 | .... |
| .... | 1055 | dep. | Uffenheim | dep. | 1720 | .... |
| 0940 | .... | dep. | Tauberbischofsheim | dep. | .... | 1840 |
| 1005 | .... | dep. | Bad Mergentheim (Bf.) | dep. | .... | 1815 |
| 1025 | .... | arr. | Weikersheim (Marktplatz) | dep. | .... | 1755 |
| 1045 | .... | dep. | Weikersheim (Marktplatz) | arr. | .... | .... |
| 1055 | .... | dep. | Rottingen (Marktplatz) | dep. | .... | 1740 |
| 1110 | .... | dep. | Creglingen (Omnibusbf.) | dep. | .... | 1730 |
| 1115 | .... | arr. | Creglingen (Kapelle) | dep. | .... | .... |
| 1130 | .... | dep. | Creglingen (Kapelle) | arr. | .... | .... |
| 1200 | 1135 | arr. | ROTHENBURG o.d.T. (Schrannenplatz) | dep. | 1700 | 1700 |
| 1330 | 1345 | dep. | ROTHENBURG o.d.T. (Schrannenplatz) | arr. | 1515 | 1535 |
| 1335 | 1350 | dep. | Rothenburg o.d.T. (Bf.) | dep. | .... | 1530 |
| 1355 | 1410 | dep. | Schillingsfurst (Post) | dep. | 1450 | 1515 |
| 1415 | 1430 | dep. | Feuchtwangen (Omnibusbf.) | dep. | 1430 | 1455 |
| 1430 | 1445 | arr. | DINKELSBUHL (Schweine.) | dep. | 1415 | 1440 |
| 1500 | 1530 | dep. | DINKELSBUHL (Schweine.) | arr. | 1235 | 1310 |
| 1520 | 1600 | dep. | Wallerstein (Sparkasse) | dep. | 1200 | 1235 |
| .... | .... | arr. | Nordlingen (Rathaus) | dep. | 1155 | 1230 |
| 1525 | 1605 | dep. | Nordlingen (Rathaus) | arr. | 1140 | .... |
| 1555 | .... | dep. | Harburg (Marktplatz) | dep. | .... | 1215 |
| 1610 | 1635 | dep. | Donauworth (Kirche) | dep. | 1105 | 1200 |
| 1655 | .... | arr. | AUGSBURG (Hbf.) | dep. | 1020 | 1110 |
| 1705 | 1740 | dep. | AUGSBURG (Hbf.) | arr. | .... | 1100 |
| .... | 1755 | dep. | Freidberg (Marienplatz) | dep. | 0955 | .... |
| .... | 1855 | arr. | MUNICH (Starnberger Bf.) | dep. | 0900 | .... |
| 1755 | | arr. | Landsberg (Hauptplatz) | dep. | | 1015 |
| 1815 | | dep. | Landsberg (Hauptplatz) | arr. | | .... |
| 1830 | | dep. | Hohenfurch (B 17) | dep. | | 0955 |
| 1835 | | dep. | Schongau (Bf.) | dep. | | 0950 |
| 1840 | | dep. | Peiting (Meierstrasse) | dep. | | 0945 |
| 1845 | | dep. | Rottenbuch (Post) | dep. | | 0935 |
| 1850 | | dep. | Echelsbacher Brucke | dep. | | 0930 |
| 1855 | | dep. | Wildsteig | dep. | | 0925 |
| 1857 | | dep. | Abzw. Ilchberg | dep. | | 0922 |

| | | | | |
|---|---|---|---|---|
| 1900 | dep. | Kohlhofen (Abzw. Wies) | dep. | 0920 |
| .... | arr. | WIESKIRCHE | dep. | 0915 |
| .... | dep. | WIESKIRCHE | arr. | 0850 |
| 1905 | dep. | Steingaden (Postamt) | dep. | 0840 |
| 1915 | dep. | Trauchgau | dep. | 0835 |
| 1920 | dep. | Buching | dep. | 0830 |
| 1925 | dep. | Schwangau (Verkehrsburo) | dep. | 0825 |
| 1930 | dep. | Hohenschwangau | dep. | 0820 |
| 1935 | arr. | FUSSEN (Bf.) | dep. | 0815 |

## Castle Road Summer Europabus Service

### between Mannheim, Heidelberg, Nuremberg, and Rothenburg

| | | | | | |
|---|---|---|---|---|---|
| | 0730 | dep. | MANNHEIM (Hbf.) | arr. | 2040 |
| | 0745 | arr. | HEIDELBERG (Hbf.) | dep. | .... |
| | 0800 | dep. | HEIDELBERG (Hbf.) | arr. | 2015 |
| | 0814 | dep. | Neckargemund (Bf.) | dep. | 1950 |
| | 0820 | dep. | Neckarsteinach (Bf.) | dep. | 1949 |
| | 0825 | dep. | Neckarhausen (Bf.) | dep. | 1945 |
| | 0830 | dep. | Hirschhorn (Schiff) | dep. | 1941 |
| | 0840 | dep. | Eberbach | | |
| | | | (Neckaranlagen) | dep. | 1933 |
| | 0845 | dep. | Lindach (Schiff) | dep. | 1928 |
| | 0848 | dep. | Zwingenberg (Anker) | dep. | 1925 |
| | 0902 | dep. | Neckarelz | | |
| | | | (Schulzentrum) | dep. | 1912 |
| | 0907 | dep. | Neckarzimmern | | |
| | | | (Rathaus) | dep. | 1900 |
| | 0925 | dep. | Bad Friedrichshall- | | |
| | | | Jagstfeld (Bf.) | dep. | 1855 |
| | 0953 | dep. | Ohringen (Stadthall) | dep. | 1824 |
| | 1003 | dep. | Neuenstein (Schloss) | dep. | 1815 |
| | 1010 | dep. | Hohebuch-Waldenburg | dep. | 1809 |
| | 1014 | dep. | Kupferzell (Rathaus) | dep. | 1804 |
| | 1025 | dep. | Braunsbach | | |
| | | | (Marktplatz) | dep. | 1755 |
| | 1040 | arr. | Langenburg (Rathaus) | dep. | 1730 |
| | 1120 | dep. | Langenburg (Rathaus) | arr. | .... |
| | 1135 | dep. | Blaufelden (Bf.) | dep. | 1715 |
| | 1140 | dep. | Schrozberg (Friedhof) | dep. | 1710 |
| 0845 | .... | dep. | NUREMBERG | | |
| | | | (Hbf./ZOB) | arr. | .... 1830 |
| .... | 1200 | dep. | Rothenburg o.d.T. (Bf.) | dep. | 1650 .... |
| 1045 | 1205 | arr. | ROTHENBURG o.d.T. | | |
| | | | (Schrannenplatz) | dep. | 1645 1630 |

# Austria
## and Hungary

### *Vital Tips for the Trains
of Austria and Hungary*

The "Osterreichischen Bundesbahnen" (OBB), the Austrian Federal Railroads, provide excellent, punctual service with a full complement of express trains (Ex), fast trains (D), intermediate-speed trains (E), and local trains (no letters).

All of OBB's express trains are name trains (Ex 263 is the "Orient Express" running between Paris, Salzburg, Vienna, Budapest, and Bucharest). Even some of OBB's D trains carry names.

You reach Austria with sixteen EuroCity trains, but that number is misleading because three call only in Innsbruck, not in the heart of the OBB, and three travel between Munich and Zurich, touching only Bregenz en route.

OBB sends fewer carriages on international routes than the railroads of its neighboring countries, but you can take advantage of several useful connections. OBB's flagship EC Transalpin takes you between Vienna, Salzburg, Zurich, and Basel. OBB's Austria Express takes you in orange-and-white OBB carriages all the way between Klagenfurt and Salzburg, Munich, Cologne, Rotterdam, and the Hook of Holland for the steamship crossing to Harwich and London (Liverpool Street).

### Hungarian Trains

The Hungarian State Railroads ("Magyar Allamvasutak," known as MAV) is a small, but capable, diesel- and electric-train operation. Trains are slow but reliable, and travel is very cheap. Each little train station in the countryside is alive with flowers and surrounded by green.

The morning EuroCity Lehar is the most comfortable and convenient train for reaching Budapest from the West. Leaving from Vienna's South station, the Lehar, the first EuroCity train to run into an Eastern country, speeds you between Vienna and Budapest in record-breaking time.

Aboard the Lehar you sit in air-conditioned first- and second-class cars of the OBB or a first-class salon carriage of the MAV. A Hungarian dining car is but a carriage away. A friendly hostess serves snacks and drinks at your seat.

Your border crossing at Hegyeshalom is shortened to ten minutes by the trick of using two-frequency electrical locomotives compatible with the networks of both OBB and MAV and by performing border passport, visa, and customs inspections aboard the Lehar. For the first time since 1932 (when the legendary Hungarian train "Arpad" raced along this route), you can travel between Budapest and Vienna in less than three hours.

The overnight Wiener Walzer (with dining) follows about two hours later through Vienna's West station, from Basel through Zurich and Salzburg. The Orient Express (not the luxury train) brings you through Vienna's West station at 4:22 P.M. from Paris, by way of Strasbourg, Stuttgart, and Munich.

Traveling to Hungary from the West, you arrive at Keleti Palyaudvar (East train station) on the Pest bank of Budapest. Statues of George Stephenson, inventor of the locomotive, and James Watt, creator of the steam engine, grace the front of the eclectic, charming exterior of the tremendous nineteenth-century structure.

Budapest's East station is connected by an escalator to a Metro station crowded with shops, where you use frequent Metro service to the city center and under the Danube to the South train station.

Be sure to go to the correct station in Budapest. In addition to East station, trains take you to Lake Balaton from Budapest's modern concrete South station (Deli Palyaudvar) in the west (!) of town, and aboard the Baltic-Orient Express to Prague, Dresden, East Berlin, and Stockholm from the spic-and-span West station (Nyugati Palyaudvar, at the head of Lenin Street just before it reaches Marx Square).

The most convenient place for you to buy train tickets in Hungary is at Ibusz (the Hungarian Travel Bureau) offices. Someone there usually speaks English. Ibusz has branch offices in all train stations, but agents at Ibusz' main office, Felszabadulas ter 5, not only sell train tickets, but make room arrangements, change money, and distribute free information and pamphlets in English. MAV requires that you reserve express trains (gyorsvonat) a day in advance, but local trains need no booking.

## Austria's Private Lines and Steam Trains

Austria, with high Alps and rolling countryside dotted with spectacularly beautiful lakes, offers adventurers a chance to leave mainline trains for local and private lines. These include trains still operating with steam locomotives on a scheduled basis, steam rack railroads climbing up steep inclines to lofty mountain tops, standard- and narrow-gauge short lines with frequent steam excursion trains, and numerous museum trains with fan trips throughout the summer.

One of Austria's provinces is a railroad operator in its own right. Austria's province of Styria runs both standard and 2 1/2-foot gauge lines under the banner of the Steiermarkische Landesbahnen with headquarters in Graz. Its longest line, the forty-eight-mile narrow-gauge Murtalbahn, runs from Unzmarkt to Mauterndorf. On Tuesdays and Wednesdays during the summer you ride steam along half of this line.

You are welcome to call numerous train enthusiast groups in Austria. For more details, contact the Austrian National Tourist Office (see Appendix).

## Corridor Trains

To cut travel time through Austria you ride OBB's "Corridor trains" almost without knowing it. In cooperation with the neighboring railroads, one takes you through West Germany, one through Hungary. To get on or off you must show your passport (you also need a visa in Hungary). Customs and police inspections are possible, but unlikely.

## Train Stations

The heart of Austria—and the OBB—is Vienna. Vienna has five train stations; two are important. You arrive at the West train station, the "Westbahnhof," unless you arrive from Italy. Vienna's West station handles all traffic from Switzerland and Germany. Vienna's South train station, the Sudbahnhof, connects with Italy, Yugoslavia, and the eastern countries.

Vienna's third station is the striking glass-fronted Franz Josefs-Bahnhof, a model for the modern trend toward integrating train facilities with commercial shopping centers. Two trains a day serve Prague, Dresden, and East Berlin from FJB, but most of its traffic is the electrified commuter service along the southern bank of the Danube and north of the Danube, including Krems (for Danube River steamers).

Vienna Nord connects the airport, the city, the small area north of the Danube, and Czechoslovakia.

## West Train Station

The highly glassed Westbahnhof is a big, well-organized structure rebuilt in 1953 to handle all electrified train traffic in the direction of Western Europe. Information for hotels and trains is available in one office in the middle of the hall. The tourist information office opens early, to accommodate adventurers arriving on the first international trains, and remains open late.

Luggage carts fitted for the escalators are available.

## South Train Station

The Sudbahnhof is a graceful station because of the moving walkways leading to two upper levels.

The top floor of this airy terminus is devoted to service to the south, "Sudbahn." There are waiting rooms and kiosks selling travel provisions ("Reiseproviant"), as well as a sit-down coffee shop.

The middle level, the "Ostbahn," serves the east, meaning the Communist-block countries. There are rest rooms, a cafe/restaurant, and a buffet.

On the expansive ground floor, you find nearly every service you need, including money changing, tourist information, train information, ticketing, lockers, a barbershop, and showers.

## Getting around Vienna

In front of Vienna's West station is the 1988 subway (U-Bahn) station. Plan to use Vienna's subway and streetcars. Their networks cover the city efficiently. They are fun to ride and the trams are good for sightseeing the city.

In Vienna you use the same tickets for riding trams, subways, buses, and the Stadtbahn. Buy single tickets on the tram from the conductor in the first car or from an automat in one of the subway or Stadtbahn stations.

A set of five tickets can be bought at a good discount from the single ticket price from the train station and Vienna Transport Authority ticket counters or from any of the tobacco kiosks around the city for use in the unattended ("Schaffnerlos") trams. Simply validate them in the automatic canceling machines aboard the train.

Take advantage of the seventy-two-hour Vienna network pass or the eight-day "Environment" ticket for an even greater savings. The "Environment" ticket can be used by more than one person.

Eurailpasses are valid on S-Bahn trains in Vienna, including the S-Bahn between the city and the airport.

Reach the Sudbahnhof by streetcar 18 from Vienna's West station or by streetcar D circling Vienna's Ring. All of Vienna's radial bus lines provide connections to the D line. The Sudbahnhof is the end of the D line, making it impossible to miss.

Streetcar 5 takes you between Franz Josefs-Bahnhof and the Westbahnhof.

## Airport Train

Ride the S-Bahn free on a Eurailpass for a direct link to Vienna's Schwechat Airport. It leaves hourly from Vienna's North train station with a stop at the Mitte and several intermediate stations. Allow thirty minutes for transportation time.

Airport buses travel hourly to and from Vienna's West station—with stops at Vienna's South station—taking thirty-five minutes.

## Using Eurailpass Bonuses

Two of the most delightful Eurailpass bonuses are described in the adventures below: the Puchberg am Schneeberg-Hochschneeberg rack railroad and the steamers operated by the Erste Donau-Dampfschiffahrts-Gesellschaft (DDSG) between Passau and Vienna. In addition, adventurers who want to go south of Salzburg into the beautiful Salzkammergut should take advantage of the free St. Wolfgang-Schafbergspitze rack railroad and the free steamers on Lake Wolfgang leading to it.

Not advertised by Eurailpass, the Steiermarkische Landesbahnen grants a 50 percent reduction to holders of Eurailpasses and OBB's postal coaches honor Eurailpasses.

Use the Austrian port of Bregenz (site of the summer lake festival) to begin journeys on Lake Constance, for which Eurailpass allows you a 50 percent reduction.

## Austrian Tourist Card

Buy a "Bundesnetzkarte" for nine days', sixteen days', or one month's first- or second-class unlimited travel on the OBB network (except between the Austrian border and Hegyeshalom, Hungary), the Schneeberg and Schafberg rack railroads, and OBB ships on the Wolfgangsee. A 50 percent reduction on Lake Constance and DDSG Danube ships and on a number of private railroads is also a benefit. (You can even buy a one-year card.) Children aged six to fourteen traveling with an adult receive 50 percent off the purchase price of an Austrian Tourist Card.

You can also buy half-price tickets. For about $90 you receive 50 percent off tickets of OBB and private lines for a year.

Anyone under twenty-six is eligible for the "Austria Ticket," for nine or sixteen days of second-class travel (only) on the lines of the OBB, some private railroads, all postal and railroad buses, the Steiermarkische Landesbahnen, the DDSG, and the ships of the OBB on the Wolfgangsee. Countless mountain funiculars give you a 50 percent reduction.

Regional Network Cards allow you unlimited travel for between four and ten days on OBB services within any one of eighteen different regions and with 50 percent reduction on a number of private railroads.

Finally, OBB offers a Kilometer Bank scheme whereby up to six adventurers total their travel mileage and receive discounts of up to 35 percent.

## Hungarian Rail Runabout Ticket

Tickets valid for ten, twenty, or thirty days ("Turista Berlet") for unlimited travel on MAV in either first or second class are available at offices of Ibusz/Danube Travel in Budapest, Cologne, Frankfurt, London, Munich, Stockholm, or Vienna. You can extend this Hungarian Rail Runabout Ticket to include the service of the GYSEV Railroad at main train stations in Hungary.

Public transportation fares are very inexpensive in Budapest, but you save inconvenience by purchasing day passes for unlimited travel on the trams, electric buses, metro, and HEV Railroad in the Budapest area. For an additional charge, buy one including city bus travel as well.

The two adventures described in this chapter are the DDSG steamers from Passau to Vienna and Austria's Schneeberg Rack Railroad.

## *Cruising the Mellow Danube*
## *Off with Your Shoes*

Passengers pull their deck chairs closer to the railings. Their maps, guidebooks, and disc cameras threaten to fall into the Danube. They read their texts aloud, compare notes, chatter excitedly, and click their cameras at the sight in front of them.

You see the castle where Richard the Lionhearted, King of England, was imprisoned by his enemy, Leopold V, Duke of Austria.

The sights of castles, abbeys, and picture-book villages and the warmth of the wine- and fruit-bearing slopes makes the Wachau district in Austria on the deck of a river steamer one of the great river adventures. To show it off, proud Austrian hosts take their foreign visitors on the deck of a river steamer for that "special occasion."

The First Danube Steamship Company, DDSG ("Erste Donau-Dampfschiffahrts-Gesellschaft"), takes you on cooling, mellow two-day,

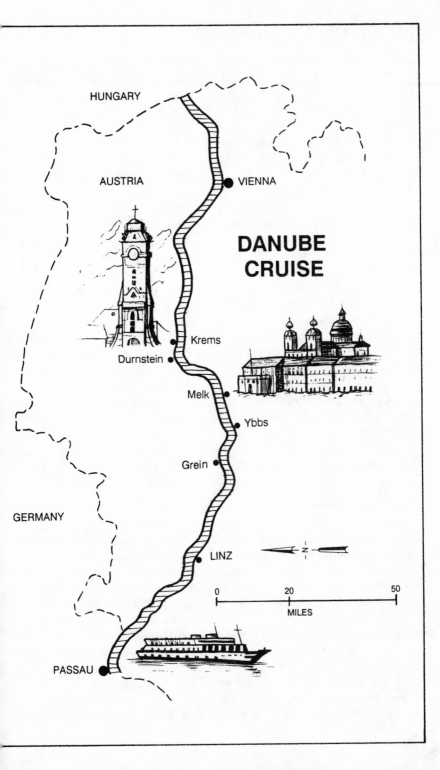

two-segment cruises along the Danube River through Austria between Passau, West Germany, and Vienna, the capital of Austria. This trip passes through the highlight Wachau district, but shorter excursions through just this stretch take 1 3/4 hours. The trips are free to Eurailers.

The Danube flows through Austria only 224 miles, but it is the most beautiful segment of Europe's second river (after the Volga). Your principal landings are at Linz, Melk, Krems, and of course Vienna. This one-eighth segment of the river is wholly navigable so you see commercial vessels, even Russian ones, all along its length, some traveling all the way from West Germany to the Black Sea.

Commerce pays your freight, so to speak. It keeps the river navigable so you can see the most picturesque sections of the Danube valley right from the surface of the river itself.

You can make this two-day trip in either direction, but there is something more rhythmic and restful about the throbbing of your ship going downstream from Passau to Vienna.

The Danube is a good river. Its color is always changing, depending on the time of day, weather conditions, time of year, whether the sun is rising and lightening it, whether it is overcast and gloomy, and whether it is carrying the spring glacier runoff or sediment. It is lined by castles, sparkles like an emerald in bright sunlight, and remains joyful for you to travel by ship. It is a real bargain when your passage is paid by Eurailpass.

DDSG's ships are all one class and shipshape in every respect. The Austrian government celebrated their 150th anniversary in 1979 by issuing three postage stamps showing ships of the company.

## Passau to Linz

Passau, the German port at the very head of the stretch of the Austrian Danube covered by your Eurailpass, occupies a beautiful site on the peninsula formed by the Inn and Danube rivers.

Reach Passau's DDSG landing from Passau train station by bus No. 5 from the steps in front of the station. Disembark the bus before it crosses the long Danube Bridge.

After the junction of the Inn River with the Danube below Passau (the Inn is the larger at this point), the Danube is wide and majestic and bordered with wooded, rocky slopes. Gravel plains along the valley were formed when glaciers receded. You sail past green meadows, marshes, and evergreen forests now covering the hills.

After your ship stops at Engelhartszell, you see the river open out into a magnificent lake. This is the reservoir of the Jochenstein Dam.

The rocky island in the river was supposedly the dwelling of a water fairy called Isa, the sister of the more infamous Lorelei of Rhine River notoriety.

Past Wesenufer, a pretty village with flowers on the balconies, you make a wide, sunken loop called the "Schloegener Schlinge," meaning "Sling of Schloegen." At the outermost point of your great U-turn, a Roman castle of the second century has been excavated. It guarded communications between Castra Batava (Passau) and Lentia (Linz).

After stopping at Aschach, where you see the surprising brown, blue, and orange colors used to decorate the villages in this area, you continue to Linz for a stopover in "The Excursion Center on the Danube."

## Linz

You embark in Passau or Linz to cruise downstream. Book a cabin from Passau and spend the night on board in Linz, but if this is too much trouble, plan to board directly in Linz, the vital capital of Upper Austria. Train connections are good here because it is a pass-through station.

Before you sail from Linz in the morning, visit Linz's showpiece main square, the Hauptplatz, only a block from the Hauptstrasse Bridge over the Danube from where you see the embarkation station for the cruise ships downstream. It is an easy walk.

You see a striking ensemble of diverse buildings on the Hauptplatz. The fascinating baroque Trinity column dominates the center of the square. Emperor Charles VI directed that it be erected in 1723 to celebrate the escape of the city from the plague, fire, and Turkish invasion. You see baroque columns of this type in many towns of Austria and Bavaria, but this is the best example.

You can use the tourist information booth and money change office right in the Linz train station. Both open at 8 A.M. If you arrive earlier, you find a warm waiting room in the station giving you the comfortable feeling of Austrian gemutlichkeit.

A streetcar in front of the train station takes you to the Hauptplatz and the DDSG pier along the river.

Linz is a convenient port for you to board for the day trip to Vienna. Downstream is lined with industrial growth, but when you see the hills grow green and wooded and the houses and barns become picturesque and when you find yourself peeping into the lives of dwellers by the river, washing and boating and threshing and piling hay into yellow haystacks, your cruise begins to unroll like a continuous reel of travelogue color adventure. You have well begun the singing, guitar-strumming, cooling swing down the Danube.

Your cruise is a marvelously soothing change from the helter-skelter madness of rush-around sightseeing, cathedrals that all look alike after a while, fortresses perched at the ends of dusty climbs, endless museums, crowded palaces, and bumpy cobblestone streets in the summer sun which finally make you believe your feet will burst into flames any minute. Your Danube cruise is fun.

## Off with Your Shoes

Shortly after leaving Linz at 9 A.M., the youthful aboard shed their shirts, shoes, and socks and gather to play guitars. Even more reserved passengers take this opportunity to slip off their shoes and socks and wiggle their toes from the ship's deck in the fresh, cooling breezes above the river.

Passengers scrape their deck chairs to the railings and compare their geography texts with the highlights of the passing countryside. You overhear no English. You are adventuring off the common tourist path, but all the deck personnel cheerfully answer your questions in English.

Downstream, about noon, you are hemmed between rocky, wooded slopes. Your approach to Grein is beautiful. This pleasant little town, guarded by its castle, lies ideally at the foot of a wooded bluff watching over the entrance to the Strudengau gorges.

From Grein to Ybbs, you pass around will-covered islands, past the ruins of the castles of Struden and Sarmingstein, and soon find yourself on a placid lake nearing the Ybbs-Persenbeug dam, a major power station.

The crew members are excited and rushed. They scurry passengers below and rope off the upper deck while the locks of the power station loom larger and larger. When the Danube is high, the clearance between your steamer and the locks is so slim that anyone poking his head above the ship's railings would be seriously injured.

When you pass Persenbeug, look for the castle where the last Austrian emperor, Charles I, was born.

From Persenbeug, at the head of a well-tilled plain where the river bends to Melk, you pass through the valley you know from episodes in *The Nibelungenlied*. You may hear echos of Brunhild and Kriemhild, Gunther and Siegfried.

Pochlarn, on the right bank, was settled in the tenth century by the Babenbergs, who began the vigorous growth of the Austrian monarchy.

## The Wachau

The stretch of the Danube from Melk to Krems, the Wachau, is considered the most interesting stretch of river landscape in Europe. You see charming villages lining the river, the ruins of fortified castles crowning the crests, and onion-shaped belfries adding notes of fantasy to the countryside.

The Wachau is a beautiful sight regardless of whether the trees are in blossom, apricots are bright on trees, or grapes are heavy on vines and every wine village is celebrating the harvest.

You are making one of the premiere excursions from Vienna. Frau Vera Kreisky, wife of the president of Austria at the time, took Rosalynn Carter on this trip on June 16, 1979, while the Austrian and American heads of state were in Vienna attending to business.

In addition to the full-day sailings of the Danube, you may take the shorter trip through the Wachau free on a Eurailpass. Pick up your boarding pass at the "Kassa," meaning cashier.

The Wachau makes a splendid debut at Melk where the buff-and-gold, 1726 Benedictine abbey rises like a vision above fine middle-class houses. You pass below the abbey's south wall, nearly a quarter-mile long, overlooking the Danube from a 150-foot rocky bluff.

Additional ships supplement this most-popular section. The smaller *Prinz Eugen*, for example, takes you on three decks, but primarily you use the rubber-mat and plastic bench vista on the top deck.

The Donauarm landing is directly below the abbey, a fifteen- to twenty-minute walk from the mainline train station served by expresses from Vienna and Linz. The deepwater Donaustrom landing used by the steamers cruising the entire Austrian Danube is across a green metal bridge and a flat, little island to where the water flows faster.

An English-speaking agent sells tickets and a simple leaflet program at the DDSG station house at the Donaustrom dock.

As you cruise out to the main Danube current, the chords of the "Blue Danube" waltz strike a romantic and unforgettable note.

Soon after casting off from Melk you see Schonbuhel Castle, which has guarded entry to the Wachau since the ninth century.

After docking at the yellow-painted village of Aggsbach, your steamer proceeds five minutes to Aggstein, precipitously below the castle, one of the largest and most formidable of the towers high on the mountain. This castle is notorious as a robber baron's haunt where prisoners were forced to jump to their deaths.

Passing Willendorf is especially interesting because the famous "Venus of Willendorf" prehistoric limestone statuette found here proved that man lived in the hills surrounding you since the dawn of civilization.

Spitz is almost the center of the Wachau, and its largest village. You see houses clustering below a hill, graceless but prosperous. The rows after rows of vines make it famous as "Thousand Pail Hill," known for the staggering amount of wine it produces in a good year.

Past Spitz on the left, fifteenth-century St. Michael appears—the oldest church in the Wachau. Thriving vineyards continue to cover the hillsides with green vines terraced in parallel rows. This region has the mildest climate in Austria.

The next picturesque village, marked by the fortified steep red-tiled roof, is Weissenkirchen, the center of the region known as "Wahowa" that gave its name to the entire Wachau.

Then, after sweeping past a broad bend in the Danube, you see the most famous scene in the Wachau—Durnstein—a historical, fortified town. As you near, you can feel its almost completely preserved medieval and baroque character.

Richard the Lionhearted in disguise was seized on his way back to his native England at the end of the Third Crusade. His faithful troubador/detective, Blondel, discovered his master here in Durnstein by strumming his mandolin and singing Richard's favorite ballad while searching through the castle.

Your next landing marks the end of the Wachau. You pass under a 500-year-old bridge at Krems, the historic wine-growing city (not village) on the left bank. At the foot of loam hills covered with prominent, terraced vineyards, you cross the famous "Iron Route," an ancient trade artery. Now a simple city, Krems was once an imperial fortress, more important than Vienna because of Danube trade.

You have completed the exciting part of your trip. Wachau steamers debark in Krems, where you take OBB's second-class-only diesel train into Vienna's Franz Josefs-Bahnhof. The Krems station is far from your ship's landing. If you are aboard a ship making the two-day trip from Passau to Vienna, you can stay aboard and alight at the DDSG's well-fitted stations in Vienna-Nussdorf wine village or in Vienna's city center.

From Krems, the Danube spreads broadly over a wide plain. It does not narrow until just above Vienna, where you pass solid, stone embankments. It will be darkening as your ship from Passau nears the Vienna Woods at Greifenstein.

Your ship docks first in Vienna at the Nussdorf landing, but you continue to the Schiffahrtszentrum, sailing under the reinforced-concrete Reichsbrucke, meaning "empire bridge" (the former one suddenly collapsed one morning in 1971 and fell into the river), and docking at the modernistic DDSG facility. Its reflecting blue glass and white concrete may remind you of the movie *Star Wars*. Proceed into the terminal's "Passagierhalle." This futuristic complex has everything including taxi stops outside and access to trams and the subway nearby.

At DDSG's information service office, you can make hotel reservations and pick up maps and directions to Vienna, the capital of Austria and for five centuries the seat of the Hapsburg dynasty.

Breakfast, lunch, and dinner are served in the ships' dining salons. Refeshments are available all through the day at the kiosks on deck.

Cabins accommodating two are available on board. You use them overnight in Linz during your journey, or even if you are boarding or disembarking in Linz. Going downstream, you occupy your cabin at 8:30 in the evening before your next day's sailing from Linz. Arriving from Vienna, you may remain overnight in your cabin at Linz until 6:30 A.M., but you must disembark at that time if you do not want to sail on to Passau.

Overnighting on board after arrival in Vienna or Passau is not permitted. Reserve cabins in advance or apply to the steward's office immediately upon boarding. The DDSG office is at Handelskai 265, 1021 Vienna (Tel. 0 22 2/26 65 36).

---

## Summer Steamer Service

### through the Wachau

| | | | | | | | | |
|---|---|---|---|---|---|---|---|---|
| 1000 | 1400 | 1530 | dep. | MELK (Donauarm) | arr. | 1335 | 1505 | 1905 |
| 1025 | 1425 | 1555 | dep. | Aggsbach Dorf | dep. | 1250 | 1420 | 1820 |
| 1030 | 1430 | 1600 | dep. | Aggstein H. | dep. | 1240 | 1410 | 1810 |
| 1055 | 1455 | 1625 | dep. | Spitz | dep. | 1200 | 1330 | 1730 |
| 1110 | 1510 | 1640 | dep. | Weissenkirchen | dep. | 1130 | 1300 | 1700 |
| 1125 | 1525 | 1655 | dep. | Durnstein | dep. | 1105 | 1235 | 1635 |
| 1145 | 1545 | 1715 | arr. | KREMS | dep. | 1030 | 1200 | 1600 |

## Summer Steamer Service

### between Passau and Vienna

| | | | | |
|---|---|---|---|---|
| 1530 | dep. | PASSAU | arr. | 1410 |
| 1610 | dep. | Obernzell | dep. | 1300 |
| 1655 | dep. | Engelhartszell | dep. | 1230 |
| 1710 | dep. | Niederranna | dep. | 1205 |
| 1720 | dep. | Wesenufer | dep. | 1155 |
| 1735 | dep. | Schlogen | dep. | 1135 |

### between Passau and Vienna

| | | | | |
|---|---|---|---|---|
| 1800 | dep. | Obermuhl | dep. | 1110 |
| 1825 | dep. | Neuhaus-Untermuhl | dep. | 1040 |
| 1910 | dep. | Aschach | dep. | 0950 |
| 1920 | dep. | Brandstatt-Eferding | dep. | 0935 |
| 2030 | arr. | LINZ | dep. | 0800* |
| 0900* | dep. | LINZ | arr. | 2225 |
| 1145 | dep. | Grein | dep. | 1915 |
| 1250 | dep. | Ybbs | dep. | 1755 |
| 1315 | dep. | Marbach/M.-Taferl | dep. | 1720 |
| 1330 | dep. | Pochlarn | dep. | 1705 |
| 1430 | dep. | MELK (Donaustrom) | dep. | 1610 |
| 1455 | dep. | Aggsbach Dorf | dep. | 1525 |
| 1500 | dep. | Aggstein | dep. | 1515 |
| 1525 | dep. | Spitz | dep. | 1435 |
| 1540 | dep. | Weissenkirchen | dep. | 1405 |
| 1555 | dep. | Durnstein | dep. | 1340 |
| 1615 | dep. | KREMS | dep. | 1305 |
| 1800 | dep. | Tulln | dep. | 1030 |
| 1940 | arr. | VIENNA (Nussdorf) | dep. | 0825 |
| 2000 | arr. | VIENNA (DDSG) | dep. | 0800 |

*Next day.

---

## Puffing up the Schneeberg
## Wieder Kaputt!

The first thing you feel is the chattering of the cogwheels. While your comic steam train pulls you slowly out of the Austrian village of Puchberg, your glimpse ahead does not promise as much as your creaky train finally delivers. The Schneeberg Rack Railroad may be your slowest, steamiest, jerkiest adventure, but may be the most fun. This diverting day's excursion is a free bonus to Eurailpass holders.

Then you hear the nasty hissing of the tough steam engine and see the black clouds swirling behind you. The Schneeberg Railroad has enough antique and functional features to turn a railfan's heart into Apfel Strudel.

What the Austrians call a "schmalspurige dampfbetriebene Zahnradbahn" is a narrow-gauge, steam-driven, cogwheel railroad. It is fired by coal from Poland and belches fumes as black as a loan manager's heart.

When you leave Puchberg am Schneeberg, south of Vienna, each chug of the steam-driven pistons shoves your little engine inches more across the highway and up onto the mountain. Chagrined, you have no doubt you can walk faster than the train can climb, but as your train

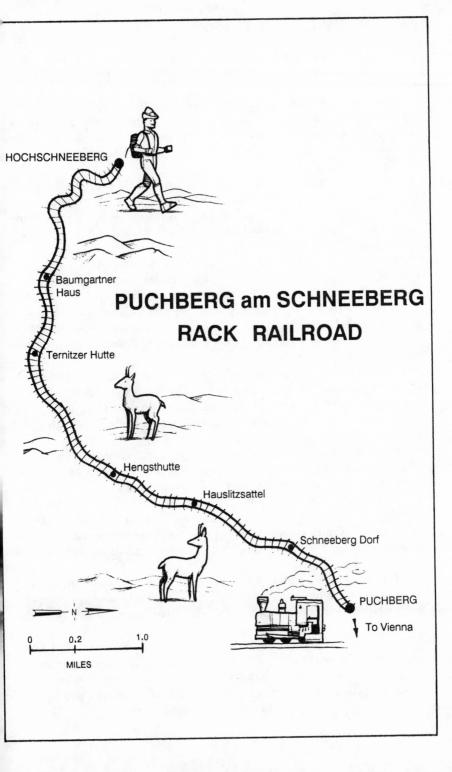

tilts upward through wild ground, the engine seems to leap ahead and virtually races past the perspiring mountaineers struggling up the nearby trails.

To reach Puchberg from Vienna, you use the Sudbahnhof (South train station). Trains to the south—all covered by Eurailpass—run via the city of Wiener Neustadt. Puchberg is a local stop bypassed by express trains, so change in the city of Wiener Neustadt unless you start your trip on a local.

When your OBB train from Vienna reaches Puchberg, you file down the platform a few feet to the carved wooden sign: "Zahnradbahn." The Puchberg terminal of the narrow-gauge Schneeberg (meaning "Snow Mountain") cogwheel railroad lies about fifty miles and 1 1/2 hours southwest of Vienna.

At Puchberg, show your Eurailpass at the counter and take a "Zahlkarte," a number for boarding one of the little wooden cars to the summit of the Schneeberg. Without a Eurailpass buy a "Wanderticket" valid for OBB transportation to Puchberg and the rack railroad's climb to the summit. Attached is a coupon ("Gutschein") for a luncheon meal. Buy these tickets at the "Inland" ticket counters in Vienna's South train station or stops en route.

Try to sit on the left going up. Your car is crammed five abreast with so many passengers the interior seems like Noah's ark. Schneeberg is considered by the Viennese as their home in the mountains. The fascination of your trip is the little, black steam locomotive with tilted fireboxes.

Passengers complain about the hard seats and crowded conditions. They give thanks for small favors: at least the north wind is blowing the steam locomotive's noxious fumes away from them.

Pushing from the rear of your train to prevent possible breakaway, the engines (built by Krauss and Company, Munich and Linz, in 1897) are nose-down into the earth like a Viennese professor peering over his spectacles. They look like their front axles have collapsed and they are grubbing for worms.

While your train scales the steep mountainsides, this odd-looking design keeps the boiler tubes horizontal to maintain heat transfer and holds the firebox level to prevent firebrands from tumbling onto the footplate.

After about twenty-five minutes you reach Hauslitzsattel (2,717 feet); your engine brakes. You see blue cornflowers, red poppies, and a dozen delicate Alpine blooms—and, for the first time, smell forest odors. This is the first of a vast system of mountain huts constructed throughout the Austrian Alps for the benefit of mountaineers.

Twelve minutes later you are high enough to see the majesty of the green valley floor below when you reach Hengsthutte, surrounded by pines. Hikers are stepping downhill with bouquets of wild flowers, sweaters tied around their waists.

You make an unscheduled stop at Ternitzer Hutte. It is considerably cooler here. Your angle of ascent is so steep, and because you perceive the interior of the carriage as being horizontal, the fir trees outside appear to be growing diagonally out of the mountainside. No one takes the stop seriously. Passengers disembark but watch their seats so as not to lose them. They are restless and wonder why the train stopped.

This is an escapist trip. Few carry a camera to burden them. They are ready for the freedom of the hiking trails above.

A ten-minute halt is scheduled at Baumgartner's new station house (4,582 feet). Your locomotive is recoaled while you go inside for refreshment or a snack. Try the prune bread loaf for a pleasant treat.

Now comes your real climb! For a short while, at least, you drive uphill on the cog-tracks through forests, wild valleys, mountain huts, and brooks gurgling down the mountainside. Then you make another unexplained stop. "Wieder kaputt!" ("Broken again!") maintains a stout Bavarian visitor wearing Lederhosen.

Suddenly, the person in front of you sees wild chamois ("Gemse") near your train. As one, fifty passengers stand, point to these small antelope, and shout, "Gemse!" The Gemse are near the first patches of snow and fleeing uphill.

Now you enter a tunnel. Passengers sitting next to the windows hurry to shut them tightly to prevent steam locomotive fumes and soot from flooding the carriage. Smoke billows between carriages.

When you exit the tunnel, condensate has covered the train windows. Passengers lower them immediately.

Shortly you enter a second tunnel. People close the windows once again, but the train stops and sits and they reopen them. "Wieder kaputt!" shouts the Bavarian.

Finally underway, the train's lights come on in the tunnel. Emerging, you are above the timberline. You see swathes of tightly bunched, gold and blue wild flowers blooming through the snow. A pinelike shrub grows in patches. To your right is the green-copper-topped stone chapel, the Elizabeth Kirche. Down the rail line to your left is the Berghaus Hochschneeberg (5,889 feet)—but eager hikers are already well on the winding way up the path in the opposite direction. The summit is Enzian paradise. This tiny, much-admired, blue flower (the gentian) is used for Alpine schnapps. Go immediately into the station house to select your "Zahlkarte" for your choice of return times.

You can cash in the "Wanderticket" coupon for a meal at the Berghaus Hochschneeberg, where they also serve a "Kaisermenu" duplicating that of the the Kaiser when he visited in 1901—or use your coupon at other locations. The mountain hotel contains a sauna and solarium.

In addition to experiencing the novel train, this excursion gives you a choice opportunity to hike high in the northern limestone spur of the Austrian Alps. The Schneeberg retains a covering of snow throughout the summer.

Trails take you around the Waxriegel peak (6,193 feet) to the Dambockhaus, where serious hikers buy inexpensive meals and sleeping accommodations.

Top off your excursion by walking (2 1/2 hours round trip) up to the Kaiserstein peak (6,762 feet) for the Alpine panorama north as far as the Vienna Woods. Or climb to the Klosterwappen summit (6,808 feet) for the view south across the ravine called "Hell's Valley" (Hollental) to the Rex Plateau, the geologic twin of the Schneeberg.

Your ride down is rocking, swaying, and squeaking like a rusty spring. It takes less time going down, about an hour, but it is more subdued because passengers are tired.

Across the street from the Puchberg train station, an idyllic lakefront promenade is perfect for picnicking. The Puchberg station has a buffet serving meals.

---

## Summer Connections
## to the Schneeberg Rack Railroad

|  |  | a |  |  | e |  |  |
| --- | --- | --- | --- | --- | --- | --- | --- |
| VIENNA (Sudbahnhof) | dep. | 0650 | 0705 | 0920 | 1000 | 1305 | 1400 |
| Wien Meidling | dep. | 0655 | 0710 | 0925 | .... | 1310 | .... |
| Modling | dep. | 0704 | 0718 | 0940 | .... | 1324 | .... |
| Baden | dep. | 0712 | 0727 | 0953 | .... | 1338 | 1417 |
| Wiener Neustadt | arr. | 0724 | 0740 | 1021 | 1029* | 1404 | 1429* |
| Wiener Neustadt | dep. | 0730 | 0752 | 1034 | 1034 | 1434 | 1434 |
| PUCHBERG AM SCHNEEBERG | arr. | 0810 | 0846 | 1130 | 1130 | 1525 | 1525 |
| PUCHBERG AM SCHNEEBERG | dep. | 0830 | 0900 | 1140 | 1140 | 1545 | 1545 |

## Summer Connections
## from the Schneeberg Rack Railroad

|  |  | b | c | d |  | a |  |
|---|---|---|---|---|---|---|---|
| HOCHSCHNEEBERG |  | (departures as required) |  |  |  |  |  |
| Puchberg am Schneeberg | dep. | 1617 | 1714 | 1804 | .... | 1815 | 1916 |
| Wiener Neustadt | arr. | 1711 | 1804 | 1854* | .... | 1854 | 2002* |
| Wiener Neustadt | dep. | 1720 | 1811 | 1908 | 1928 | 1903 | 2010 |
| Baden | arr. | 1735 | 1826 | 1925 | .... | 1916 | 2023 |
| Modling | arr. | .... | 1834 | 1933 | .... | 1923 | 2030 |
| Wien Meidling | arr. | 1754 | 1847 | 1943 | 1954 | 1931 | 2039 |
| VIENNA (Sudbahnhof) | arr. | 1800 | 1854 | 1949 | 2000 | 1938 | 2045 |

a "Schneeberg" E train (Saturdays and Sundays only).
b Mondays through Saturdays only.
c Sundays only.
d Mondays through Fridays only.
e "Fischer von Erlach" Ex train.
*Change trains at Wiener Neustadt.

# Italy
# and Greece

## Vital Tips for the Trains
## of Italy and Greece

Italy is a flashy and artistic country. Expect no less of the showpiece Italian State Railroads, "Ferrovie dello Stado" (FS). FS's 10,000-mile network is the work of a maestro.

Greece is a country of great history. It's curious how trains mirror the nature of the countries. Don't expect the trains of "Organismos Siderodromon Ellados (OSE)," the Greek Railroads Organization, to provide you with great comfort, speed, or convenience. The best travel experience in Greece is on the Aegean ferries.

The trains of Italy are as long as a Roman's nose, and just as full of character. You ride top-notch long-distance trains from the Italian Alps to Palermo on the tip of Sicily.

FS's EuroCity trains are orange-livery, identical to the trains in Austria. FS's InterCity trains on the Naples-Rome-Florence-Milan/Venice routes use 1985 and 1986 maroon-and-gray carriages and the same deluxe gray-and-white, red-striped 1973 and 1974 FS coaches that comprised former Trans Europ Express trains. They retain their superior ambience and convenience with features such as coat-hanging closets. The trains carry white-linen restaurant cars or "Self Service" cafeteria cars staffed by Wagons-Lits.

The food selection and cashier sections of the FS's "Self Service" cafeteria cars are conventional, but the facilities for eating your meal are unusual. Your dining area consists of orange formica saw-tooth spaces with swivel stools placed along the windows and separated with

233

orange dividers. Diners on one side of the train look forward; the other half looks backwards. Perhaps this is to minimize dawdling.

You ride FS's IC trains from Rome to Bari and Reggio di Calabria in green-and-white railcars of several designs. The prestigious IC Peloritano between Rome and Palermo consists of 1988 second-class gray-and-white, blue-striped carriages and the orange-livery first-class cars.

You must make seat reservations on most of FS's IC trains. If you board and find an unreserved seat, the conductor will charge you for the seat, plus a penalty!

The rest of FS's fleet takes you to villages and the seaside in an eclectic set of equipment. You ride Rapidos (R), Espressos (Expr), Direttos (Dir), or Trenos Locale (Locale), in decreasing order of desirability.

Many adventurers—especially Europeans leaving their homes—travel to Italy on overnight trains. FS's maroon-and-gray "cuccette" cars are madness-on-wheels because of overcrowding until they settle down; too many travelers arrive without reservations and have to be put off. You must have couchette reservations or take your chances.

FS's trains are clean inside and out. Train and window washing is performed in Rome Termini and Florence S.M.N. (Santa Maria Novella) stations by motorized machines that are steered past the trains.

Major FS stations have train information computer consoles to answer your punched-in questions in English—that is, if kids stop playing with them and you are going to an FS destination in Italy.

At most stops in Italy, trackside vendors with fully loaded pushcarts are eager to sell you cold drinks, sandwiches, and candy. Listen for their persistently tinkling bells. Just open your window and make your orders from the train.

## Crossing between Italy and Greece

Greece is a magnet to adventurers because of the free Eurailpass ferry transportation and the carefree stopover on Corfu's beaches.

Eurailpass holders reach Greece by the joint ferry service of the Greek Hellenic Mediterranean Lines and the Italian Adriatica Lines. Remember those names. Brindisi is alive with frauds advertising Eurailpass crossings on other lines. These tickets are not valid.

Your European acquaintances traveling on European rail passes take the train through Yugoslavia, where their passes are valid, and not on the ferries, where they are not. You can all rendezvous on the Aegean.

Hellenic Mediterranean Lines and Adriatica Lines alternate crossings. Adventurers disagree which line is more acceptable. They usually say the line they didn't take is better.

Hellenic Mediterranean uses the m.v. *Lydia* (1,215 passengers, 105 cars) and the m.v. *Corinthia* (1,100 passengers, 300 cars). Adriatica uses the m.v. *Espresso Grecia* (835 passengers, 210 cars) and the m.v. *Appia* (1,130 passengers, 150 cars).

There are two sailings a day from Brindisi to Patras and vice-versa. One stops in Corfu en route and one takes you without stop. A third sailing takes you between Brindisi and Corfu and a second Ionian island, Igoumenitsa, but doesn't continue to Patras.

When you plan to visit Corfu, board either the 2 P.M. or 10:30 P.M. sailing from Brindisi. If you want to sail without stopping over, board the 8 P.M. departure. From Patras, sail at 6 P.M. for Brindisi, 10 P.M. via Corfu.

At Patras's landing you board either a train or bus. Buses park near the ship's landing. Trains are a short walk away. Buses are not covered by Eurailpasses; trains are.

When you talk with others about this crossing, you hear horror stories. It is sensible to approach this journey with careful planning.

• Allow extra time for possible train delays en route to Brindisi. Trains run to Brindisi from Rome's Termini station or down Italy's Adriatic coast from Bologna. Station timetables indicate these trains are for "Lecce." Brindisi's Centrale station is the stop before Lecce.

Your best train for the ships is the "Parthenon" train, which carries first- and second-class carriages and second-class couchettes between Paris and Brindisi's Marittima station. It departs Paris's Lyon station at 8:06 P.M. and calls at Lausanne and Milan's Lambrate station during the night. You make connections in Bologna at 7:24 A.M. or Rimini at 8:42 A.M., arriving at 5:55 P.M. at Marittima station next to the pier, but bring food or purchase snacks from trainside vendors along the way.

Your return Parthenon leaves Brindisi's Marittima station at 12:10 P.M., arriving in Paris at 10:02 A.M. the next day.

• Dress coolly. It is sometimes stiflingly hot waiting for the ferry.

• Take your own food aboard the ships. Food served on the ships is unreliable.

• Take a cabin for the crossing. Although it is not covered by Eurailpass, you will avoid inconveniences. Make your arrangements when you board.

• Allow extra days. When you lay out your overall itinerary, allow several days for unexpected developments.

• Reserve ahead your room in Athens. Especially when you arrive late, the unfamiliar alphabet and the remote Athens train station can cause difficulties for the unprepared.

• Stop over in Corfu. Anyone who has read about Corfu or is interested in casual beach life will not miss this opportunity.

• Allow extra time in Brindisi before boarding. You pass through customs, passport, port tax payments, ticketing, and boarding bureaucracies. (The pier is about a half-hour's walk down the main steet from Brindisi's Centrale station.)

## Trains of Greece

When you reach Greece, you travel on two train networks. The meter-gauge line circling the Peloponnese Peninsula takes you between Patras and Athens. The northern, standard-gauge network connects Athens to Salonika (Thessaloniki) and the trains of the Balkans and central Europe.

Because of OSE's two gauges, Athens—which is the hub of both networks—has two major train stations in the city's northwest section connected by an overhead footbridge. There are no through trains. When you take the train from Patras, you arrive in the Peloponnese station. When you arrive via the Balkans or from Salonika, you arrive in Larissa station.

Tourist information is unavailable in either train station. The tourist information office at the National Bank of Greece building on Constitution Square has a great supply of useful information for you.

Train reservations on the international trains to the north are required. Make these at the OSE offices at 1-3 Karolou Street or 6 Sina Street.

The port of Athens is Piraeus, just five miles south. This is your gateway for the ferries to Greece's Aegean islands. Take the subway from Athens' Omonia Square.

## Italian Private Railroads

In addition to FS, there are numerous private railroads in Italy, either providing commuter service or serving rural districts and reaching villages not connected to FS. None honor Eurailpasses. Buy not the official FS timetable when you arrive, but the "Orario Generale," listing both FS and private lines, at the bookstores in the stations.

## Sardinian Connections

Your fastest crossing from Rome to Sardinia is aboard FS's connecting trains to Civitavecchia for FS's car ferry to Golfo Aranci, where connecting trains take you to Olbia and Sassari. Tirrenia Lines also serves this sea route.

Tirrenia Lines has extensive steamship service to Sardinia from the Italian mainland and Sicily. You sail from Genoa to Olbia/Arbatax or

Porto Torres, from Leghorn (Livorno) to Porto Torres, or from Palermo to Cagliari. Porto Torres, north of Alghero, is in turn connected to Alghero by diesel railcar service through Sassari.

## Using Eurailpass Bonuses

Some of the most-used Eurailpass bonuses are the free ferry crossings on the ships of the Adriatica and Hellenic Mediterranean Lines. From June 10 to September 30, inclusive, you must pay an $8 high-season surcharge. Eurailpass recommends advance reservations ($2) during July and August. You must pay port taxes in local currencies. Sleeping accommodations such as cabins or airline-type seats cost extra. Before boarding, you must check in at the shipping line's office at the pier. If you wish to stop over in Corfu or Igoumenitsa, you must so state when you receive your steamer ticket. When you ticket only to Corfu, you cannot change your mind and continue to Patras. Clearly, there is much bureaucracy involved.

Eurailpass holders do not pay FS fast-train surcharges but must pay for seat reservations where required on FS's InterCity trains. They also must pay meal surcharges on the Pendolino.

The concept of unlimited travel during a limited time frame has expanded to include discounted (30 percent) steamer travel aboard the Adriatica Line from Venice to Piraeus in Greece, Candia (Heraklion) on Crete and Alexandria in Egypt, on the m.s. *Espresso Egitto*. The same 30 percent discount applies to your travel between Italy and the island of Malta and to your traveling by Europabus in Italy.

## Italian Unlimited Rail Pass

The Italian Railroads' "BTLC" Italian Tourist Ticket is valid for unlimited travel on FS's 10,000-mile network, including the train ferries between Reggio di Calabria and Messina.

It is more comfortable traveling first class in Italy. Second-class trains are sometimes crowded and the Italian habit of lining the corridors can be bothersome. First-class passengers ride FS's 1988 high-speed train between Milan and Rome and first-class-only Rapidos.

The BTLC Tourist Ticket lets you make seat reservations free on Pendolino and InterCity trains where necessary, but you must pay the meal surcharge on the Pendolino trains.

Like the Eurailpass, the Adriatica Line allows BTLC holders a 30 percent discount on its fares between Venice and Piraeus or Alexandria. You are permitted to make such trips before validating your BTLC and within two months after it expires.

## Greek Tourist Card

A Greek "Carte de Tourisme" allows you unlimited second-class travel for ten, twenty, or thirty days on the trains and buses of the Greek Railroads. Its cost depends on the number of people traveling together, up to five, with decreasing per-person cost with each additional adventurer.

Buy them at the main train stations in Greece or at the international travel offices of other European railroad administrations, such as at the London Victoria office in Great Britain.

Adventuring in Italy takes you aboard the sleek Italian speedster, the Pendolino, between Rome and Milan, and through Sardinian highlands and beside seashores on private trains. Three great train stations serve as your bases.

## FS's Indulgent Pendolino
## The Lamborghini of the Rails

Your Pendolino from Rome skirts Florence, then negotiates the main ranges of the Apennines over a direttissima track through tunnels one after another built in the 1920s. After you whiz through busy Bologna station, you pick up speed and streak across the flat Po Valley to Milan.

FS's maroon-and-red high-speed train with the FIAT nameplate could be compared to the Concorde airplane. It is long, lean, and all first class. With a taste of speed, service, and extravagance, FS's posh 1988 Pendolino takes you between Rome and Milan in less time than it takes to visit the Vatican Museum.

FS began Pendolino service in May 1988, giving you more comfort than flying and more speed than a red Lamborghini racing down the Autostrada. You travel between Italy's two largest cities (393 miles) in less than four hours at an average speed of nearly 100 mph. This doesn't compete with the speed of French TGVs, but it is a whirlwind nevertheless.

Your bullet-nosed, aerodynamic train is officially designated Etr 450, for "Elettotreno," or electric train. FS calls it Pendolino (little pendulum) because its body tilts gently whenever you round a curve, like Spain's Talgo Pendular trains, thus minimizing the forces of gravity. It is designed for a top speed of 150 mph and service at 125 mph.

FS and Fiat previewed their Etr 401 version to GermanRail in July 1987, through the Moselle Valley and along the heavily curved InterCity line north of Munich. In April 1988, the German Minister of Transportation was so impressed with his test drive that GermanRail placed an

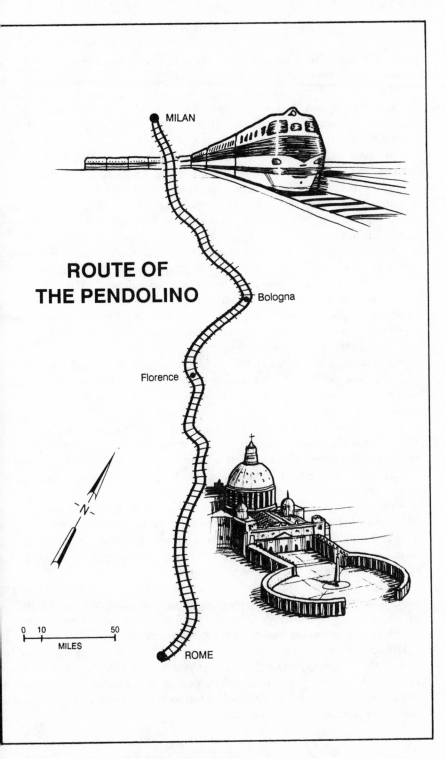

ROUTE OF
THE PENDOLINO

MILAN

Bologna

Florence

ROME

0   10                    50
      MILES

N

order for Pendolinos for use by GermanRail, with first delivery to be in 1990.

The secret for Pendolino's success in Italy is FS's modern roadbed between Milan and Rome. The new double-tracked direttissima (ultra-straight) line was begun in the 1970s, but various delays slowed its completion.

On the tracks cutting an almost straight line across Latium, Umbria, and Tuscany between Rome and Florence, FS bored new tunnels, including the 8.7-mile Adriana tunnel, eliminated all road-level cross-ings, and connected the older, more wandering route to the new line at various points. In effect, FS created a four-track system between Rome and Florence.

In roped-off check-in and departure areas at the heads of platform 20 in Milan Centrale and platform 1 at Rome Termini, blue-uniformed stewardesses and stewards hand you your computer-printed boarding pass and seat number. On board, other stewardesses offer you free Italian newspapers and bring trays to your seat with the airline-type continental breakfasts or dinners. These meals cause you to pay the required hefty surcharge for your trip.

The comfortable, fresh-smelling, blue-and-gray plush seats are two-opposite-one, with fold-down tables in the back. Your route is fast, but you see less than on slower trains because of the extensive tunneling along your route.

The windows are streamlined, longer, but not nearly so high as on older trains. You pass through fearless gangways between carriages so you don't feel terrified crossing from car to car while purring along up to 125 mph. Leave your luggage in the luggage racks near the door when you enter.

Sleek power cars front and back pull this six-car unit. It is designed like the French TGV (although the concept was not original with them). The two end cars seat thirty-eight and contain the driver's cabin. The four cars in the middle accommodate forty-six and provide the luggage space. One of these cars is reserved for smokers.

Pay for your reservations at special windows at the stations. If you don't have any rail pass, a one-way trip in the morning costs about $85, in the evening about $93. The difference reflects the meal served. Children under twelve pay $67, the basic transportation charge.

Holders of Italian rail passes pay only the meal supplement (about $18 in the morning, about $26 in the evening) to ride the Pendolino. Eurailpass holders pay this supplement and an additional $2 for the required seat reservation. Eurail Youthpass holders must also pay the difference to upgrade to first class.

Pendolinos take four hours between Rome and Milan and do not stop anywhere else. Hourly InterCity trains, stopping in Florence, take five hours and ten minutes. Slower trains take you six to seven hours.

Compare this to flying. You would spend an hour and five minutes in the air, but by the time you add an hour (more from Rome, less from Milan) at each end to get to and from the airports and then allow time to check in, the time you spend traveling from city center to city center is about the same. Yet you spend it more restfully on the Pendolino and arrive more relaxed and better fed. And, even including the extraordinary surcharge for the meals on the Pendolino, it costs about three-fourths of the airfare. Perhaps you would rather drive the Lamborghini, but you will arrive earlier with the Pendolino at a fraction of the cost.

## InterCity Service from Rome to Milan

| | | ROME (Termini) dep. | FLORENCE (S.M.N.) arr. | dep. | BOLOGNA arr. | dep. | MILAN (Centrale) arr. |
|---|---|---|---|---|---|---|---|
| IC506 | PENDOLINO | 0700 | .... | .... | .... | .... | 1008 |
| IC522 | Colosseum | 0800 | 1010 | 1019 | 1122 | 1126 | 1310 |
| IC524 | Croce | 0902* | 1110 | 1119 | 1220 | 1226 | 1410 |
| IC526 | Ambrosiano | 1000 | 1211 | 1220 | 1322 | 1326 | 1530 |
| IC528 | Naviglio | 1100 | 1310 | 1319 | 1422 | 1426 | 1610 |
| IC530 | Colleoni | .... | .... | 1435 | 1538 | 1542 | 1726 |
| IC532 | Brera | 1300 | 1510 | 1519 | 1622 | 1626 | 1810 |
| IC534 | Rugantino | 1400 | 1610 | 1619 | 1722 | 1726 | 1910 |
| IC536 | Vesuvio | 1502* | 1710 | 1719 | 1822 | 1826 | 2010 |
| IC538 | Pantheon | 1600 | 1810 | 1819 | 1922 | 1926 | 2110 |
| IC540 | Tevere | 1700 | 1910 | 1919 | 2022 | 2026 | 2210 |
| IC542 | Marconi | 1750 | 2000 | 2009 | 2115 | 2119 | .... |
| IC510 | PENDOLINO | 1900 | .... | .... | .... | .... | 2258 |
| IC544 | | 2000 | 2213 | 2222 | 2325 | .... | .... |

*Departs from Rome's Tiburtina station, having originated in Naples' Centrale station.

## InterCity Service from Milan to Rome

| | | MILAN (Centrale) dep. | BOLOGNA arr. | dep. | FLORENCE (S.M.N.) arr. | dep. | ROME (Termini) arr. |
|---|---|---|---|---|---|---|---|
| IC517 | | .... | .... | 0542 | 0646 | 0655 | 0907 |
| IC507 | PENDOLINO | 0655 | .... | .... | .... | .... | 1053 |
| IC519 | Marconi | .... | 0738 | 0742 | 0847 | 0856 | 1115 |
| IC523 | Croce | 0755 | 0938 | 0942 | 1046 | 1055 | 1312* |
| IC525 | Pantheon | 0855 | 1038 | 1042 | 1146 | 1155 | 1405 |
| IC527 | Naviglio | 0955 | 1138 | 1142 | 1246 | 1255 | 1505 |
| IC529 | Rugantino | 1032 | 1238 | 1242 | 1346 | 1355 | 1605 |
| IC533 | Brera | 1255 | 1438 | 1442 | 1546 | 1555 | 1805 |
| IC535 | Colosseum | 1355 | 1538 | 1542 | 1646 | 1655 | 1905 |
| IC537 | Vesuvio | 1455 | 1638 | 1642 | 1746 | 1755 | 2004* |
| IC539 | Tevere | 1555 | 1738 | 1742 | 1846 | 1855 | 2105 |
| IC541 | Ambrosiano | 1655 | 1838 | 1842 | 1946 | 1955 | 2205 |
| IC543 | Colleoni | 1755 | 1938 | 1942 | 2046 | .... | .... |
| IC511 | PENDOLINO | 1900 | .... | .... | .... | .... | 2258 |
| IC545 | Meneghino | 1955 | 2138 | 2142 | 2248 | .... | .... |

*Arrives at Rome's Tiburtina station, continuing to Naples' Centrale station.

# Grand Train Stations
# Islands of Order

Italian train stations are islands of order in seas of confusion. Adventuring in Italy takes you through certainly three of Europe's best stations. Use them as your centrally located bases in Milan, Rome, and Florence.

## Milano Centrale

This is the grand station of Europe, a cyclopean complex opened in 1931. The station itself is something of a tourist sight. Its grandiose, eclectic syle has been characterized as "Assyrian-Babylonian," or "Mussolini Modern." Its second-class waiting room is enormous, and its staircases—mercifully equipped with escalators—sweeping.

When you enter the upper hall you see a feature so gracious it is unique. A bubbling water fountain—its sounds fighting the cacophony of the trains—shoots above a polished rose-colored marble floor surrounded by wire-web jump seats and warm pastel mosaics.

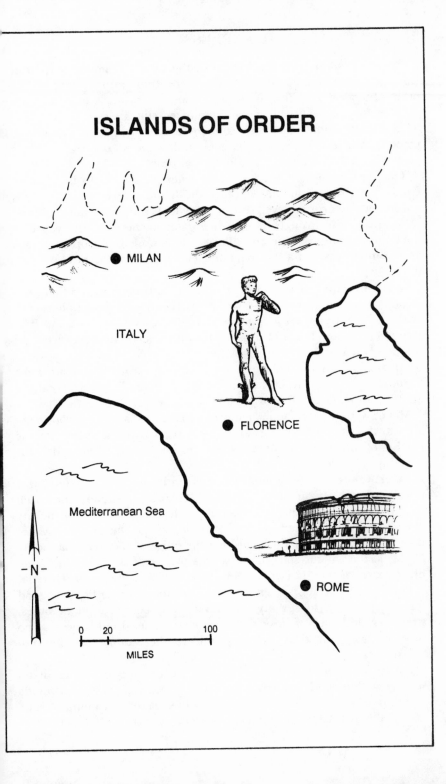

The long hall itself is highlighted by the creatively positioned "Gran Bar" at one end and "Informazioni" (for train information) at the other. Luggage checking is deviously located down a hall near the information office. Look for the illuminated suitcase sign.

FS's information office also contains a money change counter. A second bank is located on the long wall next to the sign in four languages indicating the city information office.

The "Self Service" cafeteria is located next to the "Gran Bar," down from a place for freshening up called the "Hour Hotel." A post office is outside on the ground level, conveniently tucked into the same edifice.

Once you are through the guarded gates to the platform, you find the largest "Composizione Treni Principali" console in Europe. It wraps around three walls of a stairwell and elevator shaft at the head of track 9.

Near the center of the long wall are the entrances to the first- and second-class waiting rooms. A guard restricts entrance to the upholstered chairs of the first-class lounge, so it is safe as well as pleasant. The second-class room is grand. It is clean with banks of antique, varnished wooden benches. You hear echos from its marble walls.

Milan's stations include Porta Garibaldi for local trains from Lake Como, Lambrate for trains not intended to serve Milan, Nord (near the Sforza Castle), Greco P., Porta Vittoria, and Porta Romana.

Milan's subway, Metropolitana, is more than just a way for you to get around the city with comfort and speed. It gives you a feeling for the rhythm of Milan and shows you a good example of the Italian flair for contemporary design.

Enter the subway stations at signs with the white letters *MM* (Metropolitana Milanese) in a red field. Milan's two subway lines from the outlying areas in the western and northeastern sections of the city intersect near the Sforza Castle and Piazzale Loreto. Obtain a free system map and helpful guide (in English) at the office of the transit authority (ATM) in the Duomo station, the Provincial Tourist Authority in Cathedral Square, or the Municipal Information Office in the nearby Galleria.

Public transportation is efficient and cheap. A single ticket is good for a trip of up to seventy minutes on any combination of buses, streetcars, and subway (provided the subway is used only once), so be sure to save your ticket when you leave the subway for the free transfers.

Public transportation tickets are sold at vending machines in all subway stations and at many streetcar stops, as well as at newsstands and tobacco stores. Validate them by machine at the beginning of your trip. A day ticket for an unlimited number of trips is a bargain.

Reaching Milan's Centrale station from Milan's Porta Garibaldi station is quite simple. Follow the signs to the subway, buy your subway ticket, and take line 2 (direction: "Gorgonzola") two stops to "Centrale F. S."

## Rome Termini

Rome has five train stations. When you ride a through train scheduled to connect two other cities, you stop at Rome's Tiburtina or Ostiense station in Rome's outskirts. Tuscolana and Trastevere serve trains in the direction of Pisa. But your prime destination is Rome's Termini, in the throbbing heart of the Eternal City.

Rome's Termini station is big, modern, and badly signed. You must search for features. It consists of three areas: the platform area where you catch your train, the large inner hall with tables set out for diners, and the outer hall which exits on the taxi stand in front of the station. You must have a train ticket or rail pass to enter the platform area, so the platform area is where the manager has located many valuable functions.

On both sides are luggage-checking counters. There are no lockers. Toilet facilities are by track 1, and in the "Hour Hotel." There are no luggage carts in Rome Termini, but you can find porters easily.

Waiting rooms are comfortable, more so in first class than second, but both have television monitors displaying train arrival and departure times.

The only "Composizione Treni" in Rome Termini is for night trains, at the heads of platforms. Termini is an end station and trains are waiting for you when you arrive to board.

The Provincial Tourist Authority personnel can be found at a small window facing the platform area opposite track 4. They answer questions, make bookings without charge, and give you free maps, but automation has come to the hotel reservations services in Rome.

An aluminum display case in the outer hall lists hotels in categories from one to five stars. Beside the hotel names you see the map coordinates for the adjacent city map, their addresses, telephone numbers, and red/green lights to indicate their availability. Use one of the nearby telephones to determine rates and make a booking when acceptable.

The outer hall also has ticket windows and windows 34-43 for seat and couchette reservations ("Prenotazioni VL Posti e Cuccette").

FS's train information office (with signs above the windows indicating languages spoken) is located in the outer lobby, next to FS's change bank. At the other end of the hall you use the Banco di Roma's money change office or, in the inner hall, change your money at the Banca Nazionale della Comunicazioni.

In the inner lobby you can enjoy coffee, croissants, etc., at the pleasant tables set out, or go inside (pay the cashier before ordering) for quicker service.

Adjacent, in a cafeteria ("Self Service"), you will find a complete selection of excellent food. It is enough to know that more than 95 percent of the customers speak Italian.

Rome Termini has three levels. You enter both Metro lines, Linea *A* and Linea *B*, below the inner hall on the main level. (Look for the white *M* on the red field.) The middle level is a neglected floor containing an "Hour Hotel" for freshening up and an office for long-distance and international telephoning.

The bottom level, below the "Hour Hotel," is the crossing of Rome's two subway lines. Line *A*'s orange cars take you between Anagnina station and Ottaviano station near the Vatican City with stops at Roma Nord train station, Spagna (the Spanish Steps, for the American Express office), Vittorio E, and Barberini. Line *B*'s cars run south to the EUR Center, where some hotels are located.

Deposit the correct change in the ticket-vending machines on the walls of the entrance hall or buy Metro tickets individually or in booklets of ten for a 14 percent discount at the transit authority's office. The office is located on the bottom level, between the entrances to the *A* and *B* lines.

## Florence S.M.N.

Florence's Santa Maria Novella station is similar to Rome's Termini. Probably the same architectural firm was employed. It is one of the most pleasing Italian train stations because of its long architectural lines and modern layout, and is airy with its inner and outer halls. Because there is no Metro to complicate getting around, it is easy to find your way.

When you leave the tracks the inner hall has first- and second-class waiting rooms, "Ufficio Turismo" tourist information where patient agents make your hotel reservations at the head of tracks 9 and 10, "Ufficio Informazioni" train information, and a "Composizione Treni Principali" board.

In the outer hall you find a change bank, FS change, and domestic ticketing. In a connecting hall you find counters for reservations ("Prenotazioni") and international ticketing ("Biglietti Internazionali").

The "Self Service" restaurant here is the equal of those in other grand Italian stations. It is managed well and offers excellent selections.

You will find the luggage carts convenient at Florence S.M.N. Train calls are made in Italian and English.

Florence S.M.N. is conveniently located near the center of Florence. Hotels surround it, and more hotels are located in the direction of the Arno River, the Duomo, and the Piazza della Signoria, but the city brims with adventurers during the summer so it is best to rely on arrangements by the Tourist Office.

Other train stations in Florence include Castello, Rifredi, Fiesole Caldine, and Campo di Marte, but S.M.N. is all you need.

## Compelling Sardinia
## Through the Highlands and
## beside the Sea

Rome designed fast mainline trains to scamper through Sardinia's easy central valley. They skirt the special, rough terrains and scenic, wild seashores molded by seasonal mistral winds. The stop-and-go FCS local railroad takes you to out-of-the-way, wonderful corners and backwoods.

The FCS (Ferrovie Complementari della Sardegna) is a rough railroad dating from when it was essential to bind together rural towns and shepherds' villages. It is crude. It is remote. It has next to no amenities, one coach per train, and locomotives covered with grime. Inside, passenger space is clean and comfortable.

You may miss convenience and luxury, but there is no finer way for you to discover the gracious, proud feel of Sardinia. After all, you visit Sardinia for the atmosphere, not the amenities.

Riding the narrow-gauge train through remote highlands from Mandas to Arbatax catches the honest spirit of autonomous, feudal Sardinia. This fifty-six-mile trip is a microcosm of Sardinian life and scenery.

Sardinia is Italian now. Sardinians watch mainland Italian television channels and ride mainland Italian railroads, but in their hearts, they know mainland Italians are tourists from abroad.

Neither Romans nor Phoenicians, Greeks nor Arabs ever subdued Sardinia, the second-largest island in the Mediterranean after Sicily.

The uncompromised integrity of the Sardinian way of life makes travel through the island personal and compelling. Getting around Sardinia is relatively easy. You use good, cheap trains and buses.

The Mandas-Gairo-Lanusei-Arbatax morning train twists through constantly rugged, varied, lonely, and wild country. This is the kind of countryside to harbor notorious sheep-nappers. Lightninglike zigzags

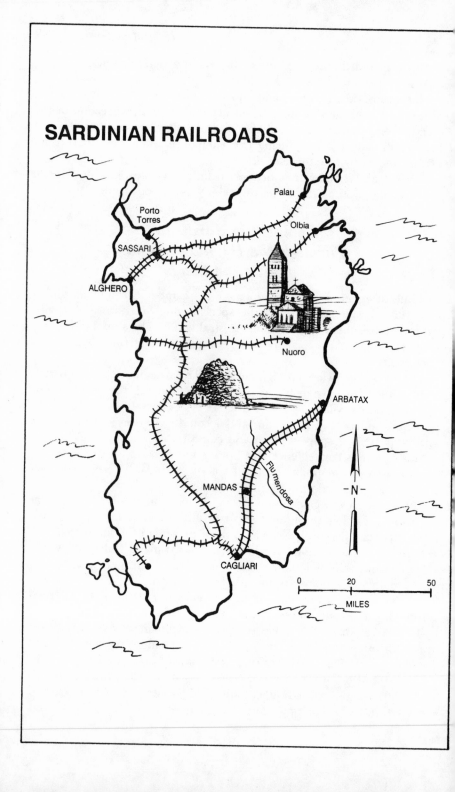

# SARDINIAN RAILROADS

Porto
Torres

Palau

Olbia

SASSARI

ALGHERO

Nuoro

ARBATAX

Flumendosa

MANDAS

- N -

CAGLIARI

0       20              50
        MILES

on your road map give clear warning of the extent of your U-turn ascents and steep descents. You pass sweeping, high-altitude panoramas and surprising stone outcroppings.

A second-class ticket costs you very little. No, Eurailpasses are not accepted on the FCS.

For the price, it is surprising that the single passenger car departs from Mandas on time. The diesel locomotive pulling it looks as dated as war-surplus equipment—covered with such an accumulation of dust and railroad grease that it looks like it just returned from battle.

Inside, the passenger coach is swept and dusted. The heating works but you lower the glass to keep close to the rugged scenery to come. Well-padded seats are small, soft, and comfortable, but your carriage is almost empty. The line suffers from such low ridership (because it is so remote) that it loses money and is in constant danger of being replaced by buses.

The first stop on your climb, Villanovatulo, is like an Alpine village, high and remote. Villanovatulo's one-room station house lies below the village at the foot of an unpaved path. The station is complete with a flea-chewing sheep dog and peasants wearing berets.

The air in Sardinia's highlands is light and sweet and the sun is bright. Your mountain site affords wide views, particularly of green Lake Flumendosa, the long, serene, artificial lake created for hydro-electric power. (Sardinia has no natural lakes.)

Soon you hear the engineer screech his whistle and see the train lights come on. You enter the first of frequent black tunnels. In the rear of your carriage, the conductor has placed his cap with gold braid beside him and relaxes on a seat next to an electric switch panel. He reads a newspaper—which is difficult because of the bouncing. Swaying and perusing his jiggling newspaper, he pushes a toggle switch on and off without glancing up from the bouncing headlines. The driver cues him with the screeches. Flip! Lights go on with the alarm. Flip! Lights go off exiting the tunnel. All the time reading the paper.

Silvery-green olive trees on the slopes vary with cork oak trees, almond trees, and small hillside vineyards. The gnarled cactuses growing as hedgerows are sheared to nourish pigs. Sardinia is greener and cooler, especially in the mountains, than one expects.

Soon you reach the pink stucco station house of Esterzili, where idlers trade humor and gossip with a conductor and stationmaster. A pretty young woman, probably from the mountains judging from her billowing pink skirt, kisses her husband goodbye.

Your train roams up and down the valleys and through the fields—the surveyors seem to have been freethinkers—averaging about 10 mph. The brown curtains beside the windows oscillate with the swaying of your coach.

After studying the dramatic, jagged rock formations on your left, it is greatly surprising to see cement-block and brick construction on the rough, rocky plateau. This is Sadali, the village of shepherds and agriculture. The slender-footed merino sheep below are white and glistening, not dingy, so that the black sheep playing among the flocks are very black indeed.

Your train is still climbing. You pass into Seui on a cut through the mountainside at the top of the village, for Seui is a settlement draped precariously down the mountain. From above, Seui looks like a maze of red-tile roofs huddled together. Only the bell towers of the white cathedral rise up to the height of your train.

Here you pause for the return train to Mandas to pass. Some of the passengers get off in Seui and board the waiting bus.

As your train approaches the summit above Seui, still running through a trench in the steep mountainside, sharp outcroppings of wind-carved stone rise next to the track. A creek far below churns round huge boulders. The road at the bottom of the valley winds like a thin gray tape with a white line in its center.

You stop for seven minutes at Gairo, a rouge-colored station with bus connections. A group of six grandmothers in brown, rough, woolen shawls and hoods mount the train. They are wearing mountain clothing— as close to costumes as you see on nonfestival days. Their loose, full aprons and skirts trail to the ground. They have wrapped their hoods/ scarfs around their heads so one can only see their wrinkled, weathered, ruddy features and the roots of gray hairs. When they smile they reveal gums only partially toothed.

The red-capped dispatcher waves his baton and several high-school-aged girls come scampering aboard. They wear faddish clothing, the kind worn in classrooms everywhere. They sit across from the veteran women so that the contrast of clothing is vivid evidence of the changes occurring on the island.

Descending, you see more merino sheep mingled with cows clanging cowbells. Closing on Lanusei, you pass a clothesline hung with diverse washing, but your eye is riveted to a blue, boy's-size, "University of Michigan" sweat shirt.

As the tracks begin to parallel the highway, your train passes the road sign: "Lanusei 5 Km." An old woman in charge of the highway right-of-way has halted a string of lined-up Fiats with her red baton.

Scotch broom and gorse turn the hillsides bright yellow on the approach to Lanusei. This is the most thickly wooded part of your adventure. The mountains are newly forested with Canadian pines. You have a long view down on Lanusei, a large village growing larger with busy construction.

Blue buses wait at Lanusei station. You see another postcard view of the prosperous village from the train station. On a good day you see a stretch of sea, seven miles below, at Arbatax on Capo Bellavista, the center of a resort area. Arbatax is the landing for ferries from Genoa, and the end of your fascinating train ride through the Sardinian highlands.

## Beside the Sea

Your maroon-and-gray, narrow-gauge diesel railcar is freshly scrubbed and glistening wet. It is now boarding for its convenient run from Sassari, on the Sardinian mainline in northwest Sardinia, to Alghero, the jewel-box port on the Mediterranean Sea.

It gives the lie to the notion that getting around Sardinia is difficult or dull. Railcars take you from Sassari's busy train station, which is seemingly lost in the center of Sassari's sea of red roofs rolling over graceful hills. But looks are deceiving, for Sassari is a bustling commercial city, the second town in Sardinia, and its train station is crowded.

The faded, Roman gold-colored terminus serves both FS (some visitors come by train the whole length of the island from Sardinia's capital city, Cagliari) and the Strade Ferrate Sarde, which has its headquarters here.

First aboard come businessmen with shiny attache cases, then gossiping nuns in black habits, peasants dressed in their Sunday best, and finally northern European adventurers carrying books of poetry.

Your railcar glides south past surprisingly tall olive trees and careful rows of trellised vineyards. Cliffs of Sardinian tufa limestone look as white as the Cliffs of Dover. Small, spiny artichokes for Sardinian antipasto flourish in the rust-red earth. Merino sheep frolic in the brown fields.

Your trip to Alghero, twenty-two miles, takes you forty-nine minutes at a leisurely pace of 27 mph, including nine stops. Your cost is very little, but not covered by Eurailpass.

At the end of your narrow-gauge railroad, Alghero is the highlight of the northwestern coast of Sardinia. Here you discover a hybrid Catalan/Italian culture and a seaside resort offering inexpensive accommodations, food, and drink.

You ride patiently, enjoying the warmth of the sun. Parochial-school children poke one another and lean out the windows. The northern Europeans put down their poetry and doze off.

Five minutes before arriving in Alghero's center, your railcar halts in S. Agostino station to discharge many of the passengers to the long lineup of waiting regional blue buses. There are two further stops, ending in the center of Alghero.

Alghero lies on a small peninsula surrounded by Aragonese fortifications. Until 1848 the town was locked tightly at night. The former entrance, at the stubby tower of the Porta Terra, is still a good place to begin your walking tour through the narrow streets. The tourist office is nearby, so pick up free color maps for your explorations.

In a sense, Alghero isn't a Sardinian town at all. It started as one, in the early Middle Ages, but Spaniards from Aragon began their Sardinian conquest by annexing Alghero in 1355. The Algherese did not prove to be docile subjects; after two fierce rebellions the Aragonese solved their problem by deporting the entire population to the interior and replacing them with Catalans from the Iberian peninsula.

Everyone enjoys the friendly Catalan atmosphere here—Alghero is now known as "Little Barcelona."

Strolling through the narrow streets of the old town protected by Aragonese fortifications gives you a sense of quiet adventure and colorful leisure. You soon discover the busy quay. Photograph scenes along the dock showing a way of life you don't find at home. Green and blue fishing boats tie up to unload crawling, creeping, and leaping Mediterranean marine-life catches. Fishermen are mending orange-colored nets on the beaches. You admire the raw pink coral destined for the exquisite cameos sold in Rome and try to avoid the leaping lobsters escaping from plastic pails.

An added attraction is Neptune's Grotto, one of Italy's greatest natural wonders, just a boat ride away across the bay to Capo Caccia.

## Sardinian Highlands Service

### Ferrovie Complementari della Sardegna (Cagliari)

| | | | | |
|---|---|---|---|---|
| 0800 | dep. | MANDAS | arr. | 1214 |
| 0832 | dep. | Orroli | dep. | 1143 |
| 0843 | dep. | Nurri | dep. | 1133 |
| 0900 | dep. | Vilanovatulo | dep. | 1115 |
| 0935 | dep. | Esterzili | dep. | 1040 |
| 0943 | dep. | Sadali | dep. | 1032 |
| 1010 | dep. | Seui | dep. | 1009 |
| 1052 | dep. | Ussassai | dep. | 0932 |
| 1058 | arr. | GAIRO | dep. | 0916 |
| 1105 | dep. | GAIRO | dep. | 0911 |
| 1126 | dep. | Villagrande | dep. | 0851 |
| 1134 | dep. | Arzana | dep. | 0843 |
| 1340 | dep. | Lanusei | dep. | 0823 |
| 1349 | dep. | Elinia | dep. | 0810 |
| 1430 | dep. | TORTOLI | dep. | 0725 |
| 1440 | arr. | ARBATAX | dep. | 0715 |

## Railcar Service between Sassari and Alghero

### Strade Ferrate Sarde (Sassari)

| | | | | | | | | | |
|---|---|---|---|---|---|---|---|---|---|
| dep. | SASSARI | 0720 | 0835 | 0950 | 1415 | 1640 | 1823 | 1950 | 2040 |
| dep. | Molata | 0728 | 0843 | 0958 | 1423 | 1648 | 1835 | 1958 | 2048 |
| dep. | S. Giorgio | 0738 | 0853 | 1008 | 1431 | 1658 | 1843 | 2008 | 2056 |
| dep. | Arcone | 0743 | 0858 | 1013 | 1436 | 1703 | 1848 | 2013 | 2101 |
| dep. | Olmedo | 0751 | 0906 | 1021 | 1446 | 1711 | 1856 | 2021 | 2111 |
| dep. | Mamuntanas | 0757 | 0912 | 1027 | 1452 | 1717 | 1902 | 2027 | 2117 |
| dep. | Punta Moro | 0800 | 0915 | 1030 | 1455 | 1720 | 1905 | 2030 | 2120 |
| dep. | S. Agostino | 0804 | 0919 | 1034 | 1459 | 1724 | 1909 | 2034 | 2124 |
| dep. | S. Giovanni | 0807 | 0922 | 1037 | 1502 | 1727 | 1912 | 2037 | 2127 |
| arr. | ALGHERO | 0809 | 0924 | 1039 | 1504 | 1729 | 1914 | 2039 | 2129 |
| | | | | | | | | | |
| dep. | ALGHERO | 0601 | 0820 | 0935 | 1255 | 1625 | 1740 | 1935 | 2051 |
| dep. | S. Giovanni | 0604 | 0823 | 0938 | 1258 | 1628 | 1743 | 1958 | 2054 |
| dep. | S. Agostino | 0607 | 0826 | 0941 | 1301 | 1631 | 1746 | 1941 | 2057 |
| dep. | Punta Moro | 0611 | 0830 | 0945 | 1305 | 1635 | 1750 | 1945 | 2101 |
| dep. | Mamuntanas | 0614 | 0833 | 0948 | 1308 | 1638 | 1753 | 1948 | 2104 |
| dep. | Olmedo | 0620 | 0839 | 0954 | 1314 | 1644 | 1759 | 1954 | 2110 |
| dep. | Arcone | 0627 | 0846 | 1001 | 1321 | 1651 | 1806 | 2001 | 2117 |
| dep. | S. Giorgio | 0633 | 0852 | 1007 | 1327 | 1657 | 1812 | 2007 | 2123 |
| dep. | Molata | 0641 | 0900 | 1015 | 1335 | 1705 | 1820 | 2015 | 2131 |
| arr. | SASSARI | 0648 | 0907 | 1022 | 1342 | 1712 | 1829 | 2022 | 2136 |

# Appendix

*Train and Tourist Offices*

Offices marked "EP" sell Eurailpasses;
those marked "BR" sell BritRail passes.

**New York and Massachusetts**

Austrian National Tourist Office
500 Fifth Avenue
New York, NY 10110
Tel. 800-223-0284 or 212-944-6880

Belgian Tourist Office
745 Fifth Avenue
New York, NY 10151
Tel. 212-758-8130

British Tourist Authority
40 W. 57th Street
New York, NY 10019
Tel. 212-581-4700

BritRail Travel International (BR)
630 Third Avenue
New York, NY 10017
Tel. 212-599-5400

CIE Tours International (Ireland)
122 E. 42nd Street
New York, NY 10168-0015
Tel. 800-CIE-TOUR, 800-522-5258
(NY), or 800-331-3824 (West Coast)

French Government Tourist Office
610 Fifth Avenue
New York, NY 10020-2452
Tel. 212-757-1125

French National Railroads (EP)
610 Fifth Avenue
Rockefeller Center
New York, NY 10020
Tel. 800-223-5252
in NY: 212-582-4813

German Federal Railroads (EP)
747 Third Avenue
New York, NY 10017
Tel. 212-308-3100

German National Tourist Office
747 Third Avenue, 33rd floor
New York, NY 10017
Tel. 212-308-3300

GermanRail (EP)
625 Statler Office Building
Boston, MA 02116
Tel. 617-542-0577

Greek National Tourist Org.
645 Fifth Avenue, 5th floor
New York, NY 10022
Tel. 212-421-5777

Ibusz Hungarian Travel Company
630 Fifth Avenue, Room 2455
New York, NY 10111
Tel. 212-582-7412

Irish Tourist Board
757 Third Avenue
New York, NY 10017
Tel. 212-418-0800

Italian Government Travel Office
630 Fifth Avenue
New York, NY 10111
Tel. 212-245-4822

Italian State Railroads (EP)
666 Fifth Avenue
New York, NY 10103
Tel. 212-397-2667/8

Luxembourg National Tourist Office
801 Second Avenue
New York, NY 10017
Tel. 212-725-2345

Monaco Government Tourist Office
845 Third Avenue
New York, NY 10022
Tel. 212-759-5227

National Tourist Office of Spain
665 Fifth Avenue (at 53rd Street)
New York, NY 10022
Tel. 212-759-8822

Netherlands Board of Tourism
355 Lexington Avenue, 21st floor
New York, NY 10017
Tel. 212-370-7360

Portuguese National Tourist Office
548 Fifth Avenue
New York, NY 10036
Tel. 212-354-4403

Scandinavian Tourist Board
655 Third Avenue
New York, NY 10017
Tel. 212-949-2333

Swiss National Tourist Office (EP)
608 Fifth Avenue
New York, NY 10020
Tel. 800-223-0448 or 212-757-5944

**Texas**

Austrian National Tourist Office
4800 San Felipe, Suite 500
Houston, TX 77056
Tel. 713-850-8888

British Tourist Authority
Cedar Maple Plaza
2305 Cedar Springs Road
Dallas, TX 75201-1814
Tel. 214-720-4040

BritRail Travel International (BR)
Cedar Maple Plaza
2305 Cedar Springs Road
Dallas, TX 75201
Tel. 214-748-0860

French Government Tourist Office
World Trade Center, No. 103
P.O. Box 58610
Dallas, TX 75258
Tel. 214-742-7011

GermanRail (EP)
222 W. Las Colinas, Suite 1050
Irving, TX 75039
Tel. 214-402-8377

National Tourist Office of Spain
4800 The Galleria
5085 Westheimer
Houston, TX 77056
Tel. 713-840-7411

**California**

Austrian National Tourist Office
11601 Wilshire Boulevard,
Suite 2480
Los Angeles, CA 90025-1760
Tel. 800-252-0468 (CA)
or 213-477-3332

British Tourist Authority
World Trade Center, Suite 450
350 S. Figueroa Street
Los Angeles, CA 90071
Tel. 213-628-3525

BritRail Travel International (BR)
800 S. Hope Street, Suite 603
Los Angeles, CA 90017
Tel. 213-624-8787

French Government Tourist Office
9401 Wilshire Boulevard
Beverly Hills, CA 90212-2967
Tel. 213-271-6665

French Government Tourist Office
One Hallidie Plaza, Suite 500
San Francisco, CA 94102
Tel. 415-986-4173

French National Railroads (EP)
9465 Wilshire Boulevard
Beverly Hills, CA 90212
Tel. 213-274-6934

French National Railroads (EP)
360 Post Street
San Francisco, CA 94108
Tel. 800-227-4813
in CA: 415-982-1993

German National Tourist Office
444 S. Flower Street, Suite 2230
Los Angeles, CA 10017
Tel. 213-688-7332

GermanRail (EP)
11933 Wilshire Boulevard
Los Angeles, CA 90025
Tel. 213-479-2772

GermanRail (EP)
323 Geary Street, Suite 501
San Francisco, CA 94102
Tel. 415-362-6206

Greek National Tourist Org.
611 W. Sixth Street
Los Angeles, CA 90017
Tel. 213-626-6696

Italian Government Travel Office
360 Post Street, Suite 801
San Francisco, CA 94108
Tel. 415-392-6206

Italian State Railroads (EP)
15760 Ventura Boulevard, Suite 819
Encino, CA 91436
Tel. 800-248-7245 or 213-783-7245

National Tourist Office of Spain
San Vicente Plaza Building
8383 Wilshire Boulevard, Suite 960
Beverly Hills, CA 90211
Tel. 213-658-7188

Netherlands Board of Tourism
90 New Montgomery Street, No. 305
San Francisco, CA 94105
Tel. 415-543-6772

Swiss National Tourist Office (EP)
250 Stockton Street
San Francisco, CA 94108
Tel. 800-443-5566, 800-633-5566
(CA), or 415-362-2260

**Florida and Georgia**

British Tourist Authority
2580 Cumberland Parkway,
Suite 470
Atlanta, GA 30339
Tel. 404-432-9635

French National Railroads (EP)
2121 Ponce de Leon Boulevard
Coral Gables, FL 33134
Tel. 800-327-9656
in FL: 305-445-8648

GermanRail (EP)
Lenox Towers, Suite 1229
3400 Peachtree Road N.E.
Tel. 404-266-9555

National Tourist Office of Spain
Casa del Hidalgo
Hypolita and St. George Streets
St. Augustine, FL 32084
Tel. 904-829-6460

**Illinois**

Austrian National Tourist Office
500 N. Michigan Avenue, Suite 544
Chicago, IL 60611
Tel. 312-644-5556

British Tourist Authority
John Hancock Center, Suite 3320
875 N. Michigan Avenue
Chicago, IL 60611
Tel. 312-787-0490

French Government Tourist Office
645 N. Michigan Avenue, Suite 430
Chicago, IL 60611-2836
Tel. 312-337-6301

French National Railroads (EP)
11 E. Adams Street
Chicago, IL 60603
Tel. 800-621-4460
in IL: 305-427-8691

GermanRail (EP)
9575 Higgins Road, Suite 505
Rosemont, IL 60018
Tel. 312-692-4209

Greek National Tourist Org.
168 N. Michigan Avenue
Chicago, IL 60601
Tel. 312-782-1084

Italian Government Travel Office
500 N. Michigan Avenue
Chicago, IL 60611
Tel. 312-644-0990

Italian State Rairoads (EP)
500 N. Michigan Avenue, Room 1310
Chicago, IL 60611
Tel. 312-644-6651

National Tourist Office of Spain
845 N. Michigan Avenue
Chicago, IL 60611
Tel. 312-642-1992

Netherlands Board of Tourism
225 N. Michigan Avenue, Suite 326
Chicago, IL 60601
Tel. 312-819-0300

Swiss National Tourist Office (EP)
104 S. Michigan Avenue
Chicago, IL 60603
Tel. 312-641-0050

## CANADA

### British Columbia

Austrian National Tourist Office
736 Granville Street, Suite 1220
Vancouver, V6Z 1J2
Tel. 604-683-5808

BritRail Travel International (BR)
409 Granville Street
Vancouver, V6C 1T2
Tel. 604-683-6896

French National Railroads (EP)
409 Granville Street,
Suite 452
Vancouver, V6C 1T2
Tel. 604-688-6707

### Ontario

Austrian National Tourist Office
2 Bloor Street E., Suite 3330
Toronto, M4W 1A8
Tel. 416-967-3381

British Tourist Authority
94 Cumberland Street, Suite 600
Toronto, M5R 1A3
Tel. 416-925-6326

BritRail Travel International (BR)
94 Cumberland Street
Toronto, M5R 1A3
Tel. 416-929-3334

French Government Tourist Office
1 Dundas Street W.
Toronto, M5G 1Z3
Tel. 416-593-4723

German National Tourist Office
1290 Bay Street
Toronto, M5R 2C3
Tel. 416-968-1570

GermanRail (EP)
1290 Bay Street
Toronto, M5R 2C3
Tel. 416-968-3272

Greek National Tourist Org.
68 Scollard Street,
Lower Level, Unit E
Toronto, M5R 1G2
Tel. 416-968-2220

Irish Tourist Board
10 King Street E.
Toronto, M5C 1C3
Tel. 416-364-1301

Italian State Railroads (EP)
13 Balmuto Street
Toronto, M4Y 1W4
Tel. 416-927-7712

Netherlands Board of Tourism
25 Adelaide Street E., Suite 710
Toronto, M5C 1Y2
Tel. 416-363-1577

Portuguese National Tourist Office
2180 Yonge Steet (Concourse Level)
Toronto, M4S 2B9
Tel. 416-487-3300

Scandinavian Tourist Board
Box 115, Station "N"
Toronto, M8V 3S4
Tel. 416-823-9620

Spanish Government Tourist Office
60 Bloor Street W., Suite 201
Toronto, M6W 1A1
Tel. 416-961-3131

Swiss National Tourist Office
P.O. Box 215
Commerce Court
Toronto, M5L 1E8
Tel. 416-868-0584

**Quebec**

Austrian National Tourist Office
1010 W. Sherbrooke Street,
Suite 1410
Montreal, H3A 2R7
Tel. 514-849-3709

Belgian Tourist Office
P.O. Box 760
Succursale N.D.G.
Montreal, H4A 3S2
Tel. 514-489-9795

French Government Tourist Office
1981 McGill College Avenue,
Suite 490
Montreal, H3A 2W9
Tel. 514-288-4264

French National Railroads (EP)
1500 Stanley Street
Montreal, H3A 1R3
Tel. 514-288-8255

German National Tourist Office
2 Fundy
P.O. Box 417
Place Bonaventure
Montreal, H5A 1B8
Tel. 416-968-1570

Greek National Tourist Org.
1233, rue de la Montagne, Suite 101
Montreal, H3G 1Z2
Tel. 514-871-1535

Italian Government Travel Office
3 Place Ville Marie
Montreal,
Tel. 514-866-7667

Italian State Railroads (EP)
2055 Peel Street
Montreal, H3Z 1V4
Tel. 514-845-9101

Portuguese National Tourist Office
500 W. Sherbrooke Street, Suite 930
Montreal, H3A 3C6
Tel. 514-843-4623

# Index